Verbal Arts in Madagascar

Verbal Arts in Madagascar

Performance in Historical Perspective

Lee Haring

upp

University of Pennsylvania Press

Philadelphia

Publications of the American Folklore Society
New Series

General Editor, Patrick B. Mullen

Library of Congress Cataloging-in-Publication Data

Haring, Lee.
  Verbal arts in Madagascar: performance in historical perspective. / Lee Haring.
    p. cm.—(Publications of the American Folklore Society. New series (Unnumbered))
  Includes bibliographical references and index.
  ISBN 0-8122-3141-4
  1. Folk Literature, Malagasy—History and criticism.   2. Folklore—Madagascar—
Performance.   3. Madagascar—Social life and customs.   I. Title.   II. Series.
GR357.H38   1992
398'.09691—dc20   91–33129
                                                                                      CIP

for Sue

Contents

Acknowledgments

THIS BOOK is based on research I began in 1975–76, when I had the honor of serving the University of Madagascar (now the University of Antananarivo) as Fulbright Senior Lecturer in American Literature and Folklore, under a grant from the United States Information Agency. Colleagues in the Department of Modern Languages there encouraged my work. Subsequent research trips to France were financed by the Research Foundation of the City University of New York. Membership in a summer seminar at the University of Pennsylvania, funded by the National Endowment for the Humanities and directed by an inspiring teacher, John F. Szwed, provided further encouragement. I am grateful for all this support, as I am for a subvention from the American Folklore Society that has permitted publication. Grateful acknowledgment is extended to the *Journal of American Folklore*, *Fabula*, and *Acta Ethnographica* for granting permission to reprint material published in earlier forms.

I especially thank Roger D. Abrahams, who has watched over this book as a benevolent godparent and intervened more than once to see it published. Readings by him and (in part) by Anthony Astrachan have benefited the writing; so have the suggestions of some anonymous readers. I am also grateful for the help I have received from Philippe Beaujard, Dan Ben-Amos, Brunhilde Biebuyck, Geneviève Calame-Griaule, Robert Cancel, Georges Condominas, Daniel J. Crowley, Bakoly Domenichini-Ramiaramanana, Jacques Dournes, Gillian Feeley-Harnik, Marie-Paule Ferry, Ruth Finnegan, Leonard Fox, Rachel Fretz, Henry Glassie, Veronika Görög-Karady, Ron and Claudia Gould, James T. Hardyman, Jessica Kuper, Susan Kus, Hazel Lanyon, Patrick B. Mullen, Denise Paulme, Philip M. Peek, Leslie Prosterman, César Rabenoro, Françoise Raison-Jourde, John F. Szwed, Pierre Vérin, and Henry T. Wright, and the staff of the University of Pennsylvania Press. My beloved wife, Susan Vorchheimer Haring, has never stopped paying me the tribute of her delighted attention, and I never stop trying to express my gratitude.

1. Malagasy Lore and Folk

No oral literature has been more obscure to an English reader than the verbal art of Madagascar, the fourth largest island in the world, lying in the Indian Ocean 260 miles east of Mozambique. What little the English-speaking world today knows of Madagascar is mostly television documentary and "folklore," in the ordinary sense of lies. A legend about a man-eating tree circulated in European popular periodicals eighty years ago (Osborn 1924:8). Farther back in time and with a better supply of facts, Madagascar entered British literary history by means of the journal of Robert Drury (1687–1745?), a cockney sailor who was shipwrecked there in 1703 and stayed for thirteen years (Secord 1961). Drury's credibility has been attacked by literary persons ignorant of Madagascar, though seldom by historians. The reason is that the transcriber, editor, and ghost-writer of his journal (1729) was none other than that prolific writer of adventure stories, Daniel Defoe. He organized the sailor's narrative, padded out the story with descriptions he found in the classic 1658 account of Madagascar by Etienne de Flacourt, interpolated some philosophical reflections about primitive religion, and did the actual writing (Brown 1979). These services would not make the book fiction if later generations had not labeled Defoe as the founder of the English novel. His most famous shipwreck story was *Robinson Crusoe*, which is usually presented to children as a classic fiction. If Defoe the novelist was Robert Drury's ghost-writer, said the literary historian Moore, every word of Drury's journal must be a fiction. Historians of Madagascar, ignorant of this reasoning, have found Drury's book invaluable as a source for Malagasy history in the eighteenth century and have reedited and translated it (Grandidier 1906, Oliver 1890). Drury's posthumous career (Secord 1961) is a case study in the mutual incomprehensibility of two interpretive communities, British literary historians and *malgachisants* (a term often used for specialists in Malagasy studies). Few people have learned much about Madagascar from this story.

Language, colonial history, and ethnocentrism have been the main reasons why Madagascar deserves more attention from English-speaking people, especially in the late twentieth century when these topics are being reexamined. For previous generations, if Africa was the dark continent, at least some of it was colonized by the British, who wrote African history and ethnography in the English language. African folktales gained a reading public, partly by being published in Britain and France, partly by being carried to the New World by slaves, who gave Americans a vague sense of connection to Africa. But Madagascar, colonized by France in 1896, had contributed few slaves to the New World and found no interpreters there. Then, too, no citizen from the great island emerged to make an impact in the West. (By contrast, a number of Basques, who began in similar obscurity, attained positions of power in South America.) Also, the Malagasy language was forbidding. Virtually disconnected from the African languages that some Europeans were coming to know, it was the westernmost branch of the Malayo-Polynesian family; its other relatives were far across the Indian Ocean. Finally, such an obscure people as the Malagasy inevitably lay under the shadow of being labeled "primitive" and superstitious. Their custom called *famadihana*, for instance—removing the corpses of their dead from a tomb, rewrapping them, and entombing them again—drew some momentary horror from the readers of Sunday supplements.

Imagined as having little technology, simple "tribal" organization, and no real law or science, the Malagasy now deserve closer attention from the English-speaking world. It comes as a surprise to many people to discover that the Malagasy have been literate for much longer than many segments of the European population, or that by the time of Napoleon the island had developed a military conquest state with a dynastic monarchy. Fortunately, much accurate information is now available in English to explain how Madagascar acquired a population from Indonesia, thousands of miles away, instead of being colonized only from Mozambique across the channel (Vérin 1981, 1986). The island's population is made up of Africans and Indonesians; the latter came along in the sixth to ninth centuries, when the Swahili civilization of the African coast was also developing. A leading archaeologist and historian remarked in conversation that the creation of Malagasy culture is like a detective novel: you know who did it, but not how. English readers have a highly readable history of the island (Brown 1979), which takes advantage of the many historical records of the Merina (Elevated People) living in the central highlands[1] to give lively accounts of the contacts between Malagasy and Europeans in the nineteenth century. In addition to the work of historians, English readers can now consult fine ethnographic studies, based on precise observation of Malagasy people today, by Bloch, Kottak, Huntington, and Feeley-Harnik. Here, therefore, I shall only sketch the few facts needed to provide a background to Malagasy folklore.[2]

Malagasy Culture

The principal fact of Madagascar's history is that the island has always been an arena for internal movement and external exploitation. But first, what is the name of the place? The island which Marco Polo called Madagascar got that name because he confused it with Mogadishu (now in Somalia). The name was a convenience for Europeans. Because the island is so big, most Malagasy people had no reason to refer to it as a geographical unit. Later, after three-quarters of a century of French presence (from 1896 on), Malagasy people invented several alternative ways of indirectly referring to Madagascar: the Great Island, the Red Island, and the Happy Island. After World War II, it was the first European colony in Africa to feel the eruption of a movement toward independence. A bloody rebellion against the French in 1947 turned the Red Island into the Bloodsoaked Island (Domenichini-Ramiaramanana 1983:19). So though its name varied internally, Marco Polo's misnomer was used by the outside world until independence renamed it the Malagasy Republic (a political, not a geographical, designation; Brown 1979:vii).

The people of Madagascar are a mixture, descended from Africans and Indonesians. In early times Madagascar was populated by several waves of settlers who started from what is now Indonesia. Much of the scholarship on Madagascar has been devoted to the question of ethnic origins, under the expectation that the uniqueness of the island's language and culture would be explained if one knew their starting-point. An absorption in origins caused some scholars, especially in the age of Charles Darwin and James George Frazer, to look backward. In fact a good deal is known about the most important parts of Madagascar's recent history. One of the world's great documents of oral history is found there, for instance—the *Tantaran'ny Andriana*, royal histories written with the collaboration of authoritative informants in 1862–66 by the French Jesuit priest Callet. Furthermore, a great deal is known about Islamic influences (Julien 1929), British missionary history (Gow 1979, Bouillon 1981), early political organization (Kent 1970), the sixty years of French occupation (Deschamps 1972), and the postcolonial years (Archer 1976). Definite information has emerged in recent years from the history and archaeology of the central highland region, Imerina (Wright and Kus 1979), and the northern parts of the island (Vérin 1986). These new facts promise concrete knowledge about how the Merina state originated, an issue of great theoretical significance for Marxism (Kottak 1977). The internal diversity among Malagasy groups I shall return to later.

The new facts show that foreign influences brought about a renegotiation of culture. In Madagascar, as elsewhere in the Indian Ocean, Indonesian, African, and Arabo-Persian cultures attempted to exert political and cultural hegemony. Indonesia contributed rice cultivation, which today supports a great majority of the people, as well as the outrigger canoe and a plucked musical instrument, the *valiha*. Africa contributed drums and rattles, pottery, and the special importance of cattle all over the island (Heseltine 1971:65–66). It also contributed something to the capacity for verbal eloquence which is the subject of this book. Arabic culture brought writing and divination to Madagascar about five hundred years ago, along with strong Islamic influences which are still visible (Brown 1979:21–23). Consequently, Malagasy culture(s) and society

> combine traits characteristic of the Indian Ocean islands, India (especially southern India), and East Africa, not to mention a considerable Arabo-Persian contribution. . . . Virtually all the countries surrounding the Indian Ocean have left discernible traces in material techniques, vocabulary, family and political structures, and religious conceptions. (Ottino 1976:3)[3]

This history should be quite recognizable to people of the New World from looking at the Caribbean. Such mixing of languages and cultures has been given the name "creolization" (Hymes 1971). Madagascar, indeed, is a creolized culture. It has combined diverse imported elements to create something discontinuous and new, which could not have been predicted from its origins and which is no mere assemblage of foreign influences. As these diverse traits came into contact in Madagascar, they were also isolated from their places of origin. No one traveled to Africa to check on how people there identified their cattle. Isolation from sources, necessitated by geography, had the effect of detaching Malagasy culture. That is why it is unique.

Then the same processes of creolization and isolation continued within the island itself. A highland plateau, arid plains, and tropical coastal regions, each with its well-adapted means of livelihood, isolated its rural societies from each other, similar though they were economically and socially. Most of them practiced rice cultivation, which was well suited to the terrain, and bred cattle for their horns, their strength, and their beautiful hides. Others raised maize and manioc. Slash-and-burn agriculture, practiced at long intervals, effected little erosion. Social structure was stratified throughout the island, though most rigid in the central highland region, Imerina. Three levels existed among many of the societies: nobles (*andriana*), freemen (*hova*), and slaves (*andevo*). The three levels were paralleled by a tripartite division in the superhuman world: a remote God, a set of spirits both benevolent and malevolent (*zavatra*), some of whom are embodied in physical talismans, and the spirits of the ancestors (the more ancient called *vazimba*) (Domenichini 1973). The most obvious result is eighteen distinct dialects of a common language. According to historian Paul Ottino, the remarkable thing about Madagascar is how easily one can see the evidence of creolization. Deep connections in life styles, family structure, political organization, and expressive culture with eastern Africa, the Arab world (especially the Persian Gulf), India, and Indonesia are still discernible. Malagasy managed to syncretize conflicting elements of these diverse traditions (Ottino 1976:3).

> The more ancient of these syncretisms were already initiated on African or Indian shores even before arrival in the Great Island. They fostered a broad phenomenon of creolization. But this was a creolization of an original kind: in contrast to what happened in Réunion and Mauritius—sister islands to Madagascar in the origin of their peoples—it could develop "naturally" according to the inherent tendencies of the societies and cultures involved, rather than following the foreign logic of a plantation economy. This brief chronicle produced the society and civilization of today, which of course are still unfinished. (Ottino 1976:8)

Not only the language, then, with its diversity of dialects within a single tongue, but the entire culture of the thousand-mile-long island of Madagascar displays regional differences within a broad unity.

Folklore and Literacy

The writing of Malagasy folklore since European contact has depended upon literacy, which Madagascar has known in both Arabic and Roman alphabets. In the seventeenth century, the People of the Banks (Antemoro) of the southeast made use of the Arabic alphabet to write Malagasy on paper made from bark and with ink they extracted from gumtrees. Their Great Writings, or Sacred Books (*Sora-be*), like so many people's early writings, record prayers, magic formulas, genealogies, memorable events, and legends—all oral materials which, through being written, came under the control of royal scribes. But they did not thereby cease to be varied; "written texts were altered all the time" (Kent 1970:91, Deschamps 1972:52—53).

The second period of Malagasy literacy began when Protestant missionaries arrived in 1818, commenced translating the Bible (largely from English), and created the first dictionary. This profoundly influential encounter between Malagasy and the West has been scrutinized by Françoise Raison-Jourde (1977). Literacy helped in molding a concept of "Malagasy culture" as a unity. In contrast with emerging nations like Finland (Wilson 1976) and Greece (Herzfeld 1982), where folklore formed a basis for national identity, Madagascar underwent transformation into client status. Perhaps missionaries David Jones and James Hastie foresaw the transformation. They, after all, were part of that larger effort of evangelization which aimed also at the British urban working class. In both Britain and Madagascar, learning to read Scripture had to come first, and to the missionaries of the first wave (1820—36), oral culture had little importance. From their side, the triumph of Christianity as religion and ideology was won in battles by civilization over native belief. Language, however, they saw differently: it was evolving from oral to written. From the Malagasy side, the reverence for writing which the Antemoro displayed to the Great Writings worked in favor of the dictionaries and grammars, though these remained under the control of mission librarians.

Literacy had a different value to the Merina monarch who welcomed the British, Radama I (1810—1828). He did not foresee any transformation; rather, he welcomed the missionaries as part of a larger accord between himself and Britain. Writing would be a necessary instrument of governing. To construct dikes for irrigation (in accordance with the system set up by his powerful predecessor, Andrianampoinimerina (1787—1810), to build his royal palace, to recruit soldiers and workers, Radama would use writing to effect the obedience and submission from the tribes outside the highlands. Thenceforward he could convince outsiders that all Madagascar was under the power of the Merina king. The Merina close to the capital would benefit from schooling, which took the young away from the local organization (*foko*), with its narrow controls, and prepared them to serve the sovereign and the state. Ironically, within fifteen years the rapid advance of linguistic science and literacy empowered Jones's pupils, who by then occupied high state and military positions, to bring on a political crisis. Literacy helped produce a new elite.

Though literacy at this stage had considerable political importance, folklore did not. Because the missionaries sought alliances with power, their folklore research put the Merina in first place (Esoavelomandroso 1978:13–14). Yet they ignored the controls exerted within the family by elders over the speech of the young. They also ignored the upward path of the people's speech toward the king, the downward path of the king's word to the people, and the crucial intermediacy of spokesmen who could recite a royal genealogy (Domenichini-Ramiaramanana 1983:499). Finally, they ignored the various forms of pronoun and of salutation that allowed any dialogue to register the rank of the speakers (Raison-Jourde 1977: 654–55). Perhaps they were aided in these omissions by their Malagasy informants. "All mutilation of a language issues from those who have inherited it as their mother tongue," said the creole linguist Hugo Schuchardt (1980:65). A gap opened between the written dictionaries and grammars and the continuing oral performance of folklore in context. In many places, folklore retained its position as the area of social consensus. The Antemoro scribes continued writing Arabico-Malagasy (Domenichini-Ramiaramanana 1977:20). Merina farther from the royal capital and the non-Merina groups maintained their traditions of storytelling, riddling, speaking proverbs, and formal dialogue (*kabary*). In all these practices, Malagasy people wrote their own culture before the letter (Spivak 1976:xxxix).

Ignored by the first generation of British missionaries, folklore maintained its force in Malagasy communities. So long as proverbs and other genres of verbal art could be orally exchanged, they could be treated as authoritative speech and internalized by each speaker. "It was in the maximum socialization of the word," writes Raison-Jourde, "in what could be considered 'everybody's language' par excellence, that the most complete internalization of fidelity [to tradition] took place" (1977:657). By apologizing at the beginning of a marriage request, political negotiation, or other debate, each speaker could reveal doubts and ambivalences, thus linking himself to other speakers. So long as decisions could be ratified by the approbation of family, community, or village, discourse could preserve its characteristic movement from the ambiguous and the hidden to a common utterance which had the force of law.[4] This movement, I shall show, is learned from riddling, in which a movement from figurative to literal serves as a model for all the genres of *fitenin-drazana* (sayings of the ancestors). "There are grasses whose name is unknown," says a proverb, "there are animals whose name must be guessed, but with words there is no guessing" (Houlder 1960:44, no. 560; Domenichini-Ramiaramanana 1970:465, no. 2630).

Several oppositions emerged which affected folklore. One was between spoken Malagasy and a unified, purified Malagasy found in grammars. At this first stage of literacy, folklore was unified, in the missionaries' eyes, by being ignored, and language was divorced from its social function. By treating Malagasy language scientifically, as a merely grammatical order, their linguistic efforts indirectly remodeled Merina society at the level of its symbolic representations. Their contact with the highland Merina and their desire to conform to current standards of linguistic science produced a purified Malagasy. Another opposition was between the unified Malagasy and European languages. It was a case of what M. M. Bakhtin observed when he wrote, "Linguistics, stylistics, and the philosophy of language—as forces in the service of the great centralizing tendencies of European verbal-ideological life—have sought first and foremost for *unity* in diversity" (1981:274, his emphasis). A third opposition was between highland and regional dialects. In nineteenth-century Malagasy dictionaries, dialect and regional variations were distilled into a bipolar division between "Merina" and "coast," which has been a potent linguistic and political fact ever since. The heterogeneity and capacity for lexical mixing in Malagasy were disguised.

Thus at this first stage, folklore took on the status of a set of symbolic representations of a dominated people who did not think they were dominated. One can see highland culture as an arena of cultural confrontation (Raison-Jourde 1977:641–43). Then, in a cultural backlash, folklore began to get some attention. In a reaction against foreign influence, the new queen, Ranavalona I (1828–1852), banished the missionaries (1836) and sought to extirpate Christianity. Seeking to disconnect the art of writing from the occidental ideology it carried, the queen may have actually enhanced the discontinuity between language and social context. When she banned all books except the dictionaries, the only road to culture became a lexical one. "From 1836 on," Raison-Jourde writes, "the social elite were in possession of a surplus of vocabulary in search of objects" (1977:661). And so, in Madagascar's first systematic transcribing of folklore, some pupils of Griffiths and Jones began to write down traditional *hainteny* (poems), which I study below. At that moment, the study of folklore became part of Malagasy culture.

British Missionary Folklorists

After the queen's death in 1861, when the missionaries were allowed back into the country, until the French conquest of 1896, Malagasy folklore collecting flourished. Through the efforts of one Protestant group, the collecting and publication of folklore formed the basis of the identity of Madagascar in the minds of English readers. An energetic group of British clergymen, sent to Madagascar by the London Missionary Society (LMS), collected and translated Malagasy tales, proverbs, riddles, beliefs, and folksongs. They founded the Malagasy Folk-lore Society in 1877, a year before its British counterpart (Domenichini-Ramiaramanana 1983:173), and published twelve numbers of a folklore journal (1886). The most active missionary folklorists were J. A. Houlder and W. E. Cousins, who collected and published Malagasy proverbs (*ohabolana*), and James Sibree, Jr., who edited the *Antananarivo Annual* (1875–1900). This informative periodical, not authorized by the London directors, was initiated only by the enthusiasm of this handful of men (Hardyman, personal communication). Not all the LMS missionaries were neutral observers: W. Clayton Pickersgill left the LMS to become the British vice-consul (Gow 1979:99), and William Ellis, historian of Madagascar, became an agent for the British crown (Brown 1979). But their articles in the *Annual* show them as keen folklorists. The LMS collecting of proverbs and other folklore was augmented by the patient researches (1872–76) of the Norwegian Lutheran missionary Lars Dahle, whose *Specimens of Malagasy Folk-lore* (1877, in Malagasy) remains the classic work in this field. It was also augmented by the oral histories collected and published in Malagasy by the French Jesuit Callet (1974). This was the time of the invention of Malagasy tradition, or what has been called the *folklorizing* of Malagasy culture (Bouillon 1981:143).

What was folklore, to the great team of Houlder, Cousins, and Sibree? Obsolescence (because of the inevitable impact from the spreading of the gospel), unchanging stability, and revelation of the Malagasy past were components of their definition. Like his fellow missionaries, who were both authors and audience for the *Annual*, Sibree understood "Folk-Lore" in the terms that his countryman William Thoms used when he

invented the word in 1846—proverbs, folksongs, and customs now threatened with disappearance (Dundes 1965:5). In his first number, Sibree
wrote, "It is most desirable that any Traditions, Legends, Fables, or Folk-
Lore that may be met with should be preserved, as throwing light on the
origin of the different tribes." Essential, therefore, to the LMS conception
of folklore was that it represented a set of survivals: "phenomena originat-
ing under a set of causal conditions of a former era perpetuate[d] themselves into a period during which the original conditions no longer
exist[ed]" (Harris 1968:164). Sibree derived the concept from the new
anthropology initiated at home by E. B. Tylor, whose work he read and
with whom he corresponded (Hardyman, personal communication). Like
Tylor's games and popular sayings, Malagasy traditions, legends, fables,
and other folklore, though threatened with disappearance by the work of
the observers themselves, were products of past history rather than evidence of dynamic processes.

By collecting and publishing folklore, Dahle and the LMS folklorists
brought the Malagasy-Western encounter a new relation which favored
themselves: the scientific treatment of tradition. Their predecessors had
evangelized language; they separated tradition as an object of study. For
the LMS folklorists, many of whom were expert linguists, Malagasy verbal
folklore posed less threat than stronger cultural symbols like circumcision,
divination, or taboos (*fady*). As their predecessors had divorced language
from its social context, so they transmitted folklore to a new audience.
Proverbs helped them learn the language and teach it to their younger
successors. Including proverbs in their sermons, they could seem more
accepting of Malagasy tradition than they actually were (Gow 1979:118–
20). Ironically, in the same breath they were accepting and imitating Malagasy oratorical style, which relies heavily on quotation. Another of their
unconscious imitations was to use local collaborators between themselves
and the people whose culture they were recording (Gow 1979:240).

The Invention of the "Malagasy Mind"

Now came a third stage of objectifying Malagasy in European eyes, with
the aid of folklore. Under colonization after 1896, British collecting came
to an end and French ethnography expanded. Its history has been written
by Antoine Bouillon (1981), who shows that cultural studies were inseparable from the normalization of the colony. A psychological approach to

"the" Malagasy, sometimes through the products of folklore, became a necessary adjunct to governing. In this third stage of Malagasy folklore studies, the data would reveal the Malagasy mind as a system of beliefs, which must be scientifically understood so as to be "normalized" or Europeanized.[5] Succeeding the dialectic between linguistic unity and diversity was a debate between *madécassitude,* the native mentality, and individuality (348–49). A third view held that the different Malagasy "tribes" had different personalities: the Merina man, for instance, has been trained from childhood to conceal his feelings and to express what others expect from him (Molet 1959:32).

Among folklorists who contributed to this debate, and who thus provide data for folkloric reconstruction, the names of Gabriel Ferrand, André Dandouau, Charles Renel (who as superintendent of schools assembled an authoritative tale collection), Henri Dubois, Jacques Faublée, and Raymond Decary stand out in the colonial period. Obviously, it was the dominance first of England, then of France, and the submission, at first imperceptible, of the great island that made it possible for missionaries, explorers, ethnographers, linguists, anthropologists, and civil servants to observe folklore in Madagascar. That relationship affected "the practical pre-conditions of [folklore]; the uses to which this knowledge was put; the theoretical treatment of particular topics; the mode of perceiving and objectifying" an alien society, and the folklorist's "claim of political neutrality" (Asad 1973:17). Folklore study became a part of colonial life which brought both sides together. The Académie Malgache, still flourishing today as a center for research, was established in 1902 in an atmosphere of collaboration between a European elite comprising goverment officers, merchants, bankers, and settlers, and an increasingly Europe-oriented Merina elite who hoped to maintain aristocratic traditions. One of its early projects to that end was the republishing of Callet's *Tantaran'ny Andriana.* For the ensuing eighty years, the *Bulletin* of the Académie has been the outstanding source for folklore reports. As on the African continent, so in Madagascar, "anthropology did not receive the same sanction in territories of French colonization [as in British]. Nevertheless, some administrators were at the same time talented anthropologists who gathered considerable masses of knowledge." (Mercier 1971:78). Since independence, both Malagasy and French scholars have become absorbed in recovering Madagascar's past. Their materials are assuredly reliable for my purposes. Today, the accounts of Madagascar by ethnographic fieldworkers (Beaujard 1983), linguists (Aly 1977), and insider spokesmen (Michel-Andrianarahinjaka

1986) are as trustworthy as any in the world, and they show a growing interest in folklore (Ottino 1986). Yet there is nothing on Malagasy folklore in English. This book aims at remedying the gap.

The Present Research

My own knowledge of this history and this culture derives mostly from the lore assembled by these scholars, rather than from the folk. When I arrived in the capital, Antananarivo (A Thousand Villages), in July 1975 to take up a year's visiting professorship in the University of Madagascar, I knew a little of East Africa but had only read about Madagascar. I hoped to study folklore, especially its connections to African folklore. Field study, however, proved to be impossible that year. A newly installed government had not yet put in place the procedures it established later to enable people like me to carry out fieldwork. It was possible, though, to study Malagasy folklore in print. An excellent bibliography was begun in 1905 by Guillaume Grandidier, son of the most famous of *malgachisants*. Extensive resources awaited me in the university library, the National Library, the Académie Malgache, and the bookshops, and university colleagues were helpful, though sometimes quizzical. A great deal of collecting had been done, but almost none of the collected materials had been analyzed. This disparity was not new to me; unanalyzed collecting characterizes the whole field of folklore, in which generations of collectors have preserved innumerable facts without asking many questions about what they meant (Dundes 1975). Like my *Malagasy Tale Index*, therefore, which assembled the information needed to study Malagasy folk narrative texts, this book relies entirely on those published folklore collections and printed sources. It attempts to bring to a reader of English some of the expressive culture of these people who are too little known—a worthy goal in itself—and to integrate that culture into the body of facts and theory constituting the field of folklore (as Americans call it; some European scholars call it ethnology). To that end I practice a kind of history writing I call "folkloric restatement," a term which I have adapted from the "sociolinguistic restatement" advocated by Dell Hymes (1966) and practiced by Joel Sherzer. Using as its materials the observations of past collectors, whether they were seekers of folklore or not, folkloric restatement reconstructs folkloric communication in other times and places. Though it can never replace field study of actual performers, it can suggest how pieces are constructed and varied. Folkloric restatement can identify the patterns of verbal art: Malagasy genres, as I shall show, overlap and depend on each other, much as Malagasy people tend to do. Then folkloric restatement interprets collected texts, in the light of other information about the culture and of the concepts of folklore and literary criticism.

My general assumptions are as follows. A unique culture makes Malagasy people different from others, but not more or less worthy than others. Their responses to environmental conditions, like people's responses everywhere, are patterned, in ways developed in the past that are still emerging in the present. Some of these patterned responses the people classify as "traditional." The particular folkloric patterns of Madagascar happen to exemplify concretely Anthony F. C. Wallace's view that culture is a "set of standardized models of contractual relationships" (41). As to the issue of comparative evaluation, a person who assumes Malagasy poetry must inherently be inferior or superior to English or French poetry must have acquired that assumption from his or her culture. No one, up to now, has known both poetries well enough to compare them. Both literatures are equally available for criticism, that is, a general interpretation of principles whereby people are making their art (Glassie 1982: 11–12). Thus the formal analyses below are part of a general program of folklore studies I derive from Dell Hymes (1974), in which the structural analysis of the cultural behavior of a community requires inductive emic analysis of cultural items and the search for their functionally relevant internal relations.

My general affiliations are to the "writing culture" movement in anthropology, the work of M. M. Bakhtin, the "formal inductive analysis" of literature practiced by Paul Goodman (1954), and the performance approach to verbal art pioneered by Dell Hymes and Richard Bauman. For the first of these, folkloric restatement in Madagascar must bring out not only the recorded texts of folklore and their context of performance, but also the encounter between performers and outside observers. The problematic nature of encounters between colonized artists ("informants") and ethnographers from the colonizing power has drawn much attention in recent years (Asad 1973). In the 1980s, anthropologists turned their skills of participant observation on the history of their own practice (Stocking 1983, Herzfeld 1987), and folklorists examined the traditions of their own group (Bronner 1986, Zumwalt 1988). Most influential on this book has been the writing culture movement, which puts the encounter between observer and observed persons at the center of its study. One major proposition of this movement is that ethnography is moving toward a greater variety of expressions and taking broader responsibility for cultural critique (Marcus and Fischer 1986). Another is that ethnography is a practice more allied to fiction and autobiography than to laboratory reporting (Clifford and Marcus 1986). And this movement itself quickly became an object of history (Rosaldo 1989). These emphases on the politics of the folkloric encounter and the rhetoric of writing folklore recur throughout this book.

As to my other affiliations, repeated references to Bakhtin will mark his influence on me. The printed texts cited here tend to make Malagasy folklore look more fixed than it is, a fixity Bakhtin would disclaim. His vision of dialogue goes far deeper than supplying a terminology and framework for understanding recorded performances. Paul Goodman's insistence that formal analysis could bring us to the heart of what makes people respond to literature underlies the analyses found here. The performance approach constantly urges me to imagine real performers and real audiences behind printed texts.

The four genres studied here justify study together because they make up a single category called *fitenin-drazana*, sayings of the ancestors. My thesis is that *fitenin-drazana* are all governed by a principle of two-sided interaction, which determines the manner of their performance, the metaphors they summon up, and their internal structure. Like the American children's folklore studied by John Holmes McDowell, *fitenin-drazana* constitute a "broad range of locutions sharing the surface structure of the riddle" (31), but in contrast, the category includes poetry, proverbs, and oratory along with riddling. Whereas American riddles, in McDowell's presentation, are a set of "enactments based on interrogation," these Malagasy genres are performances based on "solicitation," the sort of speech act which functions to elicit a response (40). The response may come in the interaction situation, as in riddling, or internally within the piece, by conveying a sense that an incomplete half needs completion. This category *fitenin-drazana*, in turn, names a selection of verbal art from the larger range of Malagasy folklore, which includes greetings, curses, gestures, games, songs, dances, instrumental music, art, costume, architecture, cookery, and religion. For verbal art, Dahle's table of contents shows the repertoire among the Merina:

Longer "art of the word" pieces [poems translated into prose]
Shorter "art of the word" pieces resembling proverbs
Riddles, "choices" [double riddles]
Songs of the ancients
Excerpts from orations
Children's games
Legends, fables, and stories

How authentic are these printed texts? Many pieces I discuss here were collected under the assumption that as a product of Malagasy cultural history, folklore is fixed and unchanging. Many of them exist in only one version, thereby raising a problem. Folklorists like Krohn, Krappe, and Bogatyrev and Jakobson have marked community acceptance and multiple existence as essential to the authenticity of their texts. Dundes frequently faults nonfolklorists for ignoring variant forms of a tale (1965:107). Can we ever assume that a saying or tale recorded only once is known to many persons in a community? "It is often very difficult," writes one authority on Malagasy proverbs, "to distinguish whether we are dealing with genuinely original sentences or with popular proverbs attributed later to a given person's creative genius." Though historical context may be authentic, it may have been reconstructed after the fact to give meaning to a half-understood saying (Navone 1977:61). This puzzle has resulted from an excessively narrow adherence to multiple existence as a criterion for folklore, as Ruth Finnegan points out for Africa.

> If one of the marks of a true proverb is its general acceptance as the popular expression of some truth, we are seldom given the data to decide how far this is indeed a characteristic of the sayings included in collections of "proverbs." We have in fact no way of telling whether some of the "proverbs" included are not just the sententious utterances of a single individual on a single occasion which happened to appeal to the investigator. (Finnegan 1970:394)

Some texts in this book come with a warranty: the Merina funeral oration, said its editor Mondain (chapter 6) "has been said and said again many times over the tombs of persons in southern Imerina; it has been heard by thousands of auditors who applauded its hidden subtleties" (1908:99). About others, we know only that they were collected in good faith. Analysis reveals that many have been built on the same structural principles as those printed in multiple versions. The problem of authenticity is resolvable by viewing folklore performance as a dynamic, ongoing process. Single texts result, in this view, from the generative processes of folklore. When Malagasy speakers adapt borrowed cultural elements and put together new structures out of the fragments, the rules they use are not fixed but variable, drawn from the same multiplicity of sources as the cultural elements themselves. Malagasy culture imparts to the speaker a skill in mediating two sets of meanings by varying the possibilities. From this "inherent variability" (Labov 1972:223–26) emerges true creation. The corpus of Malagasy narrative has already demonstrated this variability (Haring 1982). Single texts of tales or proverbs are an inevitable result of the fluidity and variability of genre distinctions. Alternative texts, and alternative rules for synthesizing new ones, are available to orators, reciters of poems, or speakers of proverbs. Elinor Ochs Keenan (1973) has recorded both the variability of marriage speeches among the Merina and the fluidity of the rules the speakers were expected to follow.

Texts are not performances. Folklore performance in Madagascar is "a dynamic process evolving through space and time." Variation in performance takes place against the background of a dialectic between egalitarian tradition and increasing hierarchization of political power. To speak of fixed genres or even of recurrent texts is, in a way, misleading, because these terms "merely seek to freeze at an arbitrary moment, and to coalesce into an arbitrary whole, phenomena which in nature are ongoing and heterogeneous" (Bickerton 1973). But because folklorists have had to freeze the phenomena into their collections, recorded texts are bound to differ. Malagasy informants have had powerful reasons for declaring their discourses to be a whole. For them, established truth consists of the inherited discourses of the ancestors. By being quoted, these discourses function for unity, binding together the many voices of the living and the dead. But the variability of performance functions to beget diversity.

Uniformity Versus Diversity in Language

The study of the verbal art of Madagascar requires a look at the island's culture, which is both uniform and diverse. Indeed, the history of Malagasy language and folklore studies can be understood as a dialectic between concepts of uniformity and diversity. Uniformity came in with the alphabetization of the language and the collecting of folklore, in the days of the Merina monarchy. In that period, scholars continually sought to explain the origin of the Malagasy people, as a whole, in some foreign population. The most influential explanation, which has been widely accepted, was also unfortunately the most tendentious, arising from an external ideology. In his encyclopedic *Physical, Natural, and Political History of Madagascar*, Alfred Grandidier (1836–1921) gave the privileged position to light-skinned Indonesians as the ancestors of the Malagasy. From them, he said, the Merina were descended. Later historians like Kent seriously questioned this view. In the colonial period, when racial stereotypes were more easily recognized and combated, the question of Malagasy origins receded. Fieldwork began to focus on face-to-face communities, whose members find differences from their neighbors more real than similarities to them.

Malagasy linguistics is pervaded by this dialectic between uniformity and diversity.[6] Majority opinion upholds the unity of the language and the variation among its eighteen dialects. Beginning with Sieur de Flacourt, who implanted a French settlement in the south of the island in the seventeenth century, foreign observers, some with more authority than others, have asserted that all Malagasy understand one another's speech. The LMS missionary lexicographers awarded to the Merina dialect of the central highlands the "destiny" of becoming the national language and the universal Malagasy. "It was the English, French, and Norwegians who presented to the Merina the elements of their own language," wrote G.-S. Chapus in 1925. These three groups all supported homogeneity. By 1925 standard Malagasy was the received wisdom of *malgachisants*.

To underline the unity of Malagasy language, and therefore of culture, standardization was the principle of grammars and dictionaries. Grammars by Webber (1853), Ailloud (1873), Basilide Rahidy (1875), Aristide Marre de Marin (1876), Pierre Caussèque (1886), G. Cousins (1882), Lucien Montagné (1931), and L. Gerbinis (1946), as well as the major dictionary by Abinal and Malzac (1888, 1893), all asserted the unity of Malagasy by contrasting it with European languages. Malzac did mention the difference between Merina and "provincial dialects," reducing variation to a mere matter of sounds. As "rational, modern" thinking spread outward from the capital, "official" Malagasy accompanied it. Although local people had already begun to create written texts in some of the eighteen dialects, they also were beginning to learn that their regional speech was *miroky*, incorrect (as Haitian creole speakers, for instance, still do). After a brief debate, the Académie Malgache, almost immediately after its founding, minuted the adoption of Merina as the island-wide language for all schools.

The teaching of standardized Malagasy in highland schools and elsewhere enlarged the opposition between official Malagasy, in the form of the Merina dialect (then called *hova*), and local speaking. "That is not a mere hypothesis," wrote one observer a generation later. "In Madagascar, the literary *hova* taught in schools is, for numerous *hova* peasants, something of a foreign language," all the more foreign to the more numerous non-Merina (Davesne in Calvet 1979). Folklore was downgraded with local speech. If folklore is born in the breach between official and unofficial cultures, then the imposition of standardized Merina as official Malagasy must have produced many new creations.

Dialect Diversity

Yet many a grammarian knew that Malagasy culture and language were not unified. There were "as many dialects as there are provinces in the Great African Island," wrote Caussèque in his grammar. From time to time, recognizing the diversity, both British and French scholars questioned the supposed linguistic and ethnic unity of Madagascar. W. E. Cousins, linguist and proverb collector, spoke for ethnic diversity.

> Although we [the LMS missionaries] are in the habit of speaking of the Malagasy as one people, this seems not to have been a familiar idea to themselves. The free use of the word Malagasy as a generic term for the people is, I think, quite modern; and even yet to some of the natives it is not quite clear what is its exact comprehensiveness. Among themselves the separating tribal names were the common designations in use. (1895:38)

Constant strife and warfare, Cousins thought, increased that sense of separateness. A similar view was expressed indirectly by his colleague John Richardson, the LMS lexicographer. Eight years after publishing his dictionary, he sent out questionnaires to local government officers on 184 words in which dialects might differ from one another. These were arranged by Sibree in the *Antananarivo Annual* into a table of 158 words from twenty-four localities. Read today, Sibree's effort to uphold standardization shows strain. He is obliged to attribute dialect differences to different racial origins and to the practice of tabooing certain words. Still, he conceded, a Merina speaker did have difficulty understanding Sakalava, Antemoro, or Bara speakers, who lived some distance away (Richardson 1897, 1898).

Also attesting to the dialectic between unity and diversity, as France moved closer to invasion, was a prickly nationalist, Louis Catat. He snarled that the British (against whom he was virulently prejudiced) had created a spurious hegemony by cultivating the Merina. Malagasy language, after all the intensive efforts of scholars, had been but poorly understood.

> Obviously in general the Malagasy language is unified. Theoretically that is true, and no one doubts it. But in practice, the Catholic and Protestant missionaries . . . have misunderstood this fact: though the Merina are the most potent tribe in Madagascar, they are still a long way from having absorbed the other peoples. While considerable account has to be taken of Merina customs, language habits, and politics in every question connected to Madagascar, it is absolutely illogical, and contrary to French interests as well as to scientific truth, to insist on seeing only this people in Madagascar. That is a trap which has been set for our policies for many years now by the British. (259)[7]

Catat was not the only witness who struggled with dialectal and cultural diversity. Soon after the occupation, another French observer, a civil engineer, was impelled to produce a comparative table of Malagasy dialects. Antony Jully seems to have regarded all of them as equally uninteresting, because the language possessed no written documents. But he had to use it. While sailing to the Paris exposition of 1900, he enlisted the aid of the Malagasy on shipboard with him as informants. In his manual, seven dialects had equal rank (Merina, Betsileo, Antankarana, Betsimisaraka, Antemoro, Antanosy, Sakalava) along with the Swahili spoken in the northwest and the nearby Comoro Islands. With the aid of his manual, a Frenchman could avoid too much contact with the natives "by doing away with that ever obstructive, sometimes perfidious person the native interpreter." Wanting the words in his lexicon to be genuinely Malagasy and to correspond to a clear idea in his informants' minds, Jully neatly systematized their denotations. Unwittingly, he also paid tribute to a Malagasy capacity for maintaining contact with fellow speakers by means of imitation. With irritation Jully wrote, "Led on by his neighbor's example, a native has often pronounced the same word as his predecessor with no clear idea of what it meant" (v). That capacity for imitation and echoing is a principal stylistic feature in Malagasy oral poetry. Jully also bore witness to the impossibility of the standard which the missionary lexicographers had tried to set up. Whether in the genre system or in the performance of a particular proverb or riddle, the performer" retains a choice among several possibilities.

Other voices also drew attention to the dialectic between unity and cultural diversity in the colonial period, though few of them spoke for folklore. One teacher, Father Raphael of the Christian Brothers school, argued for spelling reform. Behind his proposals lay real variations he had observed in pronunciation, word formation, and style. Then a more serious call came from Gabriel Ferrand. Already author of a classic folktale collection representing fieldwork on both east and west coasts, Ferrand was a major dissenter from the prevailing commitment to Merina hegemony. His selection of tales showed the diversity of Malagasy narrative by representing five distinct repertoires. Merina language, he thought, could not be fruitfully approached without knowing at least two or three other dialects, and, if possible, Malay as well. Ferrand argued for the study of Malagasy dialects, which would make use of no fewer than thirty-four distinct varieties. Comparing these to Malay languages would reveal the laws of Malagasy phonology. Ferrand's attack on the supposed uniformity of "the" Malagasy language included a critique of the reigning *malgachisant*, Alfred Grandidier.[8]

Ferrand, a folklorist as well as a linguist, clearly saw what diverse cultural forces had converged on Madagascar. The charms and magical formulas in amulets were in Arabic. The months of the year were called by two sets of alternative names, derived from Arabic and Sanskrit. In the early nineteenth century, with the rise of the Merina monarchy, the ordinary dialect of the highlands began its ascent to a national language with standardized spelling. Yet spelling as Ferrand saw it was a microcosm of what we now call creolization, for it combined Malagasy, Arabic, and English. The Merina monarch Radama I learned to write Merina in Arabic characters. When the first British missionaries put it into the roman alphabet, they borrowed the romanized spellings *ao* for the *o* sound and *o* for the *oo* sound from Arabic. The terminal *y* for *i* had certainly come in from English (it is rumored to have been chosen from the letters available in the British-made print shop). "So the British missionaries," Ferrand wrote, "were reproducing in roman characters the transcriptions previously adopted by the Islamised Malagasy of the southeast coast" (1909:xxix).

Ferrand's evidence for creolization and plea for a Malagasy dialectology fell on ears prepared to give only Merina the victory in the battle over language. Yet many observers attested to differences among dialects and to a Malagasy capacity for switching between dialects and registers. Shortly after World War I, though conceding Merina linguistic hegemony, Henri Rusillon detected important phonological and lexical differences. Merina and Sakalava speakers experienced confusion from speaking differently, though the coastal speaker would have to admire a language so much richer and more supple than his own. "The mixture of accents is so complete that it is very difficult to draw any conclusions from it" (1921:231). Among the Betsileo of the southern highlands, a long-term missionary recorded the Malagasy capacity for switching among dialects in folklore. The many proverbs collected by Fr. Henri Dubois in his twenty-five years of fieldwork included many in mixed dialects. Some were wholly Betsileo, others half Betsileo, half Merina. His best informants for proverbs made no scruple about mixing Merina forms with "country" ones. "My proverb notebooks present variants of every kind in this genre" (1296–97). Another Jesuit, not a folklorist, insisted on knowledge of the dialects outside Imerina as a precondition for plumbing the depths of Malagasy language, "as well as the related Indonesian languages (God knows if there are any!)" (Boudou 1949:2, 358–59). Yet in the same year, the grammarian Gerbinis could insist on linguistic unity: "A few Europeans claim that the Malagasy language is divided into several dialects. Therein is a profound error." These field reports suggest that Malagasy possess phonological and lexical strategies which bridge or efface the differences between sounds and sounds, person and person, group and group. Perhaps the sense of connection to a home place and a family tomb gives Malagasy a stronger sensitivity to the social distinctions arising from those cues. Their skill at reproducing heard speech is a strategy which is stylized by Merina orators, who quote incessantly, and is a principal feature of the *hainteny* poems of the Merina. The complete mixing of accents which Rusillon noticed manifests the same strategy at a less stylized level. All peoples use dialect cues to identify one another, but some, like the Sranan of Surinam, use dialect or language to elevate or lower their style or to invoke the intimacy of a time before European contact (Voorhoeve 1971). It is the role of Malagasy folklore to present such interpenetration in artistic forms.

The Idea of "Tribe"

What about ethnic identifications among the eighteen distinguishable groups on the great island? If Malagasy dialects and cultural patterns are so interpenetrated, how do Malagasy identify themselves? Who were those Sakalava who, in Antony Jully's hearing, were so imitative? Contemporary sociolinguistics holds that people identify themselves by means of choosing among various cues (Barth 1969, Sankoff 1980). Dialect, place, name, and custom may all be used, and affiliation choices are inherently variable. The Malagasy idea of tribe is as elusive as its counterpart in colonial Africa, where the stereotype of a tribe linked by language, social system, and law was a kind of collaboration between Europeans and African leaders (Iliffe, cited in Ranger 1983).

I have considered dialect; let me look at place, which Malagasy often claim as their basis of identity. Madagascar contains hardly a single group that originated where it lives today. Conquests of one group by another, emigration for the sake of better grazing land, abandonment of villages polluted by a violation of *fady* (taboo), religious conversion or enthusiasm, lack of space for cattle or people, periodic famines and droughts, and the lure of cash have made the history of Madagascar the history of movements. As an instance of the paradoxical results, let us look at Majunga just before World War II. With close to a million people in its district, the Afro-Arab flavor of this tropical port appeals to many a visitor. Though the town was well known to be the principal center of Sakalava population and culture, only about one-sixth of local people would identify themselves as Sakalava. As another instance, in Diego-Suarez (now Antsiranana), at the northern end of the island, a place well known as the center for the Antankarana (People of the Rocks), only one person in seven would identify himself as Antankarana. In a third case, researchers concluded that the region in the southeast known for the Antemoro (People of the Banks) had better be renamed for the Antaisaka (People of the Sand) (Decary and Castel 1941). Since that study, internal migration has increased. Clearly, place is a variable identifier for a Malagasy folk group.

Researchers both in and outside Madagascar have questioned the utility of the idea of tribe. One informant told Emile Birkeli, "You have to remember that today, there are a multitude of tribes erroneously called Sakalava. Only a minority of those are really of Sakalava origin" (370–71). The Malagasy case is presented in general by Jacques Faublée.

> To take as example one region which I know . . . , the Bara are an aggregate of families who came from points all over the south of Madagascar, especially the high valleys of Tomampy and Ionaivo. In those valleys, the large patriarchal families were recognized as subjects of kings from the Zafimanely family. They pushed the former populations before them, including Bara tribes from

previous migration. Once settled, the Bara kings received as their subjects Mahafaly, Tandroy, and Tanala who were fleeing from poverty or excessively harsh sovereigns. All these people who were subjects of Bara kings became Bara. . . . A Tandroy who settled in Bara country in the time of the Zafimanely kings was a Bara. Nowadays, one of his relatives who comes to join him remains Tandroy. Then whether that person is or will be considered Bara or Tandroy by the Bara is something no one can state for certain. . . . The notion of tribe gets lost among the Malagasy. (1943:209–10)

These facts (no researcher is more scrupulous than Faublée) demonstrate the variability of Malagasy identification. The ethnic map of Madagascar is a variable one, existing in people's minds. It embraces large ethnic-political entities which include an image of ways of livelihood: "Merina lands, Betsileo peasants, Sakalava herders, Southern tribes." If they do not assimilate, all new settlers in a region will have to identify them is their "original name"—another mental construct inherited from their past (Faublée 1946:99). Other people's name for them may turn out to be a misnomer. Recent research by Eggert in the southwest of the island reveals that the name for the local people, Mahafaly, "having the ability to taboo," was imposed from the outside and is used by local people only to label themselves for outsiders. Apparently derived from a designation for the land they live in, the word is strictly exoteric.[9] As the eminent anthropologist Georges Condominas has written, "In Madagascar . . . a 'tribe' contains a considerable number of villages depending on a single dialect which gives its name to its neighbor" (1980:43).

Malagasy Creolization

The dialectic between unity and diversity takes place in linguistics; folklore, in the background so far, raises the question of the relevance of creolization. Malagasy culture resulted from creolizing processes in the past, but it also displays such processes in the present. One meaning of the word creole, supported by French dictionaries, is "a child of Europeans in the colonies." Another meaning is such a person's descendants, and Madagascar of course has known such creoles. In the West Indies, the word varies between meaning whites and blacks, but as a euphemism for the offensive "native," it usually refers to persons born in the New World or "what originates in the colonial setting" (Gratiant 1957). In Madagascar, such a native-born "creole" was the greatest historian the island produced,

Raombana, whose long history of his country juxtaposed Malagasy traditions with Enlightenment ideas about reason. His very writing style was
creolized: he expressed himself in images and fixed phrases, as would any
Malagasy *mpikabary*, but drew in and remodeled materials of the English
or Malagasy Bible (Ayache 1979:204). Raombana undertook such fusing
of influences amid much political tension. Queen Ranavalona was simultaneously displaying great hostility toward foreigners and encouraging her
courtiers to record the island's traditions.

More strictly in linguistics, a creole is a new language resulting from
the convergence of existing languages. In a historical moment of intense
contact, elements are combined from several diverse linguistic and cultural
traditions. Most languages in the Indian Ocean cultural area, including
Malagasy, have resulted from creolization or display its processes now.
Languages in Réunion, Mauritius, Diego Garcia, Mayotte, and the Sey-
chelles constitute a family, with a common stock of phonemes (irreducible
sound units with distinctive features and functions). According to one
linguist, though no two Indian Ocean dialects are identical, their similarity
is great enough so that their differences may be considered matters of
choice (Papen 1978). Speakers can adjust their speaking in the direction of
someone else's speaking. Thus Indian Ocean languages display a complex
network of similarities and differences. Where speakers have choice, they
can develop strategy. "Phonological strategies" make a bridge across the
systematic separations between languages and between related linguistic
systems. The result, for the linguist, is that those rules which govern allow-
able sounds (phonological rules) and those which govern acceptable structures (morphological rules) in Indian Ocean creole languages are not
static. The rules are variable, and they are strongly influenced by social and
political factors (Gueunier 1985).

If creolization provides people with variable strategies for speaking,
it can reorganize not only language but all the provinces of culture
touched by language, especially verbal art. And not only those: the Aus-
trian traveler Ida Pfeiffer recorded with ridicule the colors of costumes in
the Merina royal court of 1857. The combination of a blue silk dress with
an orange border, a cherry sash, a sulfur-yellow bodice, and a bright green
shawl excited her laughter; so did the whole spectacle of exaggeratedly
European costumes on stocky Malagasy women. Pfeiffer credited them
with great imitative powers. In general, Malagasy folklore presents a picture much like Zoltán Kodály's rosy description of children's singing
games in Hungary.

Here, like tiny crustaceans in Lake Balaton, the motifs stick together, always in a different way; as in our dreams, when one figure shows the features of two or more people at the same time, the atoms of melodies swarm, unite, and become separated again. It is the eternal secret of folk poetry: the miraculous swarming of atomized entities and of heterogeneous elements clinging together to form new entities. (1974:46–47)

Not that Madagascar is unique in its diversity: Stith Thompson remarked on the "great variety of narrative content" among North America, where "classes of tales flow freely into one another" (1946:299, 303). Every culture presents enormous diversity at close range. Even within the Merina, a group of 1,300,000, a creolized kind of diversity exists, according to ethnographer Louis Molet. Highland Imerina,[10] he says, is permanently fragmented and constantly re-forming itself without impairing its vitality or its functioning. It mixes cosmological systems with each other, its rituals are extremely complicated, its observances and taboos are confusingly complex, and it lacks a coherent Merina mythology. Yet its culture is alive.

It all happens as if many ideas, practices, customs, and terms had entered [Imerina] from the outside from very different horizons, gained acceptance, and become assimilated without entering into any philosophical, dramatic, or mythical synthesis or any integrative rationalization on the part of the actors or participants. One has the impression of looking at disparate bits which were fused somehow by more or less ancient custom, and were finally "Malagasified." It is as if a void were being gradually filled and becoming truly common property, becoming authentically Malagasy, yet with no potentially collective idea that might seek to articulate some systematic organization of the positive assertions by turning them into a cycle of legends, a tragedy, or a discourse. Meanwhile, as in any truly living whole, the elements are ceaselessly changing, the kaleidoscope is turning, the image we see in it is changing, and reorganization continues. (1979:399)

Though Molet maintains a chimerical ideal that the culture ought to be unified by pan-Malagasy mythology or art, he has discovered the extraordinary Merina capacity for maintaining multiplicity. I believe his picture of Merina cultural creolization is true for the whole island, but many authorities disagree.

As ethnography suggests that Malagasy people have multiple affiliations, linguistics suggests that they can move between two or more dialects or registers in their common language. They can summon up "official" Malagasy, or the ritual language associated with ancestral spirits (*vazimba*), or the "speaking in tongues" (glossolalia) heard in rites of possession. In Antananarivo, the capital, and other cities, they are bilingual in Malagasy and French. In a classic instance of a folk speech functioning to resist the pressure of officialdom, the unemployed urban youth of Antananarivo have a semi-secret language known as *zoam*, which operates by reversing syllables and stresses (Domenichini-Ramiaramanana 1977:23).

Is Creolization Still Going On?

Folk speech in Madagascar contains enough evidence of variability to support the hypothesis that Malagasy have cultivated multiplicity and ambiguity as their response to cultural convergence. At the lexical level, a government publication of 1881 carried an average of one French or English word per page of Malagasy (leaving aside religious terms and names for the months). A historian noted during the occupation that "the Malagasy language sometimes hesitates between English and French forms of the same word," simultaneously adopting *militera* and *military* (Chapus 1925:151). Ministers and politicians today mix French words into their Malagasy sentences: "Ny extrémistes no atahorako," It's the extremists I'm afraid of (Calvet 1974), and they model the morphology and vocabulary of their language on French. Lexical mixing occurs too when Malagasy speakers, some of whom have learned their style from European grammars, use a proportion of active verbs that would be more appropriate to English or French than to Malagasy. The label for this mix, "speaking like the missionaries" (Vérin, personal communication), signals that Malagasy are aware of the social forces conditioning speech style.

It is primarily from folk speech that Malagasy children seem to acquire skill in switching registers. In the high bourgeoisie of today, which requires a Merina child to be bilingual, she learns to switch between Malagasy and French.

> Un, deux, trois: c'est gai!
> Et quatre, et cinq, et six: c'est gai!
> O Randria Maola [crazy teacher]
> Maola Firantsa [crazy France]
> Aza mandehandeha [don't move]
> Pas permis
> Pi pan do
> La re mi re mi re do

When the informant for this rhyme had grown up to become the leading scholar in the field of Merina oral literature, she was better able to appreciate the protest content of "crazy teacher, crazy France" (Domenichini-Ramiaramanana 1974). Like the riddles in the next chapter, the rhyme provides its speakers with a dialogic model of social interaction, in which Malagasy, French, music, and nonsense confront each other. As in the West Indies, "ambiguities of cultural reference and of associated expressive and moral meaning pervade symbolic expression and are a focus for constant play and manipulation" (Reisman 1970). The arena for that manipulation is verbal interaction; the content of that play is folklore.

Multiplicity and ambiguity were not, however, produced in Madagascar upon European contact. They were long a feature of Malagasy folklore. Alternative vocabularies, for instance, furnished two or more words to denote the same thing (Sibree 1880). The institution of slavery, terminated by the French in 1896, involved an abundant vocabulary of specialized expressions, part occupational jargon, part alternative lexicon (Molet 1974). In the first quarter of the twentieth century, at least five Malagasy ethnic groups were still observing the custom of prohibiting words that evoked the memory of a memorable person who had died. The substituted word, of course, could not be too esoteric, but it was drawn from a code of conventional metaphors employed for this purpose which each dialect group had devised (Julien 1926). The Merina of 1908–11 said, in their alternative register, that the corpse of a king gave off a pleasant odor. When they entered the chamber where a defunct prince's body was laid out, they would exclaim, "Manitra ny Andriana," The king smells fine! This expression plays on the word *Andriamanitra*, the perfumed god, one of the commonest words for God. Among the Sakalava and Antandroy, plural lexicons have long been available. "Special terms are used to reflect relative placement in a social hierarchy," especially in referring to parts and functions of a chief's or an elder's body (Vérin, Kottak, and Gorlin 1969:34–35). These tabooed words, as Arnold van Gennep recognized long ago, do not constitute a special language, for "they are tabooed only for a fixed time, a few years at most, and . . . the dead king's enemies take no account of the interdiction" (1904:111). The contrast of registers is connected to opposed gender in rural Imerina today. Some Merina men, because they are men, are expected to avoid expressing anger directly in words. Their style of speaking, at least in public, is expected to be more formal and indirect. Women in public (as in the West Indies) are allowed a much less formal, freer, more direct style of address, especially in the market. Men do know the women's register and can drop into it if they choose. But men have, as well, a third register which enables them to shift down the social scale. When driving their cattle (addressees of low status, after all), men make their indirect rejoinder to sixty years of colonial imperatives by barking orders to the cows in French (Keenan 1974).

A symbol for Malagasy creolization in modern times is the poetry of Jean-Joseph Rabearivelo (1903–37), generally esteemed the greatest poet. Rabearivelo was a truly Malagasy amalgam who fused influences from Merina *hainteny* (poems) and folksong with European romanticism. "Sometimes he simply translated well-known [folk] poems, sometimes he altered and adapted them, sometimes he seems to have created original *hain-teny*." Critics who have read no Malagasy poems tend to see Rabearivelo's sense of exile and melancholy as having been "shaped and even largely derived from his reading in French and other European poetry" (Reed and Wake 1975:xviii). It is more significant, though, that he expressed this sense of melancholy through adaptations of Malagasy originals. His first published article was an essay on Malagasy poetry; his final book of poems, "Old Songs from Merina-land," wove together classic, modern, translated, and newly written *hainteny* poems. The combination followed tradition. Any Merina *mpikabary*, man of words,[11] would give his discourse more authority by quoting, adapting, and alluding to traditional lines. Rabearivelo was always a syncretist. At the same time as he was devouring the Spanish language to read the poet Gongora, he devoted immense efforts to modernizing the Malagasy oral history texts Callet had collected in Imerina fifty years before, to make them accessible to a modern reader. As *mpikabary* have assimilated their predecessors, so Rabearivelo absorbed into himself the personalities of Baudelaire, Hugo, Rimbaud, Poe, Casanova, Mallarmé, and generations of Merina poetic reciters and singers. His dependence on his predecessors illustrates the creativity that results from the convergence of cultures. Sadly, that convergence would also kill him: when he could not win a posting to France, he committed suicide (Boudry 1958).

Through writing and publication, Rabearivelo became known to a wider world than earlier *mpikabary*. They bequeathed to him a poetic diction—a selection of words, phrases, and images, specifically associated with formal and poetic speaking (*kabary*). These words, phrases, and images serve to "key" performance (Bauman 1977:15–17). This poetic diction, called riddle language in West Africa by Geneviève Calame-Griaule, is not, in oral cultures, peculiar to poetry, as the English poet Thomas

Gray held it to be in literature. Rather, being associated with certain social functions, it is an alternative register, elicited by circumstance such as courting (Kaivola-Bregenhøj 1978) and marked in Madagascar by an alternative lexicon, a more rapid delivery, and a dignified, serious tone to detach or depersonalize the speaker. Riddle language is found all over Africa (Peek 1981) and southeast Asia (Finnegan 1970, Ottino 1966, Leenhardt 1947, Zahan 1963). What is specific to Madagascar is its tendency to appear in two-sided interactions.

Two-Sided Social Interaction

The four genres treated in subsequent chapters oppose pairs of speakers in a contestatory mode. One model for contestation is the village debate, which at least in former times tended to be two-sided. The impulse to parody, with its opposition of meaning and style, has produced in Madagascar many sayings and proverbs. It has even created mock debates among village men, who played a verbal contest to parody their elders' grave discussions. Literally its name (*mampiady karajia*) means "fighting like a drunk" or "a battle of the intoxicated." When John Richardson was compiling his dictionary, his polite informant, taking on the Protestant mentality, told him it meant "to talk and dispute for the mere purpose of wasting one's time" (Richardson 1885:317). In this game, which bears many analogies to the way *hainteny* poems were tossed back and forth, one man would get up and begin a speech. He would draw his subject from the current activities of the community, but he would also signal the parodic spirit of his discourse with poetic interpolations, in which he would invite his listeners to escape from their daily cares and anxieties. Continuing the game, a second player would reply. Then a third man would speak; presently a lively dialogue was coming from all sides. Though women did not speak, they would listen and applaud. In this setting, the younger men and women could see a model of how to throw dialogues back and forth. Such dialoguing had only to be made into a slightly more professional entertainment to become the prototype of Merina theater (Andriantsilaniarivo 1947).

The two-sided "battle of the drunks" typifies the formalized dialogues I study below and demonstrates the Malagasy habit of binary opposition. The same habit governs the classification of speech registers among the Merina. We may assume that "no normal person, and no normal community, is limited to a single way of speaking," but instead has access to several different ways of speaking (Hymes 1972:38). The Merina group these ways into a characteristically binary division, classifying their registers of speaking into two complementary heads, formal and informal. Informal, everyday talk (*resaka*), associated with women, includes greetings, gossip, requests, calling out, consultations, and discussions. Most of these are forms of dialogue; some are more formalized and stylized than their classification suggests. Formal, heightened speech (*kabary*), practiced by men, includes ceremonial orations used at marriages, burials, bone-turnings (*famadihana*), and circumcisions, as well as royal edicts. By contrasting the two headings, a speechmaker can play with the system. For example, in a formal oration, he can deny that what he is doing is really a formal speech, and call it nothing but *resaka*—private speech that would be spoken at home instead of the public, outdoor, monologic discourse he is practicing (Keenan 1974). To deny that a performer is performing is, in Bauman's performance theory, a sure sign of performance. Though formal speaking used to be dialogic, nowadays people increasingly expect that it will be a monologue by a hired orator. This tendency toward specialization is today's response to the long-growing authoritarianism that entered Merina society two centuries ago (Keenan and Ochs 1979:143–44).

The National Game

The same binary opposition characterizes Malagasy games, which as in so many places are the best models of social interaction, symbolizing values and teaching needed skills and strategies for achieving those values. In Madagascar, the basic word game is riddling; its nonverbal counterpart, which also starts two players at equal rank and also ends with a winner, is the board game *fanorona*. "The ancients . . . named it 'lest we die from blocking.'" A great king called it "God's writing" (Callet 1974, 1:276). The game is played mostly by men, on a rectangular board or flat stone divided into squares and triangles. The pieces are made of complementary materials: one player uses stones, which have been found and are the detritus of nature; the other uses potsherds, which have been made and thrown away and are the debris of culture. The game starts the players in positions of equal power. At first, to a Western eye, it resembles checkers: each player is trying to capture his opponent's pieces, and that aim appears to be integrating the rules and strategies. But metaphor reveals a relation of the players different from that in checkers or chess. I do not *capture* my opponent's pieces; I *eat* them, which suggests that I depend on him rather than destroy him.[12]

> One side eats and the other answers it, and they go on like that, exchanging blow for blow. If neither of the players has anything left to eat, they move their pieces in such a way that they cannot be captured. If it seems that neither will be able to eat, one of the two "gives rice," which means allowing one of his pieces to be taken. The one who gives up a piece in this way expects to eat others from the other side; if he moves his pieces with good tactics, he will unfailingly win the game. His opponent will not be able to move, or know where to put his eaten pieces once they are moved. He loses the game either because not a single piece remains to him or because, though some do remain, there is no more place he can put them. So he loses. (Callet 1974, 1:276)

The metaphor of eating food in *fanorona* suggests that the game is a tool of thought.

In this two-sided game, one learns two tactics for living: to block an opponent and stop his movement, and to give the false impression that one has conceded. These tactics will also be used by the Merina orator when, as spokesman for a bridegroom, he negotiates for a bride. One also learns how to cope with the state of separation entailed by losing. To restore himself to equality, the loser is provided with a rite of reincorporation as a rule of the game. He "eats the remainder," or plays another round, with or without a handicap. "If he moves his pieces well, he will not fail to win another game, or at least the two sides will be even. If they are even, the loser isn't free yet: he will be free only when he wins the game" (Callet 1974, 1:277). The sequence of separation, marginality, and reaggregation, which happens in miniature in this game, is familiar to anthropologists from Arnold van Gennep's rites of passage (1909). To Merina, it is familiar from the moral concept of *tsiny* (reproach), which weighs on a person until he is reincorporated (Andriamanjato 1957). *Tsiny* is inevitable. No one escapes imperfection. The trained speaker will apologize whether he feels inwardly culpable or not (Andriamanjato 1957:16). He will recognize that he has to be fined at least once (Bloch 1971).

Known in many parts of Madagascar in variant forms, *fanorona* is recognized as symbolic of war and associated with kings. Its significance is like that discovered in the Balinese cockfight by Clifford Geertz. According to history, one Merina prince used *fanorona* to plan for war, arranging his slaves, nobles, and freemen like pieces on the board. He is credited with modifying the game into today's best known form. Thus any player today in the streets of Antananarivo can re-enact the princely conquest of lands that will furnish food. The prince's passion for *fanorona*, however, lost him the kingdom. When his father was dying, he answered his death-bed summons by saying to the messengers, "With three [pieces] I'll take five." Appearing more promptly at the bedside of the dying king, the prince's elder brother was awarded the royal succession (Decary 1951: 173–74). Two sayings come out of this event, "Winning with three against five means losing the kingdom," and "Talk makes time lost, *fanorona* makes work forgotten." When a later king, Radama I, came to be crowned in 1810, the plain of Mahamasina below the royal palace was filled with people who had been aligned according to his favorite diagram.[13] The prince's ghost (*ambiroa*) must have been pleased.

In modern times, the great popularity of *fanorona* indicates that it symbolizes the kind of contest valued in Malagasy life. A clear statement of secular Malagasy ethics is found in the semiofficial rule book for the game.

> *Fanorona* is a game which does not necessitate speed, for there are traps everywhere. It is possible to avoid the traps by taking different paths. The philosophy of *fanorona* thus rests on the idea that in life there are always possibilities. The person to whom this relates must discover and utilize these possibilities. A player must not consider that he has lost because one path did not lead to the desired goal; another path will at least lead to a draw. *Fanorona* also teaches not to accept defeat. (Chauvicourt 1984:2)

Neither in *fanorona* nor in debate does the victor seek permanent victory, for that would mean the permanent loss of another member of the community. On this principle, the dual goal of a marriage orator will be both to control the debate and to reconcile two families of opposed interests. The outcome most prized by experienced players is a draw, which is attainable in variant forms (holding three pieces against four, or four against five). Strategy is the same as in riddling or the exchange of *hainteny* (poems): knowledgeable playing requires anticipating the opponent's countermoves. The most brilliant strategy is not direct aggression, but exposing the opponent to attack.

Other two-sided Malagasy board games also symbolize social interaction. The goal, in *fanorona*, of stopping one's opponent from moving also dominated a Tanala adaptation of chess called *samantsy*, played two generations ago or more but now apparently defunct. Though its moves and pieces were obviously of foreign origin, the Tanala (Forest People) renamed the ranks according to Malagasy social classes. They also made one alteration in the rules, which remodeled chess into a game without a loser. If the *hova* pieces (kings) were not captured, they could not capture each other (Decary 1951:174). And other board games, like *katra* (well known all over Africa under names such as *bao*), which in Imerina is played more by women, also streamline the social interactions of life into a two-sided contest. Modeling fundamental Malagasy values, two-sided board games illustrate complementarity by distinguishing two kinds of pieces and separating winner from loser. At the same time they illustrate symmetry in their strategy, since each player aims at blocking the other. Moreover, no player undertakes his risks alone. In cockfighting, which is also a popular sport for men, only two cocks can fight; in a marriage debate, only two spokesmen can actually speak. In *fanorona*, though only two players can move the pieces, several bystanders are involved as partisans if not bettors. "It's the same as with bullfights," said the Merina of a century ago. "Only two men are holding the pieces of stone and potsherd, but five or seven men are in with them. If one party loses the game, each of these many individuals gives a sum to the winner" (Callet 1974, 1:278). In both its two-sided combat and its inclusion of others, *fanorona* is a nonverbal model for achieving power.

The dialogues I shall discuss in subsequent chapters display the formal features of *fanorona*: participation by two players or voices, a challenge by one to the other, a distinct time and place for play, and a strategy guiding the performer to discover and use alternative possibilities. Riddling, proverbing, exchanging *hainteny*, and formal speechmaking are all games in the formal sense defined by Brian Sutton-Smith. Some of their formal features are also found in folktales. The marriage debate, for instance, symbolizes a setback which the bride's family poses against the groom: the family makes a show of opposing its daughter's departure. In many Malagasy folktales, the hero encounters some setback before achieving his final satisfactory condition (tales numbered 1.5 in *Malagasy Tale Index*). Most important, verbal consciousness in Madagascar always has two voices. Formalized complementary dialogue streamlines the innumerable voices of the world into a contrastive pair. Odd numbers are unlucky, because they are incomplete; even numbers, being complete, symbolize connectedness (Domenichini 1977). Art exists to stylize the multiplicity of voices into the dialogue of a pair of speakers, and to register the conflict between contestation and harmony.

2. Riddling: Question and Answer

The Smallest Dialogue

What connections might exist between the continent of Africa and the island of Madagascar, only 260 miles away? Historians such as Kent (1970) have found such connections, usually culture traits like loan words. In expressive culture, the most significant link is that Madagascar, like so many African societies, highly values the artistic uses of words. Geneviève Calame-Griaule (1963) groups these uses together as "riddle language." Malagasy riddle language is the subject of this book. Generically, the smallest, simplest dialogue in Malagasy oral literature is the riddle. Names for it are *ankamantatra*, what is to be found out, and *fampanononana*, something said to cause something else to be said. This latter term is a Malagasy folk equivalent to what discourse analysts call "solicitation" (Sinclair and Coulthard 1975). The riddle form is question and answer, or, since the first part is not always grammatically interrogative, precedent and sequent (Harries 1971). The larger dialogues, *hainteny* ("art of the word," courting poems), *kabary* (formal speaking, oratory), and proverbs (*ohabolana*) use the same two-part form, complicating but not obscuring it. Malagasy folklore possesses a unique form of double riddle, the *safidy* (choice). I discuss the riddle first because it is a kernel structure that unites dialogic performance with dialogic structure. The more complex genres separate dialogic or two-sided structure from their interaction situation, which may or may not be dialogic. The *hainteny* portrays dialogue but may be performed by two persons or one; the *ohabolana*, representing an authoritative answer to a previous utterance or interaction, is basically monologic. Into this category, known as *fitenin-drazana*, sayings of the ancestors, history has introduced a conflict between monologue and dialogue.

In performance in Madagascar as in Africa, riddling and storytelling traditionally form parts of the same communicative event. One of the LMS missionaries reported from his time in the south, "Often have I sat by the village or camp fire, as the case might be, while the men, and women also, if any were present, squatted around enjoying the early hours of the evening, telling tales (fables) and putting conundrums" (Last 1889). Another link to Africa is that a riddling session and the individual riddles are introduced by such verbal formulas as "What is this?" (Sibree 1890). Like the many west Africans studied by Calame-Griaule, Malagasy "are extremely sensitive, even in everyday speaking, to dialect differences, grammatical correctness, appropriate vocabulary, eloquent linking of sentences, and the use of metaphor" (1963:74). When language is to be used artistically, as in riddling or poetry, it becomes a means of simultaneously hiding and revealing thought so as to convey delicate and dangerous matters. Also, being deliberately beautiful, artistic speaking is a form of politeness. Through its double meanings, moreover, artistic speaking becomes a game, testing intelligence and quick wit. Those who understand it feel "in the know" and are glad to be so, while those who do not are excluded. All these features of the "riddle language" which Calame-Griaule and her colleagues have observed among the Somono, Bambara, and Peul of Mali, as well as the celebrated Dogon (Calame-Griaule 1986) and other west African peoples, are prominent in Madagascar as well. The most accessible Malagasy genre through which to observe artistic language is the riddle.

Riddling is especially practiced by children. The published literature shows its important developmental function. It directs their attention to mastering the speech code, with all the double meanings and wittiness it contains. Perhaps it is the special task of Malagasy folklore to convey messages about the Malagasy language. In addition to this metalinguistic task, riddling has a poetic function: it directs the attention of children to a certain message form comprising precedent and sequent. Particularly in Imerina, the central highland province, riddling emphasizes the closure that occurs when an answer follows a riddle question. Children learn the symbolic importance of question and answer through riddling, among other, less playful forms of interchange. So they come to see how important it is to master the art of dialogue, to have an answer ready. At marriages and funerals, they also observe the great respect given to an artistic speaker (*mpikabary*). Like other games, riddling in Madagascar constitutes a small-scale folk model for a dialogic pattern that pervades much other verbal art.

Malagasy are not alone in making use of riddling and other childlore as a learning model for the complexities of language. All over Africa and the Indian Ocean, as all over the world, linguistic routines or repertoires—sequences more complex than the sentence—are provided to children as means to develop communicative skill and as material for them to parody. The child learns not only to recall lexical items, but also to produce them in a way that is artistically marked, for instance by rhyme or by rhythmic parallelism. In many of these cultures, he or she may need to know how natural it is to switch from one code or style to another. Variation among codes is the rule rather than the exception among Indian Ocean and Southeast Asian peoples. The Thai, for example, have for many years had occasion to put up with English-speaking strangers. They practice rhyming word games that provide for their children's linguistic needs by reinforcing knowledge of both Thai and English. One of these, the rhyming translation game observed by Mary R. Haas (1957), involves displaying skill in alternating between the two languages by rhyming them. The player "gives a Thai word and its English translation. The next player must produce another Thai word which rhymes with the English translation of the first word" (174). Players who cannot master the two lexicons coexisting in their language field are gradually eliminated, as riddlers are eliminated in Madagascar and Africa. The game imparts to Thai children the mastery of two alternative codes. It makes an art of switching between the two; it rewards the capacity to do so with laughter. As riddling promotes the African or Malagasy child to higher status, the rhyming translation game initiates the Thai child into that prestigious community of those who can play with two codes. Other Southeast Asian and Indian Ocean parallels can and will be found. And others still: such bicultural competence exists among, for instance, chicano children in the United States (McDowell 1979: 164–65).

Riddle Collecting in Imerina and Elsewhere

Of the three hundred or so riddles recorded in Madagascar, at least two-thirds were collected in the central highlands in the nineteenth century (Richardson 1876, Dahle 1877, Ferrand 1893, Grandidier 1908). Thus in riddling as in other folklore genres, the ethnic group that appears to predominate is the most influential, best documented, and largest—the Merina, who make up one-seventh of the population. If this predominance is not simply an accident of folklore collecting, it is attributable to Merina social structure. This group, being more hierarchical than others, offers a test of Roberts and Forman's hypothesis (1972) that riddling is correlated with social structure. In this view, riddling is a model of the questioning process. It is invented, within a stratified society, to demonstrate, teach, and comment on how persons of higher rank interrogate persons of lower rank. Old Malagasy society, especially in Imerina, divided people into three classes, *andriana*, nobles, *hova*, freemen, and *andevo*, slaves. Inequality among classes was projected onto a superhuman ranking of God, *zavatra* (the spirits governing sorcery and divination) and *vazimba* (ancestors with special power). Inequality also governed all social relations, and traces of the class division can still be observed today (Domenichini 1973). In the central highlands, after the time of the powerful Andrianampoinimerina, the Merina imposed themselves on other ethnic groups with the aid of arms supplied by the British and French, thus putting intergroup struggle on a larger scale (Deschamps 1972:149–223). This history of vertical integration internally and conquest externally has required Merina society to come to terms with the ambiguities of status and age that crop up in any hierarchical society, for instance when persons of different classes marry each other.

Another reason the Merina are good at riddling is the verbal play which the game involves. Having been noted for their verbal skill since the beginnings of European contact, they might well be expected to enjoy this element. Even the diehard colonial Berthier had to admit that the Merina had a culture of "prodigious imagination" in the verbal realm: "On a favorite theme, they embroider at will. They speak abundantly for hours, and discuss gladly but always courteously. Their speeches, generally very long, are sprinkled with proverbs. Commonplaces and clichés abound, to the greater pleasure of the audience" (1933:26).

In other groups, interest in riddles on the part of collectors in the island has not been very consistent. One cannot tell whether all the other dialect groups (formerly called tribes) perform this genre. The Antandroy (People of the Thorn Bush; at least twenty-five thousand), Antankarana (People of the Rocks; at least thirty-five thousand), and Tsimihety (Those Who Do Not Cut Their Hair; at least four hundred thousand), may practice riddling but appear to lack this genre, since ethnographers have not told us. Collectors also have not yet adopted the practice of telling us when riddling is absent from a culture, as they might. The published data, however, have much to say, and I hope future fieldworkers will augment the data and test my interpretations.

Riddling is a distinct game. The language of riddling, with its emphasis on wit and the connecting of unrelated things, is one end of a continuum. The Merina call this indirect, formal, witty language *kabary*, the name they also use for the genre of orations and for the public occasions which elicit formal speech. In public *kabary* is usually spoken by men, who show respect to their questioners by means of polish, artistry, and emphasis (Keenan 1974). Ordinary talk (*resaka*) lies at the other end of the continuum. In conversation, when not performing riddles, Merina, like other Malagasy, have their own style of answering questions. Some people find the style too full of circumlocutions.

> To the simple question, "Did you go to the village you planned to visit on Sunday?," the Malagasy will answer immediately with the greatest naturalness, "The weather wasn't as nice as we hoped. Also we couldn't leave until the middle of the afternoon, which didn't allow us to visit my wife's cousin, who has been in bed for several days." And if one adds, "Does this cousin live far away?," he will answer without cracking a smile, "A person walking fairly fast will probably reach her house in the time it takes to cook a pot of rice." (Le Garreres and Ranaivo 1949)

This answer conveys much information, doubtless more than some Europeans in colonial days wanted to hear. The exasperation of French colonists at this lavish style of conversation probably arose from their desire to hear only the "relevant" facts. But is this exchange an instance of *resaka*, ordinary talk? The speaker's answer is relatively formal: for instance, he quotes a well-known simile for measuring elapsed time. To quote in this way marks him as someone who knows how to connect his speech with the speaking community of the ancestors. Yet in the colonial period, the unexpected formality of such speaking was sometimes perceived as a form of lying. The writers of this example state, "The emphatic tone which the 'orator' has thus managed to give his answer, forestalling even the slightest contradiction, is in his eyes well worth a little bending of the truth" (Le Garreres and Ranaivo 1949:78). Knowing how to answer a question politely, in formal style, marks the speaker as a person who commands language, whatever his social rank.

Metaphorical Riddles

Children's riddling does not demand as much sophisticated control of language as that man's answer. Still, it locates the art of clever speaking firmly in a dialogic context. Many Malagasy riddles consist of an elaborate metaphorical question and an answer that may be only one word. These riddles ask the "riddlee" to see the literal base for the metaphor.

Perfume from the forest.—Ginger.

The grease [fat] of wood.—Honey. (Dahle 1877:418, Ferrand 1893:256–57)

Such a metaphorical riddle is very familiar to Europeans. It may have been favored by collectors in Madagascar, for in continental Africa, some collections (Blacking, Gowlett) offer hardly any other structure under the name of riddle. What is being tested is the respondent's knowledge of either a single answer deemed to be traditional, or an answer the poser is willing to accept (Huizinga 1955:105–18). Within the dialogue of poser and riddlee lies a dialogue of levels of language: the metaphorical language of the question is answered by the literal language of the last word. Seen as mere intellectual puzzles, the simplest metaphorical riddles test the riddlee's capacity to recognize, in figurative language, the principal economic and ritual centers of Imerina.

Perched high with good dikes.—Antananarivo.

Perched high where there are beautiful shadows.—Ambohimanga. (Dahle 1877:417, Ferrand 1893:255)

The knowledge tested by these metaphorical riddles may be only linguistic, unless in performance they are transferred into some metaphorical context which collectors have not told us about. A related metalinguistic play appears in the following riddle from the People of the Island (Antanosy), in the south, about their neighbors to the west, the People of the Long Valley (Sakalava): "Its length and breadth can be said in one word.—Sakalava" (Richardson 1876). The single word *Sakalava* (*saka*, side, *lava*, long) meaning both the people and their territory, suffices to answer the longer question. Such is the power of the word in the right place, especially as the essential second part of a dialogue.

Metaphorical riddles proliferate in Madagascar: "Its foot is above its leg.—The leaves of the *horirika*" (Dahle 1877:59, trans. Sibree 1890:175). The *horirika* is an edible arum with a broad leaf. As its leaf is to its stalk, so is a human foot to a leg. Several riddles join plants and human beings in their metaphors.

The king's child is not slapped on the head.—The prickly pear.

The king's child looks down from above.—Bananas.

God's stick has water in its stomach.—Sugarcane.

Five men with round hats.—Fingers. (Last 1889)

The metaphors for the thorny plant and the great head of bananas hanging from its stalk connect nature and humanity. Animal and human worlds are connected in riddles too.

White chicks filling a hole.—Teeth in the mouth. (Dubois, 1938:1354)

My grandmother's ox bellows day and night.—A waterfall. (Decary 1924:358)

Malagasy riddles teach children the inevitable ambiguity and multiple meanings in language. In any riddle, "an ambivalent word, concept or item of behaviour can be considered as belonging to any of two or more frames of reference, according to the interpretation brought to bear upon it, or indeed to several or all such frames at once" (Hamnett 1967:381–82).

As a developmental device, riddling can be said to provide Malagasy with one culturally determined means of learning how to manipulate verbal ambiguity (McDowell:221–42). Riddles are especially well suited to bringing such ambiguities into the foreground by their spirit of play. Risks of reproach are confined to the verbal realm. The penalties are part of a game in which learning about ambiguities can accompany something titillating.

Something mixed up with a person's name.—Basket [*vaha*, a woman's name], or [alternative answer] sweet potato [*makinty*, a woman's name]. (Last 1889)

Either answer attests to the multiplicity of meanings. The person who gives the right answer has learned that language is ambiguous and that he can control its ambiguities. Behind the play of the game lies reference to a rule for euphemism within the linguistic code itself, which provides an alternative register. Seen from a psychological point of view, riddling makes allusion to the unmentionable (Gaignebet, Wolfenstein, Todorov 1978). This practice of metaphorical allusion receives reinforcement in Madagascar from euphemism and name-changing. In former times at least, people would allude to the name of a dead chief by means of euphemisms. Words forming part of a chief's name, either at the time of his death or from the time he took power, were forbidden. By avoiding those words and substituting others, speakers could allude to the dead without seeming to do so until the forbidden word could come back into use. When the Merina monarch Ralambo took power in the seventeenth century, the word *lambo* (boar) was forbidden, being temporarily replaced by *kazana* (shark) or *Rabiby*, Mr. Animal. "So," an aged informant told Father Callet, "he let only cattle, sheep, and goats come into the village, and the people were forbidden to speak the word *lambo* in the village" (Callet 1974, 1:124). These euphemisms were a stylistic alternative, not a permanent substitute. After Ralambo's death, *lambo* again became available.

Inevitably, it seems to me, such a regularized use of alternative language would be bound to educate members of the speech community toward a capacity for varying their speech. Euphemism is a form of style-switching governed wholly by nonlinguistic forces. Only social and political forces could bring it into play. As groups are set apart by dialect, they are also set apart by class. It used to be thought that the three Merina classes before the conquest—nobles, freemen, slaves—all had their own class vocabulary. Now, however, after examining these and related switchings, the linguist Jacques Dez has refuted that older view (1969). The reality behind what looked like a special vocabulary for the sovereign was nothing but a switch between styles. Still today, as we saw in the example of conversational answering above, what prevails is the capacity for switching. Metaphorical riddles model that capacity when they call one thing by the ordinary name for another. The choice was and is beween more polite turns of style, closer to the *kabary* (formal) end of the continuum, or less polite ones, closer to the *resaka* (informal) end. This choice is freely guided by consideration of the personality of the speaker or the subject being handled. To manage this choice, the speaker needs to command alternative lexicons which, in a playful realm, are the province of riddling.

Accordingly, in this context of allusion and style-switching, we find riddles of social commentary which use metaphor to play with what is inexpressible. Such riddles allude to social facts by referring directly to speech.

> A big ricefield surrounded by solid dikes.—Freemen [a reference to the nineteenth-century hova class, specifically to those of high rank around the ruler].

> He who stays above the town gate.—The judge [who sees and knows those who go in and out].

> Old man leaning on the wall.—Boiled rice [because it sticks to the sides of the pot].

> Ordinary marriage.—Rice and herbs. (Dahle 1877:417–18, Ferrand 1893:255–57, Dubois 1938:1353)

Mixing rice and herbs produces a humdrum but not tasty meal; like many husbands and wives, the two are of little use to each other.

Identifying Riddles by Their Structures

Studying riddling outside Madagascar, folklorists such as Ian Hamnett, Elli Köngäs Maranda, and Charles T. Scott insist correctly on defining the riddle as incorporating both answer and question. To classify the world's huge array of riddles and thus make the definition more exact, a structural definition has been devised by Robert A. Georges and Alan Dundes. This structural approach distinguishes oppositional from nonoppositional riddles and subdivides these categories. In an earlier essay (1974), I proved its utility for analyzing African riddles. The examples given above were all nonoppositional; I move now to oppositional riddles, those that depend for their effect on stating contradictions.

Structural definitions can often reveal a cultural preference, and so it happens in Madagascar. Among the subdivisions of oppositional riddles which Georges and Dundes have devised, Malagasy show a strong preference for one type. By far the largest number of collected Malagasy riddles belong to what Georges and Dundes call the privational contradictive type, in which "the second of a pair of descriptive elements is a denial of a logical or natural attribute of the first" (115). Not all contradictive riddles are privational: another kind is "antithetical," stating an opposition explicitly in words: "'Strike with the flat of your hand,' says the mother. 'Strike with your fist,' say the children.—The frond of a fern." A third kind of contradictive riddle is causal, denying an expected consequence: "Cut but no wound.—Water" (Richardson 1876).

In contrast, privational riddles shock the sensibilities by making important use of knowledge the hearer is assumed to have. Such allusiveness asserts and reinforces the sharing of knowledge between riddler and respondent. By performing such a riddle, a Malagasy speaker establishes his connection with the traditions of ancestral, dialogic discourse. For instance, the riddle will deny the main function of a common object. Everyone knows that a rock is used to dry rice; everyone knows about swimming in lakes and about common household crafts.

> God's little rock on which you can't dry rice.—A toenail or fingernail.

> God's little bag, its stitching can't be seen.—An egg.

> God's little lake, you can't swim in it.—The eye. (Richardson 1876)

It is in this sense that riddles play with cognitive boundaries, creating tension by denying the familiar function of a familiar object (Köngäs Maranda 1971, Lieber 1976). At the same time, they signal their metaphorical, alternative character in the word *kely*, little, as a reduplicated form would do in language. Privational contradictive riddles are used in Madagascar to comment on the social hierarchy. In them, children symbolize all those of low rank. Identifying with these imaginary children, the players (children themselves) are licensed to violate vicariously the normal limits of child behavior.

> Little one dwells in an iron house.—The tongue.

> Little one is bold to the queen.—A fly. (Richardson 1876)

> Little one isn't afraid to enter the king's house.—The louse. (Dubois 1938 : 1353)

Gird up the little one's loins, for he will fight.—A needle. (Dahle 1877 : 45, Richardson 1876)

In each of these riddles, the "little one," either a child or a person of low status, acts above his rank.

When the little one comes, the great one takes off his hat.—The great water pot [in a house]. (Dahle 1877 : 63, trans. Sibree 1890 : 175)

Sibree explained the literal image: for water to be drawn with a horn or tin ladle, the straw cover, made from the same material as a hat, is removed from the cistern. A similar reversal of rank is stated in: "Small thing knows how to leap.—A leech" (Dahle 1877 : 63, trans. Sibree 1890 : 175). Sibree commented that a leech seems to leap from the ground or the grass when it fastens itself to the bare legs of people passing by.

Such texts suggest that in Madagascar as elsewhere, riddling is a game in which power relationships are reversed. Reversing the ranks in fantasy, the players become aware of the stratification of the social system. Such an interpreter as William Bascom (1954) will say that this kind of folklore keeps the social order stable by providing an outlet in the game for potentially subversive impulses. A Bakhtinian interpretation will say that the laughter of riddling stands in opposition to the official class system, represented by the cognitive order, and that riddling thus permanently mocks the social order (Bakhtin 1968). The preference of Malagasy for privational contradictive riddles lends support to Bakhtin's approach, if we accept observers' statements that Malagasy people keep their subversive feelings to themselves. When the riddle portrays a dramatic scene of role reversal, the player inverts high and low ranks in a game that is safe, contained, and socially approved. But who knows, and who will ever know, what private mockery or subversion the game contained for its players?

Contexts and Frames for Riddles

Such use of dialogue for wish fulfillment is more visible when riddles are framed inside other genres such as folktales. Wish-fulfillment, of course, underlies the appeal of many an international tale. For instance, there is The King and the Peasant's Son, which was recorded six times in Madagascar between 1907 and 1956. As this tale opens, the clever boy hero is being interrogated by an adult in authority, either a noble or chief. Impertinently the clever boy answers in metaphorical riddles. The key motif, "Clever youth answers king's inquiry in riddles," is used in Madagascar (as in Africa) to establish the hero's potency by equating it with verbal prowess. In Europe, "the whole interest of this tale" for a hearer lies not in the skills of the boy, but in the content of the riddles themselves (Thompson 1946:160). In Africa and Madagascar, however, the tale shows the close connection between adult male authority and power in *kabary*. Its issue is status. Riddling behavior here is a model, not of how to ask questions, but of how to answer them if you can get away with it. Not everyone can.

One full version will show how Malagasy narrators frame riddles into a tale. From the Betsileo (The Invincible Multitude), rice cultivators living on the plateau south of the Merina, comes this version of The King and the Peasant's Son (Dubois 1938:1341–43). The name of the boy protagonist, Indevo (Slave), indicates that childhood and low rank can signify the same thing. The adult male authority figure is a courtier who has come to collect a debt from Indevo's father.

> The courtier asked him, "Where are the people of this house?"
> The boy answered, "Who is it you are looking for?"
> "Where is your father?" the courtier went on.
> Little Indevo answered, "He's looking for money, actually. If he sees a butterfly, he'll go to your house; if he doesn't see one, he won't go to your house. Success goes to the swift."
> "Where is your mother?" the courtier went on.
> "My mother is looking for a thousand captives."
> "Where is your eldest brother?"
> "My brother is doing a job that never ends."
> "Where is your other brother?"
> "He is collecting grass that has been thrown away."
> "And what are you doing?"
> "I'm standing up, I'm making something, I'm amusing myself, and what I've made doesn't suit me any more."
> "You are making fun of me," the courtier then said.
> "I'm not making fun of you," said little Indevo.
> "Because your father owes me money and I come to claim it, you are making fun of me. I am going to accuse the lot of you before [king] Andriambohoemanana.[1] I won't let myself be insulted by a brat."

End of scene 1; the boy has put himself in jeopardy by his skill with words, a realistic outcome. Any attentive hearer could tell by this point that the tale is structured like a riddle. This scene (a precedent) has posed a problem to the hero, and scene 2 (a sequent) will resolve them. The same structure of disequilibrium/equilibrium underlies many folktales (numbered 1 in *Malagasy Tale Index*; Dundes 1964:61–64). Moreover, reported speech is crucial to the hero's repeating of traditional-sounding metaphors and to the plot. In scene 2, the reporting of the dialogue of scene 1 leads to high rank for such a skillful speaker.

> With that the courtier made his way to Andriambohoemanana. "Be blessed above all the blessed! Prince, a child has been disrespectful to me, and I won't stand for it. Therefore I accuse him before you."
>
> Andriambohoemanana summoned the boy. "Did you really insult this man?"
>
> "Not at all."
>
> "What did you say to him?"
>
> "This morning, when he came to our house, he asked me where my father was, and I answered, 'He's looking for money, actually. If he finds any, he pursues it like a butterfly and goes to find you; if he doesn't find any, he doesn't go to find you. Success is for those who go to some trouble for it.' Then he asked me where my mother was, and I said, 'She is looking for a thousand captives,' which means when she finds some rice, she takes some; when she finds some manioc, she takes some. She takes what she finds. She takes a thousand captives. As for my eldest brother, I said he was doing a job that's never finished. The job that's never finished is keeping cattle, for our grandparents kept cattle, and we'll always go on keeping them. The younger one was looking for grass to lose; that's what I call straw for burning, because what comes into the house you lose and you go outside to find it. I answered, 'I'm standing up, I'm making something, I'm amusing myself, and soon I no longer like what I made.' What I meant was modeling figures out of clay."

The chief appreciates these riddles (maybe he especially appreciates that pretended obscene one at the end) and promises to pay the father's debt. The boy joins his entourage as an expert in symbolic interpretations, a kind of Joseph (Dubois 1938:1341–43). In other versions, he rebukes one absurdity with another and is rewarded for his wit (1.6.921 in *Malagasy Tale Index*).

By framing riddles into its narration, The King and the Peasant's Son realistically shows that a person skilled in the arts of metaphor and allusive speech will be rewarded by Malagasy society (Keenan and Ochs 1979:143), as he is in African societies (Blacking 1961:4). The boy's verbal prowess and his expertise in metaphor bring about his rise in status from child to man and from slave (Indevo) to servant of nobles (*ondevohova*). This is the reward of being a man-of-words. Indevo's answers are a fantastic opposite to how the ordinary child should answer questioners. To save him, metaphor in his speech must be validated by the power structure. Similarly, in "neck riddle" stories, a character saves his neck by posing a riddle only he can solve (Abrahams 1980). In life, any child riddler takes power by posing an unanswerable question.

As a context for riddling, then, this tale shows the game to be a training for authority and a comic alternative to the conventional power relations. Riddle language poses the courtier's literal questions, belonging to the realm of *resaka*, ordinary talk, against Indevo's metaphorical answers, which belong to *kabary*, formal speech. More broadly, such a tale symbolizes any person's transfer from the group he descended from into an affiliate group (Kottak 1980:165–77). The clever youth's riddling answers are feats of strength that mark the maturing of a young hero. With its dramatization of the hero's successful combat against a father figure, its inversion of power relations, the high value it places on artistic speaking, and its portrayal of the amusement of riddling, it is no wonder the tale is popular all over the island. The folktale also provides one example of the strong preference in Malagasy folklore for embedding one dialogic genre in another. Four riddles are enacted in the dialogue between the boy and the courtier. This habit of embedding one recognizable utterance in another is the favorite device of Malagasy verbal art. Riddles are incorporated into poems, proverbs are quoted in poems, and all are quoted in marriage orations.

Privational Contradictive Riddles

Though they are but one of the several kinds of Malagasy riddle, privational contradictive riddles carry more semantic weight than Indevo's metaphorical one-liners. They depend heavily on shared knowledge, which they undermine by splitting apart images that are conventionally a unity.

> Can't be cooked, can easily be roasted.—Hair.

> Has a mouth to eat, but no stomach to digest.—Scissors.
> (Richardson 1876)

A man of words usually stands before his audience to engage in dialogue.

> He who stands up, yet whom one questions in vain.—The center
> post of the house. (Dahle 1877:417, trans. Ferrand 1893:256)

The center post, though it stands before us like a *mpikabary*, can take no part in life's dialogues.

> Has many shields and many spears, but can't defend wife and
> children.—A lemon tree.

The spears and shields, Last explained, "refer to the thorns of the tree and the hard green rind of the fruit."

> Six legs and two soles.—Money scales.

Scales used for weighing money, Sibree explained, always had "three strings [legs] for each pan, which is called . . . its 'tongue,' but in the riddle is compared to a foot" (175).

This kind of riddle is preferred by Malagasy riddlers, I surmise, because its particular contradiction goes against their world view and plays with it. All African riddles evoke "contrasting classifications and conceptual frameworks" (Hamnett 1967:382). These riddles contradict the interdependence that is so important in Malagasy world view. One writer, Richard Andriamanjato, has seen in Merina thought a sense of connection to the vastness of all creation, entailing a keen sensitivity to the logical and natural attributes of objects (18–20). What is taken away, in a privational riddle, is an attribute that is necessary to that sense of connection. "A big house with no roof.—The cattle pen" (Last 1889). Moreover, these riddles constitute an artistic metalanguage, which continually declares the importance of tacit understanding, the sense of connection between speakers which life constantly threatens. People's clothes communicate their connection to one another; a century ago, people wore coarse, sometimes dirty clothes next to their skin, and put on over those the fine white cloth of the *lamba* (shawl). A privational contradictive riddle reverses that image: "Coarse rofia cloth outside, white inside.—Manioc," which, said Sibree, has "brown skin but white floury substance." Similarly, marriage contains the contradiction of spouses who don't get along: "Lying on the same pillow, but not on the same bed.—The rafters of a roof." Sibree (who had been a housebuilder in his English youth) pointed out that rafters "lean on the same ridge-piece (or pillow), but rest (that is, the opposite sides) on different wall-plates, or beds."

Other Contradictions and the Dilemma

In Madagascar, what Georges and Dundes call causal contradictive riddles, in which the expected consequence of something is denied, are not numerous. Still, the notion that actions have consequences is fundamental to Merina ethics, with its favorite proverb, "Retribution does not exist, but what is done comes back on you." Thus some riddles do play with categories of thought by denying consequences.

Living on fat, but not getting fat.—A lamp.

Buried but not rotten.—Hair.

Cut down, not withering.—Hair.

Dead before it begins to bluster.—A drum [referring to the calfskin of which drums are made].

Cut but not wounded.—Water.

Not thrown, not pitched, but going far.—The eye.

Not hurled, not twisted, but it reaches, it reaches.—The mind (or thought). (Richardson 1876, Grandidier 1908:140, Dahle 1877:60)

All these riddles are esoteric, to the extent that they refer to knowledge the riddler and riddlee are expected to share. More caustic social commentary licensed by the riddling game is found in an inversion of the life cycle, "Toothless when young, fat when old.—The moon" (Richardson 1876:247). But often the contradiction is entirely a matter of two words: "Cannot be carried but can easily be moved.—The road" (Dahle 1877:58, Grandidier 1908:140). All such riddles set ways of speaking in opposition to each other. These two exemplify what Georges and Dundes classify as "antithetical contradictive riddles." This type sets up a symmetrical contradiction between two ways of speaking. Their antithesis dramatizes contradictions in speech which, like Indevo's riddles, invert power relations.

> The mother says, "Go straight up," the children say "Let's go crosswise."—A ladder.

> The mother says, "Strike with the flat of your hand," the children say, "Strike with your fist."—The frond of a fern. (Dahle 1877:61, Grandidier 1908:140, Dubois 1938:1354)

Such antitheses could well remind a hearer of dilemma proverbs and folktales, in which a victim is caught between two courses of action, both of which bring blame. No one can avoid violating *fady*, taboo, or incurring *tsiny*, reproaches. One proverb says, "Go forward, grandmother dies; go back, grandfather dies." One favorite structure for proverbs is a kind of veiled riddle; it connects the situation being commented on with an image, then explains the image in an antithesis. "Like the eggs of the *anganga* [legendary bird]: left alone, they kill your grandfather; taken away, they kill your grandmother" (Houlder 1960:8). In performance, the opening image of eggs evokes a riddle question: "How is this life-situation or person like the *anganga's* eggs?" The explanation uses antithetical form.

The victim of such a dilemma is the suffering protagonist of a tale, which gives the origin for an antithetical saying.

> The guinea-fowl, it is said, went to visit his relations beyond the forest; but when he came to the thick of the woods he turned giddy and fell, and broke his wing. Then he lamented thus: "I would go on, go on, but cannot: yet if I go back, I long for my relations."

> So that, they say, is the origin of the proverbial saying, "Guinea-fowl in the midst of the forest: go forward, he can't; go back, wing broken; stay there, longs for his relatives." (Dahle 1877:298, trans. Sibree 1883:314; tale 2.1.121 in *Malagasy Tale Index*)

Such proverbs and tales model their two symmetrical parts on the dilemma. By contrast, dilemma tales, as performed in Madagascar and Africa, transpose their dialogism into the rules whereby they are performed. The narrator, playing the role of riddle poser, sets a problem which the audience, as respondent, must debate (Bascom 1975; tales numbered 1.4 in *Malagasy Tale Index*).

Dialogic Games

Along with these riddles, children learn another linguistic routine in life. They learn to imitate adult formal conversational devices as a game. Children always imitate, of course. Believing the Merina to be perfect imitators and expecting an undeveloped people to be highly conservative, Europeans have sometimes seen these games and amusements of Merina children as mere imitations of adult life. Indeed they are toy versions of routinized adult interactions, but in Madagascar they teach a higher register of speaking. They teach parody.

> With a handful of clay they build a little house. They imitate a little market, where they carry out transactions, sometimes very noisily, using pebbles as coins. They dig tiny ricefields complete with canals. In the game of *kifatifaty* [play death], it is funerals that are the object of amusement. A miniature tomb is built of earth. In it the boys bury a locust, in the role of the deceased, while the girls sing songs. (Decary 1951:167)

Verbal imitation accompanies the imitation of custom in a popular Merina amusement, folk puppetry.

> On the plateau [Merina and Betsileo country], boys and girls somewhat more advanced in age practice *tomabo*, the conversation game, with a seriousness worthy of adults. In this they use either round seeds and sticks of wood or, in more recent years, marbles and twisted glass rods sold in the market. The marbles represent women, the rods men. Manipulating these objects, the partners bring them closer together and farther apart, imitating a social call by carrying on a connected conversation. (ibid.)

The conversation game, like riddling, functions as a folk model for dialogue. Children will trace a playhouse on the ground by the side of the road and orient it like their own, with its main door to the west, its hearth to the north, and its ancestors' corner to the northeast. Bits of white, yellow, green, and blue glass (*tomaboko, tamaboka*) represent adults more directly than the pieces in *fanorona*. Women are represented by the big pieces, men by polished rods. The variable rules of the game allow players to take alternative roles according to circumstance or quick decision. Sometimes one piece represents one man or woman; at other times, a single pair of players will play several different parts, changing as they go along. A single player can even perform the drama alone. All these variations between monologue and dialogue have counterparts in the reciting of poetry, as we shall see below. Usually each player, holding a single piece, would imitate formalized adult dialogue.

> "Good day, madam. How is your health?"
> "Very well, thank you, and how is your health?"
> "We are all very well. And how is the health of your husband? How are your child and your little baby?"
> "Very well—they are all very well, I thank you." (ibid.)

Older persons who are watching will chuckle. Then the conversation game prescribes a metalinguistic reference to the formal code it imitates, citing a proverb.

> "And now that the greetings are over with, what is the news from your place?"
> "Everything is quiet at our place. Mrs. ____ has just had a baby."
> "Boy or girl?"
> "A boy, a very little one."
> "How happy she must be! For as the proverb says, 'To want a child and have a boy!'" (*Namiry zaza ka teradahy.*) (ibid.)

These sketches seem parodic because of their foregrounding of style. Since no information is being exchanged, the children must perform in the correct manner. Thus the observance of rules for polite conversation becomes the only object. In another sketch, two girls pay a visit to a third, who takes the role of a woman who has recently given birth.

> "May we come in?"
> "Come in, do come in, madam. How are you?"
> "Very well, thank you. We heard that God has given you offspring and posterity, and we come to rejoice with you. And, if you will

allow us, we bring you 'a bit of money to buy a little shrimp'" (*vola-kely atao rom-patsa*). (Molet 1966:15–16)

Even in the mouth of an adult, the old-fashioned folk metaphor might sound stilted; from a child, it is funny. Similarly after a funeral, children "play grownup" (*kindriandriana*), uttering the oft-heard formal expressions of condolence, and offering to the one playing the bereaved person a toy version of the ceremonial gift, called "something to dry your eyes" (*fao-dranomaso*), or, more literally, "a bit of cloth" (*rambon-damba*). All these conversation games provide opportunities outside the riddle for children to practice formal dialogue, ask the correct question, and give the correct answer. In their adult life, formalized dialogue will recur as a reliable means of maintaining social cohesion.

Performance at special times of the year had important effects on Merina childlore. Of course the dialogue of children's imitative play, at least in former times, could be heard all year round. "Making toy rice" (*kivarivary*) was an imitation of the cooking of rice, using sand and potsherds. In "playing high society" (*tsiandriandriana*), a variant of the conversation game, girls would draw a house on the ground using leaves, divide up roles with seeds and bits of crockery as their puppets, and act out a social call. In "playhouse" (*kitranotrano*), boys would build little houses, and in "pretend cattle" (*tsiombiomby*) they would play at butchering, as others would enact a funeral. The reduplication, which weakens the meaning of the roots in these names of games, classifies them as child activity. But in the days of the Merina monarchy, it was a special occasion, the "royal bath" ceremony, that brought together in good festival style the largest number of opportunities for highland children to imitate adult behavior and develop alternative modes of speech and dialogue. A ritual of reunification and renewal, as well as of submission to the sovereign, held mainly in the capital, the royal bath (*fandroana*) was terminated by the French in 1896, who tried to substitute Bastille Day for it. It is the subject of two fine monographs by Razafimino and Molet (1956) and an article by Maurice Bloch (1989). It was observed in the field by the sharp-eyed James Sibree, whose account (1890) I draw on here. During the *fandroana*, a separate day was assigned for children's activities, which followed the sovereign's purificatory bath on the first day and a large cattle-killing on the second. Customs of "children's day" included the procession of the ox, a picnic or "doll's feast," and a beauty contest. "Bringing out the ox" (*voak'omby*), a parade accompanied by singing and dancing, asserted symbolically the continuing vitality of the cattle, after a massive slaughter on the first day of the festival. The children's picnic (*tsikonina*, "not [where you] stay," hence a meal prepared outdoors by children rather than at home by mothers) was a complete family meal of rice and meat, cooked in new pots and eaten from new dishes. In imitation of adult competitiveness, children would try to outdo each other in cooking ability and in the beauty contest. Essential to all this festival behavior was the formalized dialogue of high society. Assembling in large numbers, dressed in clean or new clothes and jewelry, with some children even being carried in litters, they would carry with them

> fruit of different kinds, and small plates, bottles, glasses, and baskets, and go along singing. . . . Each party places the fruit on the plates, and fills the glasses with water. One division then calls out:—
> "May we enter, ladies?"
> The others reply:—
> "Pray walk in, ladies;
> Certainly, ladies."
> "We bring you a little feast. May you live long, ladies, in good health."
> "Yes, may God bless us all, ladies."
> and so on, imitating the formal and polite speeches of their elders when paying visits. Then having eaten the fruit, they sing and dance, during the afternoon singing a number of songs . . . . The children in the country places have a somewhat different custom, for they take meat with them to feast upon.

Children's imitative dialogue, like riddling, teaches wittiness through language and imparts the power of the word at an early age. At festival time a century ago, perhaps all year round today, formalized dialogue continually reinforces the linguistic norms of adult society. It reaffirms status relations, rations information, creates a mental space between situations of interaction and imaginary situations, and maintains a verbal form of group solidarity. Moreover, the games reinforce the connection of children to adults. They teach competence in carrying out adult social duties and roles—a courting man, a woman being courted, a woman meeting another casually on the road, a person making a condolence call. Most important for our understanding of verbal art, by learning the formulaic dimension of dialogue, the child acquires competence in verbal reiteration, in asking and answering formal questions, and in varying codes of behavior (Hymes 1974:50, Sanches and Kirshenblatt-Gimblett 1976:73). By mastering the forms of politeness required for adult conversation, the children are licensed in *tomabo* to be "more competent in the forms of speech used by adults than their normal speech would show in nonrole-playing, nongame settings" (D. Slobin, quoted in Kirshenblatt-Gimblett 1976:176).

A discourse like this, which puts reported speech in the foreground, continually tends toward parody. These imitative dialogues seem to teach children what kinds of witty speaking will draw an appreciative laugh. When Merina children play *tomabo*, their reward for stylistic correctness is adult laughter. I suggest, therefore, that the conversation games reinforce a skill of parodying. Certain of the boys will develop this skill into habits of witty allusion, irony, and citation of traditional phrases—the features of formal speech. By imitating so exactly the distribution of roles, the pace, the lexicon, and the syntax of adult conversation, Merina childlore expresses both the parallel and the separation between children and adults. Though adults leave riddling behind with *tomabo*, they retain that keen sense of style developed in childhood. "Sweet words make easy riches," they say (Domenichini-Ramiaramanana 1970:150).

This proverb leads to another stylistic link between riddling and other genres, and leads us back to the much-debated issue of the extent to which Malagasy culture resembles or derives from African cultures. In riddle language the resemblances are strong (Kuusi 1974). More particularly, the connection between the riddle and proverb (*ohabolana*) genres is as strong in Madagascar as it is in southern Africa. One large category of *ohabolana* is a pair of metaphorical sayings in parallel structure, which echo the precedent-and-sequent structure of riddles. An example:

> *Natao hitsikitsika hivavahana kanjo voromahery hipaoka ny akoho.*
> (Houlder 1960:7, Domenichini-Ramiaramanana 1970:195).
>
> You were/He was thought to be a kestrel-hawk to pray to but you are/he is a falcon who will swoop down on the chickens.

Riddle dialogue portrays the alternation of two live speakers. It is external. The kind of "dialogue" found in *ohabolana*—its antithesis or balance—can be performed by only one speaker. It is internal. Both genres, riddle and proverb, use the pairing of precedent and sequent to reveal truth and to mirror reality. What separates the two is the relation of congruence or opposition between external and internal dialogue.

The "Choice," a Unique Malagasy Genre

Malagasy folklore possesses a unique kind of riddle that dramatizes the correlation between folklore and social structure. This is a double riddle called the "choice" (*safidy*), in which two similar things are offered to the respondent in metaphorical language. He or she must both give the correct interpretation of the two precedent parts and make a choice between them. "Which do you prefer, little eyes in the rocks or big eyes in the grass?—Wildcat and ox," says one example, for which the right choice would be the domestic ox, not the dangerous wildcat. Of all Malagasy riddles, the *safidy* gives the riddler the greatest power because he can pass on the acceptability of two answers. Recognition of the *safidy* as a distinct genre in Imerina more than a century ago can be seen from the group of this and fifteen more items in Dahle 1877. Eighty years later the same example was still in circulation in a variant form.

> Which do you prefer, an animel with big eyes seen in the grass or an animal with small eyes seen between two blocks of stone?—I prefer the first, which is an ox going to pasture, while the second is a snake stealing chickens. (Molet 1953 : 103)

The endurance of the genre is equally indicated by another example, collected in two versions fifty years apart.

> Which do you prefer, an elegant cane or a muddy cudgel? —A rat's tail or an ox's tail. (Dahle 1877 : 65)

> Which do you prefer, a clean stick or a muddy stick?—I prefer a stick covered with mud, for that's a cow's tail, while the clean stick is a dog's tail. (Decary 1924 : 359)

The usual *safidy* poses two metaphors as the precedent and demands a choice between them. Collectors have not always recorded the grammatical form of the sequent.

> Which do you prefer, four little pieces or two long slashes?—Cow's udders, dog's teats.

> Which do you prefer, a girl trailing her lamba [a sign of her availability] or a young man lying down?—Chicken, cat.

> Which do you prefer, fat you can't cook with or a half chicken dripping with fat?—Quartz, yam.

Which do you prefer, disappointment at not catching a thief or sore eyes caused by a sorcerer?—Barn owl, smoke.

Which do you prefer, his head pulled out and his tail shrunk or his tail pulled out and his head shrunk?—Goat, cat.

Which do you prefer, Miss Silly trailing her lamba or Mr. Foolish weighed down by a gun?—A cat dragging its long tail, an ox carrying its horns.

Which do you prefer, a stranger with frisky head or a houseowner with head high?—Cat, hen. (Dahle 1877:64—65)

Which do you prefer, an animal that troubles the water or an animal that does not?—I prefer an animal that troubles the water, for that's an ox crossing over, while the one that doesn't trouble it is a crocodile. (Decary 1924:359)

How much power does the "choice" give its poser? Ordinary riddle rhetoric affords an opportunity to show knowledge of traditional figures of speech and to answer in a manner which the community approves; the "choice" increases that opportunity, but also the risk. With ordinary riddles, the poser always begins as superior to the respondent: he retains the power to reject or accept an answer. When two questions are put and two puzzles must be solved, the poser has a doubled opportunity to reject inappropriate answers. Reduplication increases his power by integrating two simple units into a double unit. It dramatizes social ranking by demanding that one be rated above the other, as in a dilemma tale or a law case: "Which do you prefer?" In all these ways, it reflects the increasing hierarchization of Merina society from the eighteenth century on. The genre enacts authoritarian questioning.

This "choice" genre is found only in Imerina, where political integration is traditionally firm and society is stratified. Outside Madagascar, cultures differ, of course, in the degree of variation riddle posers will accept, and this difference reflects social hierarchization. In Malaita for example, in the Pacific Ocean, Köngäs Maranda came to understand the rules for riddling among the Lau people. Then she examined the power of riddle posers. Certain answers, which she thought ought to be acceptable, were rejected by riddle posers, though not without controversy from the audience (1971:55). While reflecting social stratification, the "choice" riddle also expresses a theme in Malagasy philosophy. A correct answer will restore the balance between poser and respondent, and in Merina thought, truth chiefly consists of balance, rather than giving each person his due. The true (*ny marina*) is what is balanced, what is in equilibrium (Rajaona 1959). The "choice" genre affords both poser and respondent an opportunity to enhance their power and prestige. The right choice recreates and reasserts a value preference sanctioned by common sense, through observation, and by the discourse of the ancestors.

"Choice" Embedded in Narrative

Once again, tales shed light on riddling. The necessity for human choice appears all over Madagascar in myths about the origin of death and of the political order. Two Sakalava examples, both located in the remote past, give support to a remark of the folklorist André Jolles about myth and riddle. Of the two genres, said Jolles, myth is the one giving the answer, while the riddle emphasizes the question (1972:103). The first myth answers the fundamental question, "What is the origin of death?" Numerous African narratives depict this event as the result of an unwise choice that is regretted ever after (Abrahamsson 1951). In Madagascar, the myth puts the "choice" into dialogue and frames it into a narrative with God as the poser. I translate a Sakalava version of 1922, which leaves no doubt as to who has the power.

> In the beginning, God created a single man and a single woman and placed them on earth. One day he put this question to them: "Which do you prefer, the death of the moon or the death of the banana tree?"
>
> They said, "Lord, we don't understand you."
>
> "Do you want to be like the moon, which remains invisible every month for several days, but then reappears, or do you prefer to be like a banana-tree, which dies after having put forth its fruits?"
>
> "Lord, explain to us what that means, for we still don't understand it."
>
> "Well, look. The moon goes on existing by itself, even though it seems to die every month and then come back to life after a few days, while the banana-tree dies completely. But before dying, it

gives birth to several offshoots which take its place. Choose which you prefer, for you must decide on one or the other."

They thought it over a while, then said, "King-creator, we prefer to die like the banana tree, which leaves successors after it." Since then, they say, men die and leave children to replace them. (Dandouau 1922:95–96)

God, represented here as the first poser of a *safidy*, is so careful to make sure that the man and woman understand the terms of their choice that he explains his own figures of speech twice. Here, as in the Malagasy versions of The King and the Peasant's Son, only an exceptional being can set riddles. In Antaisaka, Betsimisaraka, Betsileo, and Tanala versions of this tale, man and woman think their choice through carefully. They are models of well-considered, deliberate behavior. They always consciously choose the death of the banana tree, to underline the widespread belief in the importance and value of children. In Malagasy terms, theirs is the right choice. Here Madagascar parts from Africa. Choice lies behind nearly every story of the origin of death, but no Malagasy story shows the first couple's choice to have been unwise. Apart from the theme, the myth has great formal interest. It embeds the *safidy* in its narration as reported speech. The embedded genre expresses the supreme importance of arriving at human decisions through dialogue.

The second Sakalava myth, which explains the origin of kings, also portrays a capacity for choice among alternatives. The solitary hero, a figure of authority, personifies the power to make value determinations analogous to those in *safidy*. In the myth, a certain judge is so wise that the people bring him all their disputes. He gets the name King of the Word, but, he points out, when the people share the fines, he gets none. They grant him all the land, people, and power. That is how kings are made (Birkeli 1922:354–55, tale 1.2.10 in *Malagasy Tale Index*). If the distinction of Indevo in the folktale was his power over metaphor, the king's distinction in this myth is a capacity to evaluate the relative importance of the claims people present to him. Thus he speaks for hierarchy. He receives the sobriquet of *mpanito*, cutter of words. His verbal skill is part of his political power, standing for the whole. People exercise the same capacity when they answer *safidy* and in their debates following dilemma tales. What defines a just man such as this judge is his moral equilibrium. He is "like a sacrificial stone," says a proverb, posing a riddle in its first phrase. How is a just man like a sacrificial stone? we ask, and the proverb answers,

"Wherever he is placed, everything is balanced" (Domenichini-Ramiaramanana 1970:510). Because he recognizes that a certain amount of vice will always be found in virtue, he "can keep the balance between good and bad. Morality can consist only in the harmonious balance of virtues and defects," says a modern commentator (Rajaona 1959).

Again framing the "choice" into a larger genre is a tale from the Bara in the south, whose society is far less stratified than that of the Merina. Ethnographers report that Bara land belongs to the king by inheritance or right of conquest. It is from him that new settlers must demand lands and to him that they present first fruits. The myth provides a charter for this arrangement. Like the two Sakalava tales (and like so many riddles), it portrays an exchange of question and answer between lower and upper ranks. Human beings ask God the key question, "Who owns the land?"

> God sent down cattle, edible plants, trees, and land, and when God sent all that down here from up there, the freemen received the cattle, the magicians received the trees, and the king, Zafitui, received the land.
>
> "Here is what is yours," said God. The king got the land, the freeman got the cattle, the magician got the trees, the farmer got the nourishing plants.
>
> "So," said the king, "the freeman has the cattle, the king has the land, the farmer has the crops. Then who is the real owner of the soil?"
>
> "It is this way," said God. "You are the owners of the soil."
>
> "And thus," said the king, "everything here on earth is mine."
>
> "Yes," said God, "all the things here on this soil which you have received are yours."
>
> So, kings own everything here on earth. (Faublée 1947:206–7)

Through the dialectic of this exchange the need for balance between the parties finds expression in a hierarchy of ownership and of answering a question. The king's role shows the rise of authority in Malagasy society. As the representative of humanity to deal with the spirit world, credited with superior verbal prowess, the king voices man's question to God. In this riddle, only the right answer is acceptable. The result gives all power to the king, the respondent. The whole tale, with its royal edict, resembles the quasi-dialogue of Merina kings as recorded by historians. Since such quasi-dialogue is one meaning of *kabary*, the tale connects riddle, myth, and history.

Many, perhaps most *fitenin-drazana*, including proverbs, poetry, and oratory, are shaped on riddle structure. It serves these miniature dramas much as the expanding and paralleling of images serves African storytelling (Scheub 1977). Future field study can test this hypothesis, which promises to shed light on the comparison of rules for narrative and non-narrative genres. With a larger corpus of collected texts, moreover, a future scholar could discover whether certain key analogies found in riddles are expanded by accumulating more and more details of the correspondence between two things. This supplementary hypothesis was put forth by Elli Köngäs Maranda after analyzing metaphor in 3,500 Finnish riddles. Köngäs Maranda concluded that riddle-making was "a systematic investigation of the 'native classifications'" of a culture, brought into existence by exploring and exhausting all the similarities between sets of terms (1971:138). Whether such systematic investigation is culturally variable remains to be seen. Perhaps Malagasy riddle-making has other principles for creating new pieces. Finally, future investigation could discover more about the ways in which these four genres blur and overlap.

Limited though it is by available materials, folkloric restatement demonstrates the dominance of dialogism in Malagasy folklore. The pattern of precedent and sequent, which we see on a small scale in the riddle, has shaped verbal arts for all the important expressive interactions of Malagasy life, especially in Imerina. As they moved into adulthood, people observed the debates of village elders and learned to parody them. Then they began to duel in *hainteny*, which spoke of courtship and love and drenched ordinary social interactions in eroticism. This genre imparted great complexity to the dialogic pattern, by employing multiple codes, settings, message-forms, dramatic situations, and characters. Variant forms came into existence when speakers adapted known poems to specific occasions of dueling, with a view to defeating another player. At the time of marriage, the *kabary* debate used the dialogic pattern again. Like a gigantic riddle, the marriage debate posed a question, "Will you give up this girl to us?," which the bride's family answered in oratory and by delivering the bride. Finally, at the end of life, funeral speakers made use of dialogue in their eulogies, first through quotation of proverbs and other words of the ancestors, then by citing riddles. As my final chapter will show, the Malagasy riddle has been given a place of honor in funeral oratory. Such pervasive reliance on formalized dialogue for all the crises of life is no idle habit of style. Dialogism in folklore is a theatrical performance. In the domain of Malagasy discourse, it dramatizes a conflict between balance and equilibrium on one hand and *tsiny* and inequality on the other. In this drama, monologue tries to contain dialogue, and truth, knowledge, and reality emerge from the struggle between the two.

3. Proverbs: Dialogue in Monologue

Why should anybody read or read about proverbs in Madagascar? Who can read a numbered list of sentences with any pleasure? Any folklorist would turn away from them in despair, convinced that proverbs gain their only reality from their occurrence in conversation. In the absence of information about the backgrounds of proverb speakers, or about the communicative events which constituted their speaking, how shall today's folklorist see anything of importance in strings of sentences?

It was not always so. Examining the published collections, one could think proverbs the most important genre of all, because so many have been collected. The LMS missionary Houlder pointed to their importance at home, around the hearth, in the marketplace, and in public speeches. Of all Malagasy genres after the folktale, this one most attracted zealous, patient collectors (Linton 1927). Proverbs—in Malagasy, *ohabolana*, "measured speech"—have always proved tempting to collectors of Malagasy folklore, being brief, memorable, and easy to ask about. They collected thousands, interpreting proverbs to reveal primitive Malagasy philosophy, to illustrate linguistic usages, and to infer traits of national character. Some even thought proverbs to be a secret language. The history of proverb collecting suggests that this genre promised a shortcut to the Malagasy mentality. The very search for proverbs called forth a large number of the sentences that collectors recorded. But hardly any proverb publications from Madagascar give us information about speakers, occasions, situations, or contexts.

Therefore it is with this genre that folkloric restatement faces its greatest challenge. Fortunately a great critic, Jan Mukařovský, has formulated a theory of proverbs as quotation which is highly appropriate to Madagascar, and a fine scholar of African folklore has applied Mukařovský's theory to proverb use among the Owerri Igbo of Nigeria (Penfield 1983). The properties of Igbo proverbs which Penfield has identified are shared by Malagasy *ohabolana*, even in print. They depersonalize a message that would otherwise be too personal. Their foreignness to the interaction situation draws a hearer's attention. They ring with the authority of the ancients; they refer to shared social norms and ideals, and they bring prestige to the man or woman who uses them well. What I sketch below about the uses of *ohabolana*, especially in Imerina, suggests that here as in West Africa, "conflicts are managed in 'speech events' which may seem less formalized than the court system in the Western world but which nevertheless have traditional rules and regulations specified by the culture informally" (Penfield 1983:50). Even without many details of performance, Malagasy data uphold Mukařovský's approach as Penfield applies it.

On these hypotheses, I shall define the genre and then look at the history of collecting, trying to discover why *ohabolana* interested so many investigators. Then, by analysis of the sentences, I shall show that Malagasy proverbs, seemingly monologic, are simultaneously a kind of dialogue.

Definition

Proverbs in the great island fall into classes familiar to the folklorist (Brunvand 1986:74–83, Dundes 1975). There are literal proverbs, or aphorisms: "An unguarded mouth brings misfortune." There are quotations whimsically attributed to an imaginary speaker, which Anglo-American folklore calls Wellerisms: "It was only its voice, as the blind man said when he touched the cannon." There are literal imperatives not to do something: "Don't be self-willed"; "Don't have too few friends." There are folk similes or proverbial comparisons, sometimes containing slurs: "Big but clumsy, like the dogs of Avaradrano."[1] There are folk metaphors or proverbial phrases: "Big bird with small eggs." And there are thousands of what folklorists call "true" proverbs—grammatically complete sentences, often metrical, which speakers apply as metaphors to situations of social interaction: "A *kabary* [here a meeting for decision-taking] can't be made with a white *lamba* [garment; i.e., a decent appearance is no substitute for discussion]. One man alone can't force an ox."[2] To classify *ohabolana*, collectors have usually grouped them by their literal subject, rather than by the classes I have listed.

With the groupings, three assumptions about the genre appear in the literature: great antiquity, fixity of phrasing, and usefulness for moral teaching. To define *ohabolana*, folklorists in Madagascar have always accepted their informants' attribution of proverbs to the ancestors. They have also assumed that the proverbs are fixed in phrasing and transmitted so accurately through time that they represent an earlier stage of culture. An oft-quoted example is the Merina aphorism *Ny maty aza te-ho maro*, Even the dead wish to be many, often interpreted as evidence of the importance attached to friendship and kin relations. To many Malagasy and to their European observers, such a proverb epitomizes the word of the ancestors, *tenin-drazana*. Collectors have also accepted the authoritativeness of the sayings as axiomatic, and have even tried to systematize them into a Malagasy philosophy (Navone 1977, Dama-Ntsoha 1953).

To name this genre, the English word "proverb" more or less successfully translates the Malagasy term *ohabolana*, measured speech. Bakoly Domenichini-Ramiaramanana has argued that the translation is misleading. Admittedly, every definition of *proverb* in a European dictionary differs from every other, as she says. Admittedly, every definition can be illustrated by a distinct Malagasy example. The twenty-seven examples that prove this point to her (1983 : 47–90), however, prove to me only that the genre of *ohabolana* in Madagascar comprises numerous varieties. The European dictionaries she cites can tell us little about Malagasy oral genres, for cultural, not lexical reasons. Five centuries after the rise of print culture, proverbs have much less force in France or England than they have in Madagascar, where oral communication still has more force. Why not use the English word, and specify it by reference to Malagasy culture? Malagasy *ohabolana*, indeed, exemplifies all Mukařovský's attributes for proverbs. They speak indirectly, they evaluate the situation by means of third-party intrusion, they operate by means of desubjectivization and community acceptance, and they receive great respect.

In Madagascar, the proverb genre is superficially part of dialogue. To perform it, to speak a proverb, one steps into a role of authority and addresses measured words to his listeners, which they understand as being quoted from the ancestors. In that external sense, *ohabolana* are dialogic; they form part of a conversation. "Even those who belong to better-off or more educated classes never fail to express themselves by studding their point with proverbs," one observer writes. More to the point, two voices are sometimes needed to complete the performance. A European, the same observer continues, "can even try the experiment of beginning a proverb and deliberately leaving it unfinished; one's [Merina] interlocutor will invariably complete it" (Michel 1957 : 174). Similarly, for Betsileo, an *ohabolana* ordinarily comprises two parts, and to utter the first almost automatically elicits the second part dialogically from an informant (Michel-Andrianarahinjaka 1986 : 120). Jean Paulhan recorded one illuminating interchange from his stay in Madagascar (1908–11). A father said to his son, "You must decide to take a wife; you are of an age to get married." To reply to this directive style (and probably wanting to close the conversation), the son quoted, "Oh, father, I don't want people to say, 'In a hurry to marry, then in haste to divorce.'"[3] Paulhan was surprised to hear that the saying was to be interpreted not literally but metaphorically. It preached the undesirability of all haste (1925:31–33). What demanded a reply, then, was not an idea, not a sentence, but a turn in conversation. The dialogic exchange was analogous to a riddle: the first utterance required an answer. The Bara of the south may be an exception: they avoid using proverbs in running conversation as the Merina do (Michel 1957:174–75).

Proverbs are also dialogic, or at least bipartite, internally. They provide a resolution of the tension between private thought and public utterance, which is expressed in the saying *Ny ta-hilaza aretena koa ny ta handre maharare*, The need of speaking is a sickness and the need of listening is a pain (Michel-Andrianarahinjaka 1986:105). One's dangerous private thoughts should be hidden. Information must be controlled (Keenan and Ochs 1979:138). *Ny kibo no be eritreri-dratsy, ka ny vava no mahazo*, It is the mind that's full of evil thoughts, but it is the mouth that gets the blame (Houlder 1960:11, no. 121). Yet since one's thought must be communicated without calling down reproach (*tsiny*), the proverb, like gesture language, offers a controlled, publicly acceptable code in which to do so politely. In the 1960s, Maurice Bloch found repeatedly that his highland informants answered his inquiries about behavior with statements of ideology in the form of *tenin-drazana*, words of the ancestors, which were often attributed to Andrianampoinimerina or some other dead monarch (Bloch 1971:38). One fits oneself into society's way of speaking by learning this polite code. The beautiful, controlled language of the proverb, which by its quotations echoes the many voices of the past, constitutes an implicit theory among Malagasy that reality includes both the authority of the ancestors and the immediacy of the speaking event. Malagasy proverbs are internally dialogic in another sense which I shall analyze below: they realize a limited number of two-sided structures, which they share with the riddle and the folktale.

Yet these sentences mean to stop the conversation. They derive their monologic authority from the social control implicit in being inherited from the ancestors. One speaker seeks to exert authority over others by means of *ohabolana*. The sayings are monologic in this thematic, ideological sense: the speaker imposes an authoritative interpretation in a single voice. Watching proverb performance among the Merina, Paulhan found listeners submissive. No one would interrupt a proverb speaker or an orator during his performance. The speaker would shift into performance mode, physically or vocally marking the saying. One speaker would spread his arms and lean forward to mark his proverbs; another would shift her tone as if announcing some bit of sad news, such as an accident or a death; another would stand up every time he uttered a proverb (Paulhan 1925:29). Everyone would focus attention upon his intoning (Domenichini-Ramiaramanana 1978), theatrical though it might be, to encourage him. Thus the speaker assumed greater authority, indicating the monologism of the genre.

In literary criticism, Bakhtin named this coexistence of dialogism and monologism a twofold orientation. At the same time that the sayings form part of a conversation, they are "oriented in life" by selecting certain images, rhythms, and themes in order to make ideological statements (Medvedev/Bakhtin 1978:130–31). It was the ideology, in its various manifestations, that fascinated students of Malagasy national character. Just so, Bakhtin asserted, a novelist like Ivan Turgenev speaks through his characters in only one voice (Bakhtin 1984:191). Moreover, if paralinguistic markers like posture and intonation suffice to let audiences recognize *ohabolana*, the words chosen could be indistinguishable from any other words, yet still be authoritative discourse from the point of view of those who hear them. What makes these utterances proverbs, at least in part, is the new attention elicited by the speaker's behavior. Whether or not the words are fixed, then, the performance of *ohabolana* necessitates shifting into alternative channels of gesture and attentiveness.

In a more fanciful sense, furthermore, *ohabolana* have been heard in another two-sided conversation. European missionaries and colonials engaged a mysterious, verbally fluent people in a conversation which they hoped would penetrate Malagasy national character. The center of the history of folklore in Madagascar is the interactions of mostly European collectors with Malagasy informants. I retrace it briefly.

Proverb Collecting in Madagascar

The first important collectors were the men of the London Missionary Society (LMS), who turned up proverbs in large numbers once they were allowed back after the death of the hostile Queen Ranavalona I in 1869.

Their renewed efforts at evangelization, which the queen had prohibited, led to the first major collecting effort. "In the year 1871," wrote their best folklorist, Sibree, "the Rev. W. E. Cousins and Mr. J. Parrett published a small volume of 76 pp., containing 1477 Malagasy Proverbs, a branch of native traditional wisdom in which the language is very rich. A second and much enlarged edition of this work was published in 1885, containing 3790 proverbs arranged in alphabetical order, so as to be easily found" (1889:29). The Cousins and Parrett collection was addressed to Europeans, especially the missionaries themselves, as a tool of study; it was not meant to reflect Malagasy for Malagasy readers, most of whom could not read it. The impressively large number Cousins and Parrett amassed in such a short time dwarfs the four hundred or seven hundred accepted as a considerable collection in the pan-African surveys made by Bascom and Finnegan. By a century later, the collection of Father Paul de Veyrières could number 5,633 *fitenenana*, "sayings," twice the number of such a notable collection as Matti Kuusi's from Namibia (Kuusi 1970). From the beginning, then, collectors have predicated that a great repertoire of proverbs exists in Madagascar.

Fixed-phrase folklore such as *ohabolana* and *fitenenana* fitted the cultural notions of these men, who expected a relatively primitive people to express itself gnomically. They could also see in Malagasy proverbs a reminiscence of the Christian Bible. Moreover, if proverbs in Madagascar were so numerous, the LMS folklorists could use them to teach Malagasy to their new recruits, to converse with their parishioners, and most of all to include in sermons. There, as one of them wrote, the proverbs could inculcate friendship, diligence, or thrift. *Manantena lambo hiakatra, ka tsy midina any an-ala*, You expect the wild boar to come up [out of the wood], so you do not go down into the wood. *Aiza no dia ho anao avokoa ny valala manatody sy ny fandria-maraina?*, How do you expect both to get the locust with eggs [esteemed a delicacy] and to lie abed in the morning? (Clemes 1877:29). This missionary and his colleagues knew that in citing proverbs, they were imitating the best Merina oratorical style. "In all public speaking," he went on, "the natives use their proverbs very freely, and many Europeans find them of great use in enforcing truths that would otherwise find small acceptance with their hearers." The social control built into *ohabolana* served the evangelizing goal. Proverbs also fitted their sense of social and cultural superiority. "Socially exclusive," as Gow writes, they "felt innately superior" to their parishioners, for they inevitably accepted the prevailing social attitudes of Victorian Britain. Once resident in the island, they used their connections with the *andriana* to raise their social status far higher than they could have known at home (67).

From that position, they could objectify their parishioners, assimilate them to their concept of the folk, and discover the Malagasy national character through folklore. In 1877 they founded their Malagasy Folk-Lore Society. Inevitably these men defined the Malagasy proverb as stable, preserved through time, and revelatory of national character. "And in the year 1882," Sibree writes, "the Rev. J. A. Houlder completed a work upon Malagasy proverbs, arranging them according to their subject under a number of heads, giving also racy English translations and numerous illustrative notes" (1889:29). Houlder saw proverbs as expressions of both universal wisdom and national character and therefore revealing the oriental strain in Malagasy origins. Rather than investigate actual communicative events, he wrote a scenario imagining how two men might exchange proverbs (Houlder 1881:48). Like Cousins and others, he was certain that the culture they were faithfully recording was being fundamentally transformed. The proverbs, dating from old times, revealed the "Malagasy soul." S. Clemes spoke for them all: "These proverbs are the truest pictures we have of the thoughts of the people here generations ago" (1877:31). Expert linguists though the LMS folklorists were, they lacked comparative data about other proverbs (Gunson 1978:264, Gow 1979:85). Nor could they have been responsive to ambiguity and variability. When Dahle, also a Protestant missionary, saw double entendres in poems and tales, he did his best to root them out of his texts (Dahle 1877:vii–viii).

The preeminent French observer of Madagascar, Alfred Grandidier, agreed that *ohabolana* had proliferated. Though not much interested in verbal art, he noticed how often fixed phrases turned up in conversation. "At every instant they quote proverbs which express very well, in lapidary style, their feelings and thoughts; they also enjoy making ingenious comparisons." He also saw the connection between verbal metaphor and some nonverbal improvisations which illustrated stories. "When they have some event to narrate or description to give, they often take little pebbles or bits of straw they find at their doorway and arrange them so as to make their story clearer or their demonstration more obvious" (Grandidier 1908:119). French and British folklorists, therefore, agreed on beginning a dialogue between collectors and men of words, *mpikabary*, which was to continue for a century. Missionaries and colonial officers made continual efforts to penetrate the Malagasy soul through proverbs. *Mpikabary* kept them supplied by quoting and generating sentences.

The Invention of Malagasy Monotheism

Along with their conviction of social and cultural superiority, the missionaries based their proverb research on another discovery. Old Malagasy religion, they found, had much in common with Christianity. Cousins saw in *ohabolana* such notions as the divine creation of man and the world, the existence of life after death, the punishment of forbidden acts, and the human relation to supernatural forces. These anticipations of Christianity motivated his collecting, for proverbs embodied "a tradition that a purer religion had once existed, and that the ancient faith of the people had been a simple theism" (Cousins 1895:76). Cousins's special contribution, with which Sibree agreed, was to unite the statements of his informants that *ohabolana* "have come down from ancient times" with his discovery that "many of them contained a recognition of God, and some knowledge of his attributes and character" (1895:76–77). In asserting that primitive Malagasy religion was theistic, Cousins put forth a view that went back to the seventeenth-century colonist Flacourt. Alfred Grandidier also promulgated the supposed Malagasy monotheism (1888); it continued to be debated throughout the colonial period, always with the aid of proverbs. Meanwhile linguists and grammarians kept them in print (Marre-de Marin 1876, Abinal and Malzac 1888).

The eleven sayings that proved to Cousins that "God did not leave Himself without witness" were augmented by eighteen more from a colleague. They used the word *Andriamanitra*, the perfumed god, often translated "creator" by missionary collectors. One of his converts stated, "In all these, and many more like them, [it was not the old Merina idols that were alluded to, but] the one God, Who exists eternally and is the author of all blessings, even He only was thought of in these proverbs" (Andrianaivoravelona, trans. in Clark 1885).

Cousins found another persuasive use for Malagasy proverbs to aid the evangelizing effort. He found sentences demonstrating that some Malagasy were skeptical about their own belief system.

A favorable declaration of the *sikidy* (divination) is not an occasion for dancing, nor an unfavorable declaration an occasion for weeping.

An offering is not a death preventive but something to prevent regret.

Like a Tanala [tribesman] who lost his talisman (*sampy*), getting a new one is quick work.

Like the diviner asking too much, that a sick man should dance. (1875:6, translations revised)

French observers, also champions of Christianity, agreed with Cousins that some of the natives lacked absolute faith in the efficacy of sacrifices. Alfred Grandidier cited the proverb, "If an offering doesn't prevent you from dying, at least it does you no harm." One of Grandidier's informants, an old diviner of much authority from early in the nineteenth century, conceded as much: "There are times when the rain falls right after this sacrifice, and other times it doesn't come at all" (1908:119). Gustave Mondain, fifty years later, traced proverbs to a remote time when clever Malagasy were courageous enough to exercise their powers of observation at the expense of diviners and astrologers; he gave twenty-five examples of skepticism (Mondain 1953). Cousins, Sibree, and Grandidier were sincere in their interpretation, but Malagasy eloquence is so prolific that they could have proved several other philosophical positions from assembling *ohabolana*.

The Invention of National Character Through Proverbs

British and French folklorists invented this factitious Malagasy monotheism as part of their agreement that proverbs were a direct route to understanding Malagasy national character. Many European folklore collectors in the colonies agreed on this point (see, for instance, Westermarck 1930:51–52). All were engaged in reclassifying religion as superstition and culture as mere folklore. In the French vision of the Malagasy soul that now began to take shape, these people had no instinct for religion. "The Malagasy is not a religious animal, he is a poetic animal," wrote one influential pair of authorities. "His superstition is the flowering of an intense poetry" (Leblond 1946:233). Others, however, acknowledged the utility of *ohabolana* in native life. A recurrent situation that elicited proverbial speaking in Madagascar, as in Africa, was the court trial, documented for modern Nigeria by John C. Messenger. The Sakalava used proverbs in this setting. A person accused of rumormongering would assert his good faith, if not his innocence, by bringing before the judges the person who was his source for the rumor and saying, "I'm blind—if you give me an eel, I eat it, if you give me a snake, I eat it." In trials, judges would remind witnesses to tell the whole truth by saying, "Don't half-cook the meat, the food will curse me" (Rey 1913).

Observations like these prepared the way for Jean Paulhan, Madagascar's most sympathetic spokesman, who created a new definition of proverbs by paying attention to the performances that constituted this genre of artistic communication. Around the time (twelve years after the conquest) when those proverbs were being spoken in a Sakalava court, this Frenchman of twenty-four was listening to proverbs and exchanges of *hainteny* (poems) among the Merina and discovering new truths about Malagasy national character. Later to become one of the most important literary and cultural figures in France, Paulhan was then living in the capital, Antananarivo, teaching school and collecting folklore as a means of penetrating another form of thought through language (*Cahiers Jean Paulhan* 2, 33). With the same aims as many other Europeans, to put together an image of the Malagasy soul, but aiming too at defining himself, Paulhan gave his best attention to folklore. Writing about his Madagascar sojourn in 1925, Paulhan was disarmingly ironic about his youthful attraction to *ohabolana*. He preferred, he says, those with a touch of the malicious or the paradoxical to those that seemed simply obvious. If he could find as few as 30 percent that matched his expectations or tastes, he could convince himself that these were the veritable Malagasy proverbs, that they expressed the moralistic, subtle, and critical Malagasy soul. He began to connect and compare Merina sayings with European ones and to try incorporating proverbs into his conversation.

Thereby, Jean Paulhan independently invented a performance-based style of ethnography. Instead of listing proverbs, he would speak them—despite a recurrent sense that a French peasant, already in possession of proverbs, would master them more easily than he could (1925:50–53). Endeavoring to share the labors, cares, and thoughts of his Merina family, Paulhan found that like other Malagasy he knew, they insisted on the importance of proverb context. Whenever he asked a Merina friend to explain a saying, his friend would say, "But where did you hear it? What was going on?" When Paulhan would not or could not narrate the circumstances, his friend could give an explanation only by inventing a narrative context for the quoted sentence. Having gotten at the meaning, Paulhan, stubbornly the European, would say, "Why didn't you tell me that straight away?" Paulhan's researches thus pay tribute to the differences

in cultural expectations and anticipate a contextual approach to the study
of verbal art. "To give meaning to the proverb," he wrote of one informant, "he first had to situate it, surround with the very words that the discussion stirred up. Outside those relations, he could not imagine it"
(1925:41). He began to see what folklorists today confirm: it was performance that constituted the art (Bauman 1977:11).

Paulhan also discovered an essential element of the Merina definition
of *ohabolana*, which his predecessors had failed to notice. This was its
objectivity. It took him more than a year, he writes, to arrive at a satisfactory understanding of the real status of proverbs among The Elevated
People. As he learned to include proverbs in his conversation, he says, he
rid his language of a monotony and lack of conviction that embarrassed
him earlier. He began to believe, as the Merina did, that the fixed phrases
of polite apology which he was saying—the linguistic routines which he
had memorized—were true. Like a Merina, "I was glad to hide behind
the success of my words. I withdrew; I almost asked to be excused for
being so much in the right; I was glad to let it be understood that it was
not my fault, that it was things that were as they were" (1925:59). He was
beginning to absorb Merina ways of thinking; he was participating more
than observing.

Then Paulhan came upon the corollary of his discovery. Trying to
apply proverbs, he would change them, complete them, or adapt them to
particular speaking situations. This attempt, so natural to a nascent European writer, brought him only failure. Despite its utter dependence on the
particulars of a speaking situation, he found, the wording of the *ohabolana*
could not be varied. *Ohabolana* were so objective that they could not be
changed, at least not by a European like himself. Near the end of his three
years in Madagascar, Paulhan became convinced that the proverb of the
Merina was not a linguistic unit like other sentences. "When [the Merina]
spoke about the proverb in general, they envisaged something quite different from a given sentence formed out of certain words and suitable for
conveying certain facts. Exactly the opposite of a sentence, it was an event
independent of all words, a fact to be expressed" (1925:73).

In contrast to his initial, Eurocentric view that proverbs were words
to be adapted to the needs of a particular speaking situation, Paulhan came
to see the *ohabolana* as wholly objectified. With that realization, he could
begin to imitate a *mpikabary*, while affirming the status of the *ohabolana*
as a fixed folkloric artifact. So he came round to the belief the British
missionary collectors had started from: proverbs existed in fixed phrasing.

Still forming an image of Malagasy national character, a few years later, among the Betsileo, Henri Dubois reached similar conclusions. As the resuscitated voice of the past, the proverbs were the supreme authority which Betsileo could call on (Dubois 1938:1259–60). They manifested common sense and everyday wisdom, but they were so condensed as to be nearly untranslatable. "Each word or phrase contains a whole world of allusions to facts, traditions, customs, beliefs, and situations. Initiates get along without difficulty among these, but the foreigner is lost unless someone provides him with commentaries" (Dubois 1938:1261, 1296). Dubois's long residence on the plateau as a missionary also taught him how symmetrical many proverbs were.

The confrontation of European and Malagasy cultures gave new energy to the search for national character in *ohabolana*, though the result was like the orientalism dissected by Edward Said. One of the most distinguished of Malagasy folklorists, Reverend Maurice Rasamuel, a mission school graduate, claimed great importance for proverbs as a means of contrasting European and Malagasy cultures. "Occidental" expression relies, he said, on adjectives and adverbs for enhancing its message; the "oriental" (Malagasy, perhaps only Merina) flatters the ear with similes and turns of phrase from nature, animals, plants, and meteors. These similes Rasamuel found in poetic examples like this:

Ny tendrombohitra fandrian'ny zavona;
ny lohasaha fandrian'ny moka;
ny helo-drano fandrian'ny mamba;
ary ny mpitondra fandrian'ny adidy.

The mountain is the resting-place of the fog;
    the valley is the resting-place of the mosquito;
        the creek is the resting-place of the crocodile;
            and the chief is the resting-place of responsibility.
                        (1928:4)

To a Western reader, however, this sequence of metaphors scarcely seems a proverb. A lengthier variant of it had been printed as prose by Dahle (1877:38), who labeled it a *hainteny*, literally word play, a traditional oral poem. It was translated by Sibree in prose under the title "Every Thing Has Its Place":

The whitebird (a species of egret, *Ardea bubulcus*, which feeds on the flies and parasites of cattle) does not leave the oxen, the sandpiper does not forsake the ford, the hawk does not depart from the tree, the valley is the dwelling of the mosquito, the mountain is the home of the mist, the water holes are the lair of the crocodile. And the sovereign is the depository (lit. "resting place") of the law, and the people are the depository of good sense. (1889:38)

This and other *ohabolana* resemble or overlap the oral poetry of the Merina in structure, metaphors, and occasions for speaking. Dahle, Sibree, and Rasamuel assumed the genre to be fixed in phrasing and conserving the Malagasy mentality more or less unchanged through generations of oral transmission. Rasamuel's vision of that mentality tended to be somber: six *ohabolana* in his essay remind us that our own actions come back on us, and four more that we are vulnerable to betrayal by a friend. Only at the end did Rasamuel include one proverb stating that difficulties can always be overcome. His version of Malagasy worldview complemented a general expectation by Europeans that the Malagasy were a fearful people who would neither dare much nor achieve much.

Further polarizing Malagasy and European character, another influential Malagasy folklorist insisted that proverbs were ancient and revelatory. J. B. Razafintsalama became better known, after he converted from Christianity, under his Buddhist name of Dama-Ntsoha. Dama-Ntsoha was even more an orientalist than Rasamuel. To him, *ohabolana*—always stable, a window into the past—proved that from earliest times, the Malagasy had been oriental thinkers. In his fanciful history, which depended upon interpreting proverbs, the Malagasy owed their cultural unity to a synthesis of Buddhism and Shaktism. Before settling in Madagascar, they would have to have lived together in some one place for a time, which he placed in the east.[4] Dama-Ntsoha located that time near the end of the tenth century. Subsequently, the Malagasy absorbed the Buddhism that was expanding into Java and Sumatra, then moved to the great island at the beginning of the twelfth century. When, at the beginning of the historical period, the great Merina king Andrianampoinimerina established the system of community organization (*fokon'olona*) its leaders were manifestations of God. The Merina state was a triumph for secularized Shaktism. Common to all Malagasy tribes at this early date, he said, was the fundamental conception of spiritual perfection (1928, 1938, 1953).

In Dama-Ntsoha's tendentious, anti-Europeanist search for the essence of *malgachitude*, it was the proverbs above all, the treasure of the past which popular memory had safeguarded, which demonstrated the Malagasy synthesis of Buddhist doctrine with Tantric monotheism. Through their irony and humor transpired the Buddhistic qualities of essential lucidity of mind and practical seriousness. To marshal evidence, he rearranged the 1918 edition of the standard Cousins and Parrett proverb collection into sections that corresponded to Indian thought. So many *ohabolana* had already been printed that he could find dozens to support his unlikely interpretation. He made them demonstrate that Malagasy adhered to the Buddha's second Noble Truth, which states, "The cause of suffering is rooted in desire"; he arranged other proverbs to illustrate Buddhistic conceptions of death, pessimism, universal charity, and personal responsibility. He even reconciled the Merina belief in *tody*, retribution, with the Hindu notion of *karma*. He concluded that Malagasy proverbs were simultaneously statements of ancient Hindu and Buddhist doctrine and revelations of Malagasy national character. The taste for sententious utterances, which had been inculcated by the ancestors, had not diminished, he said, with the passing of time. Unlikely though his version of history was, Dama-Ntsoha's vision of an ancient Malagasy essence created a manifesto for the growing sense of cultural uniqueness in Madagascar after World War II and the bloody rebellion of Malagasy against the French in 1947.

Succeeding collections of *ohabolana* in the colonial period by Emile Birkeli, Pastor Olsen, Hubert Deschamps, Dr. Fontoynont and Raomandahy, and Louis Michel have supported the prominence of proverbs in Malagasy folklore. Through proverbs, Roger Le Garreres and Flavien Ranaivo found Malagasy character to be basically monotheistic, attached to the past, and welding God together with the ancestors as a single concept. Transferring them from the oral to the written realm had happened just in time, said one colonial officer:

> Though almost all *ohabolana* have been enumerated, there are some of the most ancient ones whose exact origin, and sometimes even whose precise figurative meaning, is not known. They are hardly used nowadays in current parlance. The present generation of Malagasy, inclined as they are to put the speech of their elders behind them, often know only the formula for proverbs without being able to give a sure explanation of them or apply them correctly. Written literature, itself too recent, does not offer sufficient information on the matter. Only very aged Malagasy properly educated in their own language are capable of informing us. Yet most of these elders today are dead. One can easily count on the fingers of one hand those who possess the dual qualities of age and knowledge and are still available to enlighten us. Yet we must hurry to find and question them, for in a few years this last possibility will have escaped us. (Bruniquel 1951:360)

Naturally a colonial administrator would sound the theme of the imminent disappearance of tradition, so familiar to folklorists. After independence, another official, Charles Ralinoro, urged proverbs as a means of persuading citizens toward change and development.

Print, in modern times, has been the principal weapon against their disappearance. G. H. Julien (1923) cited over a thousand examples from the Cousins and Parrett collection to extract from the Malagasy literary patrimony decisive arguments against their supposed barbarism, and to justify France's confidence in them (though doubtless he referred to nothing more elevated than the right of Malagasy men to be conscripted and killed in World War I). Successive reprints and reworkings of the Cousins and Houlder collections have climaxed in a definitive, comprehensive reedition of previous printed collections by the preeminent Malagasy folklorist of our time (Domenichini-Ramiaramanana 1970). Her formidable study in textual and cultural scholarship compiles 3,679 items in an ingenious classification extending Houlder's ideas, complete with concordances—a monument to the transposing of oral culture into print.

The methods and assumptions of this collection grow out of a century and a half of literacy and a century of printed Malagasy folklore. The editor assumes that each item is fixed by oral tradition, distorted through transmission, and as much in need of restoration as a written poetic text from an earlier era. What each item needs, in this view, is a reconstructed historical context that would name a first speaker of some sayings (a famous king, for instance) and posit one for others. By comparing variant readings and remembering the metrical rules, she sought "the true *ohabolana* before it was used in conversations, speeches, tales, poems, and so on" (Domenichini-Ramiaramanana 1983:xxi). Each saying, according to the values of print culture, once was like Rousseau's natural man, enjoying a primordial freedom which it lost every time it entered into discourse (see Chomsky 1965:3).

From the point of view of performance theory, however, the fixity of Malagasy *ohabolana* in oral culture is only one more statement. It is a metafolkloric belief, a piece of folklore about folklore (Dundes 1966). A concept I draw from the work of M. M. Bakhtin helps us understand the belief. Malagasy sayings, poetry, and oratory exemplify what he called authoritative speech. He might have been giving an ethnographic report on the Merina when he wrote, "The authoritative word is located in a distanced zone, organically connected with a past that is felt to be hierarchically higher. It is, so to speak, the word of the fathers. Its authority was already *acknowledged* in the past. It is a *prior* discourse" (1981:342). Bakhtin's phrase "word of the fathers" nicely translates the Malagasy term *fitenin-drazana*, which comprises proverbs, poetry, and oratory. Most coincidental, he draws a distinction in theory which Jean Paulhan arrived at through fieldwork.

> It is not a free appropriation and assimilation of the word itself that authoritative discourse seeks to elicit from us; rather, it demands our unconditional allegiance. Therefore authoritative discourse permits no play with the context framing it, no play with its borders, no gradual and flexible transitions, no spontaneously creative stylizing variants on it. It enters our verbal consciousness as a compact and indivisible mass; one must either totally affirm it, or totally reject it. (Bakhtin 1981:343)

Malagasy folklore confirms Bakhtin's insight into the social base of language. Although informants repeatedly assert the fixity of *ohabolana*, the printed collections themselves present sufficient variant forms to cause a reader to question it. Today, despite the lack of evidence about performance, folklore theory suggests a different proposition. *Ohabolana* have never been known or described historically, nor can they be, apart from some oral utterance (or a written utterance on an oral model). Every one of those 3,679 sentences was spoken, in conversation, speech, tale, poem, or collector's interview. Therefore it was subject to variation; printed collections show the variant forms. Proverbs may seem like heirlooms—pieces of furniture which each generation adds to or discards, displaying some prominently and putting others away into the attic. But they also resemble houses that have been assembled from the fragments of other, older houses. It was legitimate for earlier collectors, given their assumptions, to disconnect these sentences from their communicative context and locate the single meaning of each one in its words (Fish 1980:150). It is not legitimate to do so today. Though printed proverb texts still furnish evidence to those who speculate on precontact philosophy (Rogers 1985), many Malagasy *ohabolana* furnish evidence also for a generative theory.

Context

Alfred Grandidier's observation that the Malagasy quoted proverbs at every turn reminds us that *ohabolana* are never isolated. Twentieth-century collectors, seeking to give more information about the surroundings of the sentences, have shed light on their situations of interaction and their overlap with other genres of verbal art. Maurice Bloch observed the importance among the Merina of a saying like "Those who live in one house should be buried in one tomb" as an ideal frequently violated in practice (1971:166). The Antaisaka (People of the Ford) of the 1930s, for instance, possessed six such genres: *ohabola*, sayings; *tangahitri*, short tales; *tafaseri*, legends; *tantara*, historical narratives; *velatri*, religious invocations to the gods and ancestors; and song lyrics (Deschamps, "Folklore antaisaka").

Other dialect groups have other genre systems: the Bara, whom Faublée studied shortly after, used the word *ohabola* to mean proverb, but sometimes also to mean tale. "The proverb summarizes the tale, or the tale comments on the proverb," he writes. The saying often takes its normal meaning from an unspoken part of this context. Allusiveness gives it so much power that the shorter form can substitute for the longer. "Informants asked for a tale sometimes say only the few words of a proverb or a saying" (1947:15). The same allusiveness refers to historical or quasi-historical narratives. After the nineteenth-century noble Baraka refused his share of cloths distributed by the first Europeans in his coastal town of Farafangana, his attitude became proverbial: *Mandiny ny an-tsambo akoa i Baraka*, I prefer to wait till they send the next boat, like Baraka (Fontoynont and Raomandahy 1939:31). The same allusiveness is practiced by Betsileo speakers, who assume that their hearers will recognize particular expressions in folk speech (Michel-Andrianarahinjaka 1986:125–26). When a Merina woman uses the expression *Mihiratra ny volana*, the moon is full, she means she is already menstruating, without having had to wait for the full moon, which, some believe, brings on menstruation. Many women consider the full moon as the last date beyond which they can think that their period is merely late.[5] One *ohabolana* shows the contradiction between her true feelings and her public image: *Mihambo tsy tia, ka nony mihiratra ny volana mitomany*, She pretends not to be in love, but when "the moon is full," she starts weeping. The context which gives this proverb meaning was too steamy for the missionaries Cousins and Parrett; they deleted it from their 1877 collection once their Malagasy collaborators explained it to them (Domenichini-Ramiaramanana 1983:203). This allusiveness gives the proverb its power to evoke unspoken associations and also to exclude those outside the interpretive community. What Dubois (1938:1259–60) said of the Betsileo may stand for the Merina and others: as a shortcut answer to every problem, the *ohabolana* translates the speaker's opinion or advice into the impersonal, even sacred words of tradition. If it is pointed enough, a European will find it difficult to grasp, whereas a Malagasy hearer will grasp its entire significance and direction, make out all its allusions, and (if he is a good Christian) put himself on guard against its salacious innuendoes.

In oral culture, where and when were these sayings said? In Madagascar, as everywhere else, proverbs tend to mean most in the "interaction situation," the moment in social space-time when a person speaks a saying. In that moment, the proverb points the hearer's attention to a "context situation" which she or he will interpret according to the metaphor in the proverb (Seitel 1977:76–77). In this view, everything surrounding the words—the speaking situation, the identity and relation of the speaker and listeners, the rhetorical purposes of the moment—actually determines the words. The sentences we find in printed collections may have been not quoted, but recreated and generated by speakers who knew the rules. An instance of such generation occurred before the very eyes of the colonial officer quoted earlier, who called for finding and interviewing old Merina informants. A European missionary had brought his purebred cat to Madagascar, where he fed it so well it didn't catch rats or mice. People used the cat for comparison: a person was like "Iparitra's cat; nice-looking but no rat-catcher." The structural model for this, Topic/Comment 1/Comment 2, has existed for centuries. In another case when a saying was generated, a Catholic missionary's servant broke the wine bottle he was carrying. The priest quipped, "When the Father's demijohn gets broken, we both lose our wages, my boy" (Bruniquel 1951:244).

The Malagasy *ohabolana*, therefore, varies in its genre, its structure, and its interpretation. Though usually defined as one genre, fixed in phrasing, ancient, and authoritative, its limits blur (as do those of so many genres). The *ohabolana* overlaps the longer, more elaborate poetic genre of *hainteny*. Moreover, it varies in structure. The numerous structures and message-forms for these sayings have yet to be inventoried. A third sort of variability appears when collectors transcribe and translate the sayings. Working among Sakalava in the northwest, Emile Birkeli translated three words, *Tama valy telo*, in three different ways: "Sterility with three wives," "Accustomed to one's three wives," or "Three wives accustomed to one another." The last meaning was too far out of the ordinary for him; he preferred the first but gave no helpful context. He was obliged to use multiple translation again for *Mena maso ka mpamorike*: "Red eyes like a singer [who calls market people together]" or "like a sorcerer," perhaps the commoner meaning (Birkeli 1922–23:396–417). A wholly accurate definition of *ohabolana*, in fact, should rest upon exhaustive enumeration of structures, which might please a Westerner. No Malagasy, I presume, will ever accept such finality.

Multiple Existence

Proverbs, of all the Malagasy genres, pose the strongest challenge to what I call folkloric restatement. Easy as they have been to collect, they have never been collected according to the scientific criteria advocated by twentieth-century Africanist folklorists (Bascom 1964). The many isolated sentences in proverb collections tell nothing about how they were used. Collectors give abundant examples of the message forms they heard, but none about the identity of speakers or hearers. They tell the non-Malagasy reader what conclusions they reached after gathering these dozens of condensed, pithy utterances but nothing about the effects of the utterances on any individual Malagasy. They report innumerable items, but hardly ever the recurrence of the items in different contexts. They seek to know proverbs as fixed sentences but show no interest in the fixing process. Like students everywhere, they reduce the knowledge of their topic to digested and portable form, an enterprise to which this genre lends itself with alarming facility. Although folklore collectors in Madagascar have amassed an impressive catalog of the words said during heightened speech acts, they have left it entirely up to us to consider what theory would connect these acts to one another, or what might explain the choices speakers would make. Yet a discipline of folklore concerned with the problems of representing other people's cultural experience wants to answer these unanswered questions.

   Still more puzzling, in studying the history of collecting, is a contradiction between the time-honored definition and the printed books. If *ohabolana* are recurrent and fixed in phrasing, why do they not recur more often? Few of the *ohabolana* in printed collections seem to be variants or versions of already collected texts. By contrast, Kuusi (1970) found 4,631 texts of only 2,482 Ovambo proverbs. Of course, many Malagasy texts were reprinted from one book to another; the tradition of printed *ohabolana* initiated by Cousins continues up to Domenichini-Ramiaramanana's reedition. But apart from the continuity established by reprinting, no significant number of oral texts represent independently collected versions or variants of the same item. Thus, though informants and collectors agreed to define the *ohabolana* as a recurrent, fixed-phrase text, its existence in print shows it to be nonrecurrent or perhaps unique.

Regional dialect variation, in this huge island of dialect differences, helps to explain some of this discontinuity. When Dr. Maurice Fontoynont, the progenitor of Malagasy medical education and a dedicated *malgachisant*, and his collaborator Raomandahy (1938) print a proverb from Vakinankaratra, the highland region around Antsirabe and Betafo, they often give a French analogue to suggest one of its possible meanings. But they do not give equivalents from outside that region (for instance, by referring to the Cousins collection). Few of their proverbs, they explain, had equivalents elsewhere in the highlands.

Many *ohabolana* appear only once. Some of these allude to historical contexts in which they are supposed to have been created. History tells us that the greatest of Merina kings, Andrianampoinimerina, often cited proverbs in a strongly authoritative, monologic mode. His pronouncements always elicited an answer. Once, explaining how the community council (*fokon'olona*) was to operate, he declared that whoever failed to appear at a convocation would be condemned. "It is a commitment you have undertaken, my subjects; it cannot be changed. Cattle are fastened by the horns, people by the tongue." At the conclusion of this oration, "the people" gave formal thanks to Andrianampoinimerina for his careful administration, as if his whole speech were an utterance that required an answer (Callet 1974, 3:131). A proverb scholar may well wonder, is this a "real original sentence," or an accepted proverb which has been attributed later to the creative genius of the king? (Navone 1977:61). After his death, "tradition reports no royal speech, no appeal to the people without its little bouquet of *ohabolana*" (Domenichini-Ramiaramanana 1970:xviii).

This discontinuity strikes at the heart of the concept of tradition in folklore theory. How important is multiple existence as a component of the definition of *ohabolana*? What if Malagasy proverbs do not, in fact, recur in different contexts in the same words? If many collected texts are unique single examples, how can we be sure they were ever recurrent? And if they do not recur, are they real folklore? Folklorists and readers often assume that "acceptance on the part of many" creates a "sanction," which makes a saying into a proverb (Westermarck 1930:1), but they assume so without evidence. For Madagascar as for many countries of continental Africa,

> If one of the marks of a true proverb is its general acceptance as the popular expression of some truth, we are seldom given the data to decide how far this is indeed a characteristic of the sayings included in collections of "proverbs." . . . We have in fact no way of telling whether some of the "proverbs" included are not just the sententious utterances of a single individual on a single occasion which happened to appeal to the investigator. (Finnegan 1970:394)

The problem requires shifting our notion of tradition away from product toward process. "A proverb may be traditional even if it is innovative, as long as it conforms to the traditional patterns of proverb form and content" (McDowell 1979:14). If *ohabolana* are less stable than collectors assumed, instead of being "handed down from generation to generation," they have been generated from models that were learned by expert speakers. This approach to proverbs, advanced by European scholars (Kuusi 1972, Permiakov 1979, Peukes 1977, Voigt 1970), seems especially appropriate to Malagasy culture, which values verbal fluency and creativity. Moreover, Paulhan, an outsider, did learn some of the models. "The mind of a slave: to destroy" became his model for "The mind of Iketaka: to play coquette" and "The mind of a child: to think of nothing." Paulhan also found this two-part structure in sayings like "If the teeth get broken, the head gets the blame," which became his model for "If the hair is gray, the head gets the blame." "It happened as a consequence," he writes, "that the abstract framework, the armature common to a whole family of proverbs first presented itself to my mind: this framework was then adorned with words" (Paulhan 1925:50).

The generative binary principle for *ohabolana*, which Paulhan discovered, has been confirmed by more recent fieldwork among the Betsileo, for whom proverbs usually comprise two parts. Saying the first part elicits the second almost automatically, yet variations in wording often occur (Michel-Andrianarahinjaka 1986:120–21). The same two-sided pattern generates the performance of other fixed-phrase genres like riddles and *hainteny* (poems), which streamline the multiplicity of human discourse into two voices. More obviously monologic in performance and intention, *ohabolana* and oratory (*kabary*) attempt to contain the two voices in one authoritative "last word." This dialectic between dialogue and monologue reflects the rise of a hierarchical state in the central highlands.

Generative Structures, 1: Symmetry

> He whose wife is ugly
>> and whose rice has been ravaged by the boar
> is somber in the field
>> and joyless in the village
>>> (Olsen 1929:57)

Though *ohabolana* are spoken by a single speaker, who need not say the sentence all the way through, their form, as this example shows, may be as antithetical as the riddle and as balanced as the *hainteny*. *Tsy vantotr' akoho baranahiny aho, fa vorombazaha misy mpiandry*, I am no chicken left to run free, but a duck who has a guardian, says a young woman having been asked for in marriage (Fontoynont and Raomandahy 1938:205–6, no. 38). Antithesis and balance in such examples enact internally the external symmetry of two-sided dialogue. In the simplest model, the second half of the utterance answers the first, as if the gestalt would otherwise be incomplete.[6]

> Fahadalam-pietrana:
>> fahendram-pisondrotana.

> Foolishness abases (you),
>> wisdom raises (you) up.

> Anasanisana ny ratsy
>> hihavian'ny soa.

> Bad is told
>> so that good will appear.

> Tia ihany
>> ka be malo.

> You love,
>> yet you are too shy.

> Mody tsy tia,
>> koa lefaka.

> You pretend to dislike,
>> but (still) talk sweet.

Nahoana no ho tia vao
  ka manary kolokolo?

Why say you love the new,
  yet throw away the aftergrowth of rice (the old)?

Laha hianao manoto mahasaky,
  iaho mamaly tsy magnahatse.

If you are not afraid of me
  I have no reason to be afraid of you.
                (Houlder 1960: nos. 1626, 95,
                190, 191, 189; Michel 1956:175)

This use of balance has been observed in many highland proverbs. Dubois thought the numerous examples he collected showed distinctive traits of Betsileo mentality (Dubois 1938:1259–97). One of the most haunting and authoritative Merina proverbs, at least to the ears of philosophy-minded listeners, makes its statement on the model of the antithetical contradictive riddle: *Ny tody tsy misy, fa ny atao no miverina*, There is no [such thing as divinely appointed] retribution, but what is done returns. The concept of *tody*, retribution, is often viewed as fundamental to Malagasy thought (Andriamanjato 1957, Rajaona 1959). The two-sided form makes this saying turn into what the American literary critic Stanley Fish calls a "self-consuming artifact." The second half (which may also be translated "what you do comes back on you") states the definition of the concept of *tody* which was annihilated in the first half. Thus the proverb contradicts itself with its sham equilibrium, leaving the hearer no place to stand. A variant form frames it with an admonition.

Aza homehy lavo,
  fa ny tody tsy misy
    fa ny atao no miverina.

Don't make fun of the fallen,
  for there is no retribution,
    but what is done does return.
                (Houlder 1960: no. 1718)

Of the thousands of *ohabolana* collected in Madagascar since 1877, many have been generated from this two-part riddlelike model. Kuusi has given the name "proverb-riddle" to this characteristically African genre, which combines the structure of a riddle with the function of a proverb. Precedent and sequent are "completely or almost completely parallel in structure" (Kuusi 1974:9). Whether this balanced structure be called proverb or riddle, many Africans know it (Harries 1971, Messenger 1960, Simmons 1958). When a conjunction comes between the clauses, the added syllable changes the meter.

> Ketsa vaventy,
>> ka sarotra atao lahirodona.

> [When] young rice-plants are fat,
>> then it's difficult to double them up [in the same hole].

> Arim-batana,
>> fa tsy arin-karena.

> Big in body,
>> but not big in wealth.
>>> (Houlder 1960: nos. 1377, 1466)

The Importance of Symmetry

Malagasy men of words did not, of course, invent the rhetorical structure of antithesis, nor did Malagasy artists invent symmetrical design. Malagasy proverbs and *hainteny* share these features with African proverbs (Finnegan 1970:395–403) and Asian poetries (Raffel 1967, Dournes 1976:123–85). Malagasy proverbs display great fondness for close, punning parallelism: *Tsy nahabe fa nahalava*, They don't raise their children, they lengthen them (Fontoynont and Raomandahy 1939:32, no. 5). Reliance on a form like question and answer as a means of structuring a monologic, authoritative saying takes on special meaning when homeostasis and balance enter into opposition with the multiplicity of voices. Recent philosophers of Malagasy national character have used proverbs as evidence to emphasize the importance of balance and equilibrium. Both *tody*, retribution, and *tsiny*, reproaches, are explained by Richard Andriamanjato as departures from equilibrium which must be rectified. "The good one does is a treasure one has laid up," he quotes; "the bad one commits is a misfortune that threatens him. When it's you who speak, it's God who moves you, but when someone else speaks, it's *tangena* poison[7] thrown out the door" (1957:27). The Malagasy notion of truth, as expounded by Siméon Rajaona, advocates balance and equilibrium (Rajaona 1959).

Folktales utilize a corresponding structure to the symmetrical *ohabolana*: the two-part story which begins in disequilibrium and moves to equilibrium. A familiar myth about the origin of marriage takes the very shape of these proverbs. *Precedent*: God makes a statue and places it on the road. *Sequent*: Two men who come along attempt to turn it over without success; one leaves to look for a lever; the other turns over the statue and claims her for his wife, and God ratifies his claim (tale 1.1.48 in *Malagasy Tale Index*). In the analytic terminology developed for tales by Vladimir Propp (1968) and Alan Dundes (1964), the precedent may be called a lack, and the sequent the liquidation of the lack. Another widespread Malagasy creation story shows that human life requires two creators. One makes man's body but lacks the knowledge of how to animate his figure. A second creator gives man life, but will reclaim him when he dies (tales 1.1.11–39 in *Malagasy Tale Index*). The same two-part structure underlies the popular swallowing monster story which Madagascar shares with Africa. A monstrous snake eats whole villages (lack, or disequilibrium). A hero destroys the monster and releases its victims (lack liquidated, or equilibrium) (tales 1.3.1–11 in *Malagasy Tale Index*). Hundreds of tales and hundreds of *ohabolana* consist of a lack and its liquidation.

Generative Structures, 2: The Symmetry Doubled

The second prominent structure for *ohabolana* doubles the parallel units, setting one symmetry beside another.

> Izay mahavangivangy
>   tian-kavana,
> malemy fanahy
>   tratra am-parany.

> Those who visit often
>   are loved by their kinfolk,

the gentle-hearted
  are long-lived.

(Clemes 1877: 28)

Mandedandeha,
  be raha hita,
midoboky,
  be raha lany.

Traveling,
  you see much,
staying at home,
  you spend much.

(Fontoynont and Raomandahy 1939:31)[8]

To double or multiply the symmetry exerts further control over the
medium. Perhaps the joy of the *mpikabary* begins here. Linguistically, reduplication of syllables has the effect of attenuating meaning. Similarly,
children's versions of adult activities have diminutive names. In *ohabolana*,
however, the doubling of symmetry produces the dilemma of an oscilla-
tion between two reported contradictory voices:

Manasa ny be kibo,
  ka ny vary no lany;
mananatra ny adala,
  ka ny vava no visana.

Invite the Big-Gut,
  then your rice is eaten up;
advise the foolish,
  then your mouth gets tired out.

Ny lehibe no manaiky, ny henatra;
  ny kely no manaiky, no tahotra.

The great give way to shame,
  the little give way to fear.

Malahelo mivoaka maraina,
    ataon'ny olona hangalatra;
mivoaka hariva,
    ataon'ny olona hisakana.

Poor man goes out in the morning,
    people say he's going to steal;
he goes out in the evening,
    people say he's going to rob.
                    (Houlder 1960: nos. 1595, 1386,
                    1454)

The symmetry itself expresses the pain of an inescapable dilemma. A university student in February 1976 confirmed the force of such dilemmas when he cited to me the proverb *miala an' Ankatso Ambohidempona*, "You flee from a bad place and get into an equally bad one. This proverb," he went on, "is said quite often, about anything at all nowadays, or nearly so, whereas originally it had a very heavy meaning" because so many Ankatso people had been killed by colonials.

Generative Structures, 3: The Priamel

Some dilemmas find no resolution. Others find their resolution in a last line which gives an answer. Men of words among the Antaifasy (People of the Sand) seem especially partial to this structure.

Tsy an-tany
    tsy an-trano,
        akoa viavy molan-drafy.

Not in the field,
    not in the house,
        like a wife soured by her rival.

Lambo an'ala
    vahatra an'ala,
        ka tsy mifanola-tomboka.

> A boar in the forest,
>> a shrub in the forest,
>>> they aren't caught by their feet.
>>>> (Fontoynont and Raomandahy 1939:
>>>> nos. 61, 71)

A closely related third structure arranges lines in order of climax. Two or more symmetrical units are a precedent; they find their resolution in a final phrase with the authority of a riddle sequent. In its simplest form, this kind of proverb is a series of clauses.

> Ny anankiray natao hoe "andevo namidy";
>> ny anankiray natao hoe "nifindra fihinana";
>>> ary ny anankiray natao hoe "andevo tsy fiompy";
>>>> ary ny anankiray natao hoe "andevon-drazana."

> One man was called a "sold slave";
>> another was called "changed his dinnertable";
>>> and another was called "a slave not kept";
>>>> and the other man was called "a slave from the ancestors."
>>>> (Houlder 1960: no. 1577)[9]

These descriptions show the hierarchy of relations between slaves (*andevo*) and owners (*hova*) in former times, who regarded the last-named, closest slave more or less as part of the family. Like the earlier example, "The mountain is the bed of the fog," a sequence like this can be inserted into an oration, with varied meaning according to context. The literary counterpart is the priamel, a series of aphorisms often improvised (Taylor 1931:178–80).[10] The Malagasy priamel resembles a riddle:

> Raha revom-potaka, rano no malala;
>> raha revon-teny, vava no manala;
>>> raha revon'alahelo, ny havana no ifarainana.

> When covered with mud, you wash (remove) it with water;
>> when covered by words, you remove them with your mouth;
>>> when covered in sorrow, it's your kinfolk you turn to.
>>> (Houlder 1960:16, no. 184)

Mizara be mahahendry;
　mizara kely mahadala;
　　mandidy taolana mahadombo antsy.

Passing out much (goods), you are made much of;
　passing out little, you are belittled;
　　cutting bones dulls the knife.
　　　　　　　　　　(Houlder 1960:138, no. 1621)

Here the dilemma of the first two lines is resolved in the last, as a riddle answer completes the incomplete half (though someone ought to tell us what it all means). In this and other priamels, the authoritative tendency of *ohabolana* results from a structure in which the "last word" is a distinct grammatical and metrical unit.

Generative Structures, 4: Topic-Comment

The three structures isolated so far—the symmetry, the symmetry doubled, and the symmetry concluded in a phrase—manifest the opposition in *ohabolana* between two voices and one voice. A fourth structure, closest to the riddle and encountered most often of all, contains the same opposition. Its essential components are the riddle topic, something named, and a comment, an assertion made about the topic (Georges and Dundes 1963). The topic-comment structure contrasts with the riddle by inverting the order in which topic and comment are spoken. "An iron hammer and an iron file: one friend makes another." "The heart is like hot water: a quick temper is no friend" (Houlder 1960:15, 32). In a related form, the English "reverse riddle," the poser gives the referent (topic) first, and the respondent is to guess the basis for comparison (Abrahams and Dundes 1972:136–73).

　　Folkloric restatement allows some insight into the importance of this more authoritarian form of *ohabolana*. The movement, in such a saying, from disequilibrium (lack) to equilibrium (liquidation of lack) must be evident in performance. A speaker refers to a present or absent person as *Sotrobe lava tango*, a ladle with a long handle, posing an implicit precedent, "Why is Soandso like a long-handled ladle?" When the speaker supplies the comment, "*Mahay atsy, mahay eroa*, He dips here, he dips there," the resemblance is explained: this person can get along with anyone, even people hostile to each other (Houlder 1960:39, no. 494). Because the metaphor represents a shift of channel or tone in the conversation, it creates disequilibrium. Giving the answer creates closure. This sort of proverb is not unique to Madagascar (Mieder 1982), having been found for instance in Yiddish proverbs. The first half states a connection, "A guest is like rain," and the second half explains it: "if he stays too long, he becomes a burden" (Silverman-Weinreich 1978). The topic-comment structure may be no more than a transformation between one form and another (Kuusi 1972:16). For Russian proverbs, G. L. Permiakov (1979) demonstrated the existence of affirmative, negative, ambivalent, and interrogative transformations. The large number of Malagasy examples, however, suggests that the form takes some force from a characteristic inversion in word order. Linguists point out that placing the subject first, in an ordinary Malagasy sentence, marks it as emphatic, sententious, and solemn. *Ny olombelona mora soa sy mora ratsy*, [It is] Men [who] are easily good and easily bad; *Andriamanitra tsy tia ratsy*, [It is] God [who] does not like evil. These proverb examples utilize the same order as conversational utterances like *Rakoto marary ka tsy afaka*, Rakoto is [unquestionably] ill and isn't coming (Rajaona 1963). In *ohabolana*, the topic receives the same emphasis:

Tsingala sy dinta:
  raha miray trano loza,
  ary raha mifanaikitra, antambo.

Water-beetle and leech:
  if together in house, trouble,
  but if they bite each other, calamity.
          (Houlder 1960:26, no. 319)

Adin'ombilahin' ny mpianakavy:
  ny mahery tsy hobina,
  ny resy tsy akoraina.

Family members are fighting bulls:
  the strong you mustn't applaud,
  the weak you mustn't jeer.
          (Domenichini-Ramiaramanana 1970:
          no. 1875)

Androngo milanja lolo:
   be am-pitondroha fa kely am-pihinana.

A lizard carrying a butterfly:
   it's big to carry but small to eat.

Mason-tana:
   be hamontirana
   fa kely am-pahiratana.

Chameleon's eyes:
   they stick out a lot,
   but they're not much to see with.

Amboa nivahiny:
   tonga tsy mahafaly,
   lasa tsy mampalahelo.

A strange dog:
   his coming doesn't make you happy,
   his leaving doesn't make you sad.

   (Houlder 1960:112, no. 1348, 114, no. 1372,
   124, no. 1483) [11]

As riddles have been interpreted by Roberts and Forman as expressive models for interrogation, the topic-comment form of *ohabolana* may be interpreted as a model for authoritative speech. It suits an interaction situation in which someone (whatever his or her age or rank) asserts authority and control over others by means of its shift of channel or of tone. In Madagascar as in West Africa, the direction of proverb speaking is usually down the social scale, from elder to younger and from more skilled to less skilled, but anyone could learn examples like these and try to exert control with them. Their authoritarianism could be playful or ironic as easily as coercive or forceful.

Embedding the riddle in the proverb, the comments of such proverbs reproduce riddle contradictions. Both the antithetical and privational contradictions which Georges and Dundes found in riddles appear in the comment section of Malagasy *ohabolana*. An antithetical contradiction poses a dilemma: "Throwing it [the pot] away is shameful, keeping it dishonors the house" (Houlder 1960 : 127, no. 1511).

> Toy ny amboa:
>   anana, mahavoafady,
>   tsy anana, mahavoafady.

> Like dogs:
>   if you have them, you get blamed,
>   if you don't have them, you get blamed.
>   (Houlder 1960 : 125, no. 1487)

> Toy ny hanina omena andevo:
>   tian-kano
>   tsy tian-kano.

> Like the food given to slaves:
>   if they like it, they eat it,
>   if they don't like it, they eat it.
>   (Houlder 1960 : 133, no. 1564)

The other sort of riddle contradiction embedded in the *ohabolana* is the "privational," which denies, in its second part, some expected attribute of the first part. The chameleon's eyes "stick out a lot, but they're not much to see with." "Like a duck, he has wings but he can't fly" (Houlder 1960 : 123, no. 1465). As when one speaker reports another's speech, an opening formula like *aza manao*, "Don't act like . . . ," can frame a reproof that would be too direct if unframed:

> Aza manao tsitsik' ombin' Ibetsileo:
>   ny ombin Ikoto an' Ikoto ihany,
>   ary ny ombin' olona an' ikoto koa.

> Don't act like the Betsileo with cattle:
>   Ikoto's cattle belong to Ikoto,
>   and other people's cattle belong to Ikoto too.
>   (Houlder 1960 : 126, no. 1501)

This more authoritarian formula also introduces refinements like doubling the contradictions.

> Aza manao ombilain' Ibosy:
>> ampiadin-tsy miady,
>>> ampihosen-tsy mihosy,
>>>> hanin-kena, mafy hena,
>>>>> avela ihany, manoto ny madinika.

> Don't act like Ibosy's bull:
>> make him fight, he doesn't want to,
>>> make him tread the fields, he refuses,
>>>> (try) to eat him, his flesh is tough,
>>>>> leave him alone, he gores the children.
>>>>>> (Houlder 1960:148, no. 1732)

If the speaker wishes to enforce his authority further, he can end the topic and comment with a terminal phrase.

> Parasin' Ambohimanoa:
>> ny vavy be loha,
>>> ary ny lahy no kibotaina,
>>>> ka samy mahalala ny anjarany.

> Lice of Ambohimanoa:
>> the females have big heads,
>>> and the males have big stomachs,
>>>> so they both know their faults.
>>>>> (Houlder 1960:129, no. 1523)

Do Speakers Learn Structures?

These structures, with their symmetries and doublings, have been derived from print; they are a text-based discovery. Are they also part of the psychological preparation of a man of words? They seem easy enough to learn. Published texts show that they have served Malagasy speakers as models to generate thousands of new sayings. Adolphe Bruniquel's illustration, "Iparitra's cat: beautiful but no rat-chaser," stands for hundreds of occasions when creation of a proverb was made possible by the widespread topic-comment model. When Jean Paulhan finds seemingly proverbial lines in a poem, he is identifying the punning parallelism, not necessarily identifying a specific sentence often quoted (Paulhan 1913:168–89). The symmetrical, doubled, and topic-comment structures I have isolated do not exhaust the possible patterns by which *ohabolana* can be assembled, but they demonstrate how easily generative structures can be found by folkloric restatement, and how easily they could be learned. Probably hundreds of the single sentences in the Cousins and Houlder collections represent not recurrent fixed phrases, but rather the patterned utterances of speakers who had absorbed the rules for formal speech performance and who were performing for their investigator. Speakers who gave those texts to collectors had learned riddles in childhood, later contested with each other in *hainteny*, and held forth in *kabary* at weddings and funerals. The four proverb structures were very probably part of what they learned. In Madagascar as in other Indian Ocean cultures, proverbs, poetry, and song all overlap, and so do their fundamental devices like quotation. Swahili songs, for instance, cite proverbs as often as Merina poems do (Knappert 1979:45–51). One Malagasy informant has insisted that *hainteny*, formal oratory (*kabary*), and *ohabolana* are "completely the same," though acknowledging that the overlap creates problems for the scholar.

> The *hainteny*, the various forms of *kabary*, the *ohabolana* are things that seem to present numerous points in common. What I have in mind is . . . "undulation" [*fanonjany*], or an image that rises up from the heart of a phrase. . . . Manifestly there are links among [the different genres] . . . . As a result, the person who can manage the art of *hainteny* well can also immediately practice *kabary*, and the one who manages the art of *kabary* well can also practice that of *hainteny*. (Rajoelisolo in Domenichini-Ramiaramanana 1983:341)

Malagasy poetic genres certainly overlap with each other, and with other folklore. Some of the classic "longer oratorical flourishes" (Sibree's designation for *hainteny*) use the symmetry and parallelism of the proverb for a genre I have not mentioned, the charm.

Raha ho faty aho, matesy rahavana;
    ary raha ho faty rahavana, matesy ny omby.
Ary raha ikiaky sy ineny no ho faty,
    dia tongava ny fanafody mahavelona.
Ary raha izihay sy ny zanako no hisaraka,
    dia mikatona ny tany aman-danitra.

If I must die, may my kinsmen die instead;
  but if my kinsmen must die, may my cattle die instead.
And if father and mother must die,
  then may I find the remedy to make them live.
And if my children and I must separate,
  then may heaven and earth join together.

(Dahle 1877:38, no. 116)

Formulaic charms like this are quoted by folktale characters, thus involving another genre in the interrelations. An insistence that distinct genres are "completely the same" links Malagasy verbal art to that African tradition in which "patterning of imagery is the most visible artistic activity" (Scheub 1985:4). To systematize a seemingly systemless process of folklore variation, the notion of the *ohabolana* as a product, which reached its extreme in Paulhan's formulation "an event independent of all words," must be coupled with its dialectical opposite, the dynamic process of interactions in communicative events. Patterns mediate these opposites in *ohabolana* and also in the *hainteny* that are the subject of the next chapter.

4. Proposition and Response: The Merina *Hainteny*

Is It Poetry?

The Merina *hainteny* is an elusive though formalized utterance. Now it seems like a riddle, then like a proverb, sometimes like part of an oration. Sometimes it is long and flowery, extended by embedding one speaker's words in another's. At other times, the poem may be as brief as an *ohabolana*, though invariably more dramatic. Here, a man's first wife speaks:

> Kotsakotsa rambon-damba
>> Rano saiky nosotroiko
>> Notsipitsipihan'ilay sahona

> The fringe of my shawl is damp
>> into the water I was about to drink
>> a frog jumped
>>> (Paulhan 1913:230–31, 1938:60)

Her shawl (*lamba*) is damp because she has been drying her tears with it. Yet she denies having wept. It is only that she has been splashed by a frog, the young second wife for whom her husband is neglecting her. Like a similar piece which Ezra Pound translated from Chinese, "the poem is especially prized because she utters no direct reproach" (1963:194). Direct reproach would bring *tsiny* (reproach) upon her. Internally the poem uses two riddle devices: dialogic structure, posing its puzzle and then answering it, and indirect metaphorical language. Externally it is dialogic too. The reciter of such a poem, like the character in it, is using indirect expression to convey some message to his or her hearer.

To contrast with that monologic example, here is a narrated dialogue, complete with narrator and sexual metaphors.

Mialà, miesora, raondriana mpihambo tsy tompony, fa aza misoso-
soso foana toa vinanto kely tsy mandre fosa; fa hianao dia tsy mba
kivy, ary tsy mba ketraka hoatry ny mitari-bady tsy lasam-bodiondry,
sy ny homan-kena tsy lasam-bidy. Koa dia mialà, miesora hianao; fa
vato tsindry hahazana, ka raha maloka ny andro, dia atsipinay hianao.

Fa hoy kosa izy: Tsy misy vato tsindry hahazana, fa samy vato naorin-
kivavahana; ary tsy misy saonjo fatsaky ny kitra, fa samy saonjon' ny
an-alan' ambo. Ary tsy misy vato setrin' ny tavolitra; fa samy tompony, ary samy manana. Ka raha sofiny hianao, dia mba tandrony
aho; ka raha mikopaka hianao, dia mba mihodina aho; ary raha
manao fofonaina mifanerana hianao, dia manao fitia mifandanja aho.
Ary raha manana fitia manan' amby hianao, dia mba misy fitia
manantombo aty amiko; fa raha hianao mitsipaka, dia izaho kosa
manosika.

(Dahle 1877 : 28, trans. Chapus and Dandouau
1940 : 105)[1]

She: On your way! Go, milord, who are a pretender and no owner,
and do not presume foolishly
like a son-in-law ignoring gossipers.
You should not be discouraged
like one leading away a wife without giving the "sheep's rump"
    [bride price],
or one who eats meat without paying.
So, on your way, depart,
for you are "a stone holding down the laundry,
when daylight darkens, we throw you away."

But this was his answer:
"No stone holds down the laundry.
We both are stones set up for prayer.
No stunted herb-plant.
We both are herbs deep in the forest.
A potsherd can't take the place of a stone.
We are both our own masters, our own owners.
If you are the ears, I am the horns,
if you turn from side to side, I'll go in a circle,
if you exchange breaths with me,

I'll give you good weight.
If your love grows,
then my love grows along with it,
but if you kick me,
I'll push you away."

Different though it seems, this second *hainteny* is as typical of the repertoire as the first. Perhaps it is more so, with its two voices in dialogue, its drama of love, and its quoting of well-known sayings like the one about a stone holding down laundry to dry. Both pieces depend on dialogue internally and externally. In text and in performance, most *hainteny* are dialogic exchanges of traditional metaphors, some of which circulate independently as monologic proverbs. But are they poetry? Dahle obviously did not think so. Genre classification has determined how *hainteny* were interpreted.

The "Art of the Word"

The name of the genre means word science, word play, or, in some usages, traditional saying. One etymology connects *hainteny* with its homonym *ainteny*, breath of the word or life of words. "In traditional poetry, the word is simultaneously animated and dominated by *inspiration*, by the breath. Breathing determines both the measure and the melodic line of the verses, just as their rhythm often creates balance, parallelism, and symmetry" (Domenichini-Ramiaramanana 1978:103–6). This etymology marks the genre as poetic. A more accurate translation of *hainteny* is "the art of the word." In its name and nature, it functions in the same ways as artistic language all over Africa (Peek 1981) and indeed throughout the Indian Ocean. Paul Ottino (among others) has observed that it is characteristic of Malayo-Polynesian cultures, including that of Madagascar, to make use of ambiguity and plurisignation. A brief allusion can refer to something external to the words, the words can reveal a symbolic significance behind their manifest meaning, or the terms of a verbal message can possess several different or even opposed semantic values. In highland Madagascar, Ottino says, verbal artistry expresses a maximum of thought with a minimum of words, makes constant allusions to proverbs and folktales, and relies continually on metaphor for the sake of dissimulation or obscuring another meaning (1966).

These features of Malagasy verbal art are epitomized in the genre of *hainteny*. Here is an example juxtaposing several metaphors of desire in a balanced dialogue.

Irony tendrombohitra atsimo irony
Fandrian-javona fandrian-tsidintsidina
Any ambany atsinanana any
Misy ombalahy iray mitoreo
Ao ambany avaratra ao
Misy kibobo roa manan-jara
Tsy havan'ikaky tsy havan' ineny
Ka mahamanina ahy

(Paulhan 1913:204–5, 1960:130, trans. Fox 1990:150–51, no. 90)

She: Those mountains of the south
are a bed for fogs, a bed for swallows.
Farther off, towards the east,
a bull groans sadly.

He: Over to the north
are two happy quail,
no kin to my father, no kin to my mother—
They give me pangs of love.

Such a poem is typical of *hainteny*: the represented speakers both hide and reveal their thought, and the person reciting the poem would be doing so as well. The metaphors of *hainteny* link Madagascar with West Africa, where riddle language enables a speaker to hide and reveal his thought at the same time. Such enigmatic, figurative speech, which has been culti- vated in Madagascar especially by the Merina, is the vehicle for delicate, dangerous things. As riddles all over the world dramatize the secrets of the society for children (Wolfenstein 1954, Gaignebet 1981), Merina *hainteny* always have a not-so-secret meaning. Flavien Ranaivo, a great creator in the genre, has told me that a sexual meaning is always present when adults hear *hainteny*. They have also had a political meaning ever since they emerged into popularity with the rise of monarchy. Those who under- stand *hainteny* are glad to feel themselves an elite. Those who do not are as much excluded as the small children in a riddling session or the popu- lace outside the palace. Socially the genre is a form of politeness; aesthetically it distills the most beautiful language into elegant forms. In addition, as a dialogic game of double entendres, it tests the quick wit of the player (Calame-Griaule 1963). In these ways, the *hainteny*, like other Malagasy genres, uses the style of poetic language all over the African continent, and indeed all over the Indian Ocean.

Poets consider *hainteny* to be poetry. Flavien Ranaivo derives the name of the genre from *haitra*, fantasy, stating: "They are genuine poems. Not all of them are within everyone's reach. They were composed and created by a specialized class of persons, whom we today call poets, but who in most people's eyes were simply fantasists of language and thought" (Ranaivo 1949:61). But *hainteny* have not always been considered poetic. Before Jean Paulhan published 160 texts with French translations in 1913, Malagasy folklore collectors, whatever their origin, treated *hainteny* as prose. Reviewing Paulhan's book, Gabriel Ferrand—Arabic scholar, folk-tale collector, ethnographer of Muslim communities, linguist, historian—denied them the title of poetry. His reason was that in the Malagasy language, what distinguishes poetry from prose in Arabic, Greek, Latin, or French does not exist.

> Without rhyme, meter, or measure, a literary creation can not claim to be taken as *poetry* in the usual meaning of the word. In fact, the Malagasy language has remained at the stage where, from the European point of view, poetry and prose are insufficiently distinguished from each other for us to be able to say exactly "this is prose" and "this is poetry." Let us merely say that hain-teny is a literary composition of a special genre in which a poetic sentiment becomes manifest, more apparent in inner meaning than in form. (Ferrand 1914:155)

Some Merina agreed with Ferrand. "How can you think the *hainteny* are poetry?" one expostulated. "They have no rhyme, and it's only ignorant Malagasy who know them" (Paulhan 1913:46). Despite these views, their reliance on meter and their performance as song classify them as poems.

The Discovery of Poetry

The perception of *hainteny* as poetry retraces, in the history of European consciousness, what Propp called a donor sequence in folktale. In this recurrent sequence of incidents, a hero is tested, he reacts, and he receives a magical agent (Propp 1968:39–43). Recurrently through post-Renaissance history, European readers have been tested in their perception of non-Western literature. At the outset they know full well what universal literature is: it is the poetry that derives from Homer, Vergil, and Horace. Then they are tested: they confront a foreign poetry. In eighteenth-century Britain, for example, James Macpherson presents to them "Fragments of Ancient Poetry collected in the Highlands of Scotland, and Translated from the Gaelic or Erse Language." Or Thomas Percy introduces to them an extraordinary jumble of folk ballads, poems by the Elizabethan Earl of Surrey, political song lyrics, and poems by the editor himself and his friends. The European audience responds to the test: they invent a new category, the "effusions of nature," the "barbarous productions of unpolished ages" (Percy's term for the contents of his *Reliques of Ancient English Poetry*). This category, which the British called "natural" poetry, they could experience as alien and exotic. Universal poetry, with its "labours of art," now stands opposed to natural poetry. No one questions the assumption that their two aesthetics must be different (Wellek 1955:126). Their reward is that they are provided with a magic object, the transforming wand which the French call *folklorisation*. Henceforward they decide to perceive the non-Western poetry as something less than, or quite outside, real poetry. There is much wisdom in this decision. After all, when folklore is not coarse or obscene, it is often incomprehensible to an outsider. If non-Western poetry is to be apprehended by European culture, it must be translated. If England were to confront Celtic folk culture, that culture would have to be trivialized. Continuing this process, the Grimm brothers analyzed Irish and Scottish mythology, T. Crofton Croker inflated a "kernel of spoken legend into a full story," and others created Scottish and Irish dialect stereotypes (Dorson 1966:vii). And both French and Malagasy readers devalued *hainteny*.

We have a better opportunity to see them clearly. Since the 1950s, advances in linguistics, more humanistic interests among anthropologists, and a well-established movement in literary translation have come together, at least in the United States, to produce significant discoveries about non-Western poetry. The decisive novelty was probably the theory of oral formulaic composition, devised by Milman Parry and Albert B. Lord to explain the composition-in-performance of the West's most highly esteemed poet. Oral formulaic theory was formulated for Yugoslavian oral poetry—hardly a canonical body of work from the point of view of comparative literature. The theory defined heroic songs in terms of features and relationships valid for Yugoslav culture. These were then adapted to a reading of Homer (Lord 1960, Foley 1988). Then, too, the willingness of anthropologists to record folklore, the emphasis by folklorists on face-to-face communication, the interest of poets and critics in "primitive" or "archaic" poetics, and a renewed responsiveness among Western audiences to the aloud reading of poetry all have heightened interest in what those outside Euro-American tradition were doing. Members of these diverse interpretive communities have begun to notice each other.

In response to the trivialization which *folklorisation* represents, indeed, the discipline of folklore offers a more equitable and tolerant alternative. It offers to "formulate a theory of the special case" of a non-Western poetry, defining *hainteny* (for instance) "in terms of features and relationships valid for the individual culture" (Hymes 1981:276). So Harold Scheub, returning from fieldwork in South Africa, could arrive at a formulation resembling, but distinct from, oral-formulaic theory. The Xhosa performers of *ntsomi*, a longwinded fantastic narrative, were relying on a "*core-cliché* (a song, chant or saying) which, with a few related details, forms the remembered *core-image*, a distillate of the full performance which is expanded and fleshed out during the actual process of externalization" (Scheub 1977:40). Scheub's theory is formulated for this special case, Xhosa poetry.

All over the world, poetic features have been found where none had been seen before, and poetics have been formulated for special cases. J. L. Fischer found quantitative meter in Micronesian dance songs, in the "chants" accompanying men's stick dances, and in narrative poems. Meter, apparently one poetic option among others, had largely gone out of use by 1949–53, when he did his collecting. Fischer saw acutely the reason why no one had noticed Trukese meter before: "The investigators were looking for a type of meter like their own or like that in some other European language with which they were acquainted" (1959:51–2). Studies of meter in Ob-Ugri poetry, on the basis of the metrical foot derived from Greek, were unsuccessful until Robert Austerlitz (1958) found that the pattern of organization in this poetry was not meter but grammar and that its structure was grammatical rather than phonological. In southern India, Murray B. Emeneau (1964) recorded more than 250 song texts in "a stereotyped two dimensional poetic language," which required the performer to rely on a stock of paired phrases, parallel to each other in structure and quantity. As in *hainteny*, though much more rigidly, the first half automatically evoked the second. Emeneau found the orality of Toda poetry to reside in three characteristics which *hainteny* share. "Every performance, even of what purports to be the same song, is a free composition." Moreover, Toda poetic language differed as much from ordinary talk as Thomas Gray asserted for English in 1742: "The language of the age is never the language of poetry. . . . Our poetry . . . has a language peculiar to itself" (1742:635). And finally, said Emeneau, Toda poetry relied on oral formula more than Homer or any other oral poetry. All these features of Toda poetry are shared to some extent by *hainteny*.

The most fully developed example of these new trends, in its revelation of a literature previously unacknowledged, is the retranslation and analysis of Native American poetry. Franz Boas in the 1890s and Edward Sapir before World War I collected Native American stories, which they translated in conformity with the poetic styles then fashionable. Inevitably their translations went out of style. Linguistic research also showed them to be distorting the patterns of repetition which were essential to the poetic effect. In Kwakiutl songs, for instance, nonsense words seemed to have no meaning. When Dell Hymes retranslated these texts, his linguistic expertise enabled him to reveal patterns, structures, and metaphors obscured in the earlier translations. Near the same time, the two anthologies by Jerome Rothenberg, *Technicians of the Sacred* (worldwide non-Western texts) and *Shaking the Pumpkin* (Native American texts) brought the poetry to the attention of a literary world accustomed to the modernist expression of Ezra Pound, Charles Olson, and William Carlos Williams (Rothenberg 1968, 1972). The influential translations by Dennis Tedlock (1972) of the Zuni stories he collected introduced further decisive evidence that Native Americans were casting their narratives in forms that could only be called poetic.

The Malagasy story follows the same outline. The poetry of *hainteny* could only be recognized after a period of devaluing them as prose.

Collections

Ny rombiazina no mamerovero an-tanety
Ny tongolo no manitra voasary
Ka raha nandre ny fameroverom-pitia aho
Dia te-hividy ta-hanakalo
Ny vava soa toa sakafo

(Paulhan 1913:80–81, 1960:73, trans. Fox
1990:90–91, no. 3)

He: The hill has a fragrance of sage,
       the onion smells of lemon.
She: When I smelled the odor of love,
       I wanted to buy, I wanted to trade.
       A tender word is like a meal.[2]

The fierce pride of Ranavalona I, the Merina queen, brought about the first significant recording of *hainteny*.[3] Oral history also began to be recorded at this time, for similar reasons (Delivré 1979:143, n. 4). Literacy in the roman alphabet was new then. Ranavalona's husband and predecessor, Radama I, had sponsored the introduction of writing by British missionaries, seeing how useful it would be for registering his underlings and for keeping accounts of foreign commerce, as well as for enhancing Merina prestige (Raison-Jourde 1977:644). Though at first Ranavalona encouraged the missionaries to create a dictionary and to continue teaching literacy, she abruptly forbade their evangelizing efforts in 1835. "I will oppose any attempt by my people to change the customs of my ancestors," she declared. But already two of her court secretaries had begun writing down folk poetry—or, more precisely, texts which we now know to be poetic. They wrote them as prose. Evidently there was a limit to what a person could learn in the missionary school.

The queen favored this project of preserving the ancestors' words. "Hide them in writing," she said, remembering the secret Arabico-Malagasy manuscripts preserved among the Antemoro on the east coast. "These texts pleased her because in a way she was a woman who incessantly kept up a passion for games," said one authority in 1966 (cited in Domenichini-Ramiaramanana 1983:338). The queen's game with *hainteny* was to protect her delight in poetry by concealing them. She voiced a powerful cultural sanction against revealing secrets, which helps to explain why outsiders know relatively little about this genre. But the manuscript begun by the two court secretaries was continued by three more; some of these men were later famous; their manuscript was luckily preserved. Unlike many other manuscripts of Malagasy history and folklore, which are kept as family treasures, it has been published (Domenichini-Ramiaramanana 1968). Much of it has been translated into French by its editor and into English by Leonard Fox (1990).

Later collectors of *hainteny* included the Norwegian Lutheran Dahle (1877) and the French Jesuit Callet (1908). Some of Dahle's texts were quickly translated by James Sibree (1889). Since all the collections overlap with others, they show us particular *hainteny* in recognizable, varying forms. These missionary folklorists again treated *hainteny* as prose. The *hainteny* evidently presented Dahle with problems of taste and morality. His 144 long and 302 short texts illustrated too well "the language, imaginative powers, and characteristic ideas of the people" (Dahle 1877:vii). Determined though he was to bowdlerize them, he still faced the consequences of their sexual allusiveness. "In spite of all care I am still not quite sure that in some places an unnoticed impure thought may not lurk underneath, as it is sometimes so extremely difficult to find out what notions and associations may, in course of time, have gathered round a seemingly quite innocent word or phrase" (1877:vii–viii). Allusion and association, indeed, were essential to the effect of any *hainteny*. Levels of meaning were always multiple. Despite Dahle's embarrassment, the allusive *hainteny* claimed pride of place in his collection, preceding riddles, folksongs, games, and narratives.

Translating Dahle's texts, always as prose, Sibree found the main interest of *hainteny* to be their archaic language. Moreover, he could use them to construct an image of Malagasy national character.

> Very frequent allusions are made to fidelity in friendship, which is a strongly marked feature of the Malagasy character, as shown by the practice of brotherhood-by-blood covenants. Here is an example, entitled,
>
> MUTUAL LOVE
>
> Let us two, O friend, never separate upon the high mountain, nor part upon the lofty rock, nor leave each other on the wide-spreading plain. For, alas! that this narrow valley should part such loving ones as we are; for thou wilt advance and go home, and I shall return to remain; yet if thou, the traveller, shouldst not be sad, much less should I, the one left. I am a child left by its companions, and playing with dust [a children's game] all alone; but still, should I not be utterly weak and given up to folly, if I blamed my friend for going home? (Sibree 1889:33)

If this piece illustrates any character trait, it is surely the fear of isolation; it also poses a dilemma, a favorite theme among the Merina. But Sibree's reader, confronting the inflated pathos of the translation, could not be blamed for accepting the translator's definition of *hainteny* as "oratorical flourishes and ornaments of speech, which are occasionally expanded into an Allegory." "Mutual Love" is oratorical because Sibree translated it as Dahle had transcribed it, in prose. It is mere ornament because it has been wholly removed from any context of performance that would let us see its function.

After colonization, Madagascar, now a conquered province, entered a new stage of history. With the aid of print, writing became what it was in the European Middle Ages, "one of the means whereby a community could assuredly recognize itself, but not one whereby it could communicate in the full sense of the word" (Zumthor 1987:123). Madagascar, at least in the region of its capital, was becoming literate. The Académie Malgache, founded in 1902, sponsored a reedition of Dahle's collection. Quaker missionary John Sims took responsibility for editing it for a new audience. Perhaps he visualized a reader who had come through the mission schools, one less interested in reminiscing about precontact days than in having some classic Malagasy literature to read.

Whoever his reader, Sims declared his aims as if he were a Malagasy nationalist. He aimed, he said, at protecting ancestral customs from being forgotten, improving people's knowledge of Malagasy, and showing the mind and spirit of the ancestors (Sims 1908:1). Ancestral custom and classic literary style must have been receding out of reach. It must be necessary to study the ancestors as a remote people. To realize these goals, Sims broke up some of Dahle's material and changed his headings. He brought Dahle's spelling, antiquated within a single generation, up to date to conform to the Malagasy being taught in the mission schools. Under French influence, several grammars had now been published, and a consensus was emerging on syntax and orthography (Dez 1978). Passages that seemed obscure he altered for the sake of clarity. With these changes, Sims still adhered to Dahle's outline: *hainteny* first, then proverbs, riddles, "advice given by the ancestors" (i.e., homiletic excerpts for speechmakers), games, and finally "Legends or Fables." Now the book was given a title to clarify the separation between the world of print and the culture of oral performance: *Anganon'ny Ntaolo*, Legends of the Ancestors.

Sims's reedition of Dahle remained continuously in print throughout the twentieth century, under his name but not as he left it. It is the best-known Malagasy folklore book. Print is the only context in which its many readers know *hainteny*. But the book they know, published by the Lutheran printing house, contains editorial changes far more fundamental and extensive than Sims's. Beginning with the fourth printing (undated), one or more anonymous editors reorganized the book in a way Sims might have hesitated to sign, though they kept his preface in a condensed form. They devised new sections, to which they gave headings such as "The Foolish," "Distrust," "Actions," "The Causes of Things," "Boasting," "Dying," and "Misfortune." Into these categories they brought poems

Dahle had seen no reason to connect, arranging them by what they believed to be the content. When read consecutively, the *hainteny*, still in prose, even seemed to come from the same anonymous speaker, who sententiously preached to the reader a strangely Christian-sounding morality.

Thus *Anganon'ny Ntaolo* became the official printed version of verbal art among not merely the Merina but all Malagasy. Whatever variable meanings the *hainteny* had in live performance, their new context of print converted them into prosaic declarations of a pallid morality. To make *hainteny* into written texts was to launder them for the mission-school-educated reader. This bowdlerization by rearrangement by the anonymous Protestant editors, a subtle form of censorship, remained unnoticed until I described it in 1985.

The first to see the *hainteny* as poems was Jean Paulhan (1913, 1938). On the page, his translations look like the contemporary poems of Guillaume Apollinaire. Later authorities such as Bakoly Domenichini-Ramiaramanana credit Paulhan as the translator who most successfully understood the multiple meanings and poetic textures of the form. Under his influence, the most celebrated of Malagasy poets, Jean-Joseph Rabearivelo, published several traditional *hainteny* as well as creating in the form himself (1967, 1975). His example has been followed by Flavien Ranaivo (1975). Among the few commentators outside Madagascar who have been interested in this poetry, the outstanding name is Léopold Sédar Senghor (1948; see also Koshland 1960).

A Merina Genre and Its Analogues

These poems constitute a distinctive creation of the Merina. Their monarchic state, which asserted hegemony over the island from the beginning of the nineteenth century, clearly separated its classes into *andriana* (nobles), *hova* (freemen), and *andevo* (slaves). Political power belonged to an oligarchy, and royal marriages were kept within the dynasty. An elaborate system of dikes for rice cultivation had been created by means of *corvée*. Such a distribution of power fostered riddles and *hainteny* as folk models for the asking and answering of questions. There was always an association between language and power in Madagascar. The older Merina kings had been known as *tompon-teny*, masters of words, in their public speeches. The sobriquet was a pun on their status as *tompon-tany*, landowners. It equated property ownership with power over language. The tension be-

tween monarch and regional ruler was enacted in Merina formal dialogues, *kabary*. Moreover, the question-and-answer pattern of the many
hainteny that depict man-woman dialogue reflects the relative equality enjoyed by Merina women.

Some other dialect groups, like the Bara of the south, have learned
examples of the genre (Dominichini-Ramiaramanana 1983:297–98). Related genres have been collected among Tsimihety to the north (Dandouau 1913, Michel-Andrianarahinjaka 1968) and Betsileo on the southern
part of the same plateau (Gueunier 1973, Michel-Andriarahinjaka 1986). By
contrast, groups like the Antandroy (People of the Thorn Bush), farther
south, believed strongly enough in the inferiority of women not to bor-
row the genre from the Merina (Michel 1956).

Although it was the Merina who developed courting dialogues most
fully, a cognate genre was practiced by at least one other dialect group, the
Sakalava, who also had a military conquest state. Their counterpart genre
is called *saim-bola*, word play. The most favored Sakalava form is an erotic
poem, the *filan'ampela*, woman-chasing, in which a man is making advances to a woman. The tone is assertive:

> tsy kotrokotro tsy hanina am-bilany.
> > tsy mila antety, fa mila ambany.
> > > (Hébert 1964:238)

> Don't rinse it if there's nothing to eat in the pot.
> > I'm not after what's on top, I'm after what's down below.

Merina *hainteny* are more delicate and indirect.

> Haody haody Rasoahagohago
> Mandrosoa Randriamatoa
> Hovelarako tsihy madio
> Tsihy hadio tsy tiako hitoerana
> Zoron-dambanao no tiako hitoerana
> > > (Paulhan 1913:100–101, 1938:83, trans. Fox
> > > 1990:104–5, no. 30)

> "Do I disturb you, beautiful precious?"
> "Come in, come in, handsome,
> I'll put out a clean mat for you."
> "It's not a mat I want to sit on
> but a corner of your shawl."

The sexual associations of the *lamba*, the Malagasy shawl (which in variant forms of the poem is a loincloth) make it a locus of desire.

Outside Madagascar, oral forms of stylized dialogue have been developed by many African and Asian peoples. In Senegal, the Peul have practiced the *mallol*, an allusive manner of utterance involving hidden meanings and quoted proverbs (Calame-Griaule 1963:83). In Burundi, a kingdom as hiercharchized as Imerina, a range of speech levels and styles is learned by all who have to address their superiors or inferiors (Albert 1972). In Kenya, the Mbeere "pose problems to one another in formal discourses which they do not term 'riddles' but which are, structurally speaking, riddles as defined by folklorists," dialogues using semantic opposition or contradiction to distinguish those who know the answer from those who do not. "The Mbeere differentiate these dialogues from *ndai* [riddles] because they lack a riddle frame," write Glazier and Glazier (1976:210). "Moreover, we find that these dialogues also share a narrative quality and length not found in riddles as defined by the performers." The Mbeere dialogues resemble *hainteny* in their length, elaboration, association with courtship, and dialogic structure. In Southeast Asia, Vietnamese girls and boys would sing aggressive, challenging songs to each other at the springtime festival. Again riddle language was brought out for courting. Rich families or village nobles used such songfests as occasions to present publicly their unmarried daughters. The young men would try to evoke some reaction from the young women, disclaiming the vulgarity of their words all the while with the formula "they say, they say." The concrete imagery of their songs and the strict adherence to formulaic rules counterbalanced the temporary departure from social correctness (Nguyen van Huyen 1933). In Malaysia, the *pantun*, a four-line oral poem, makes the same use of internal dialogue as the *hainteny*: the first distich calls for a second in reply, or else a first quatrain is answered by a second (Faublée 1982). And finally, in China, courting dialogue was as intentionally ambiguous as in highland Madagascar. Chinese poems, Marcel Granet found, were performed as a game or duel for honor and courtliness. But reading a single poem, Granet faced a difficulty that confronts us also in *hainteny*. Was the text a woman's monologue or a debate between two speakers? Granet had the advantage of having read Paulhan's 1913 collection (1929: 261–71).

European poets too have made poems as *hainteny* are made, embroidering and expanding proverbs and placing a familiar phrase in a new context. In sixteenth-century England, at a time when orality and literacy existed side by side, somewhat as in nineteenth-century Imerina, there arose "a witty poetic tradition of devising whole poems and songs from these sayings." As the literary epigram was "almost surely the most important influence on the development of the heroic couplet" in English, so was the Merina proverb the most important prior genre for *hainteny*. As in English, so in Malagasy, "binary construction and balanced phrasing . . . assonance and alliteration, conciseness, metaphor, and occasional inverted word order" were principal devices for the poetry of proverbs (Abrahams 1972 : 118).

Hainteny, indeed, show most clearly how far the four Malagasy genres of *fitenin-drazana*, sayings of the ancestors, interpenetrate. Formally, in performance, *hainteny* resemble riddles: they continually rely on a question-and-answer form in which the second half balances or caps the first, and they call for a *setriny*, comeback.

> Mandrosoa etsy aloha
> Etsy avaratra ray bodo
> Ray fihiratako
> Ry sombinaiko manokana
> —Mitsanga-miankina hiany
> Fa menatra ny efa nisaraka
> —Aza menamenatra foana hianao
> Fa raha tsy afa-po mifamerina
>
> > (Domenichini-Ramiaramanana 1968 : 110–11,
> > trans. Fox 1990 : 392–93, no. 447)

> He: You be the first to go
>   there to the north, my baby
>   my plaything
>   Little bit of my life set apart
> She: I will only stand here leaning
>   I blush that we part so soon
> He: Don't blush over nothing
>   for if our hearts are not content, we can begin again

In performance, a *hainteny* is also like a proverb, functioning to size up a situation and name its outstanding ingredients by means of metaphor (Burke 1957 : 3, Abrahams 1968). It is also like an oration: it strings together smaller units, either proverbs or shorter *hainteny*, and it is meant to be authoritative and impersonal. Yet these resemblances do not make the *hainteny* into anything but itself. It remains the elusive queen of Merina folklore genres. Like the most famous queen, Ranavalona I, it is hostile to Europeans, repelling and even destroying their efforts at penetrating the Malagasy soul (Brown 1979:167–88, Gow 1979:1–38, Domenichini-Ramiaramanana 1983:279). Let us approach this genre respectfully, bringing it, as gifts from home, the riddles and proverbs we already know.

The Performance Situation

The performance of *hainteny* is a stylized version of taking turns in conversation. One speaker's words are followed and answered by another's. For instance, during the reign of Queen Ranavalona II (1868–83), two celebrated poet-reciters met face-to-face at festival time in the capital. Noticing that the audience seemed torpid, one of them, nicknamed Ibiby (Animal), aimed a satirical song at his adversary:

> The sleeping cat acts sluggish,
> the nursing calf acts sluggish too.

As a comeback, his rival Raivo-Ramianoka sang, punning on his adversary's nickname,

> The sweet-potato pest is still a pest,
> also the herb pest is still a pest.
> (Randafison 1980:191–92)

This challenge and reply was a classic exchange of *hainteny*—metaphorical, antithetical, contestatory. There was a real situation of interaction, a symbolic deflation of the opponent, and figurative language to accomplish the deflation. In performance, real speakers and situations are always present, and their exchange is always a contest. In the repertoire of Malagasy contests, their closest analogues might seem to be cockfighting, *fanorona*, or even bullfighting (Domenichini-Ramiaramanana 1983:370–75), but being a verbal contest, they are much more like southern African riddles. These too are a contest that has often been performed in the evening after a meal, as a prelude to storytelling. As one of their social functions, *hainteny* transpose a real or imaginary quarrel of the speakers into poetry. "Frequently having amorous quarrel as their theme," Gabriel Ferrand wrote, "[the *hainteny*] is also a method of regulating differences of a juridical kind, such as the claiming of a debt, or a fee whose amount is debated or debatable. Thus it has considerable social importance" (1914:154). For if the quarrel is real, the speakers will have preserved the social fabric from rupture by transforming war into poetic exchange. "The Malagasy people have extended their refinement and reserve so far as to replace wars with poetic jousts, in which the adversaries address and answer each other in verse" (Rolland de Renéville 1944:136). As Kenneth Burke has pointed out, to present human interaction in terms of two-sided conflict is both to purify the conflict of its destructiveness and to pay tribute to the essentially conflict-ridden nature of humanity (Burke 1945: 330–31). In performance, then, *hainteny* are as dialogic as riddles.

Debate is not only the characteristic performance situation of this genre, but often its very plot, brought to us through a narrator who recites a monodrama. I translate a lengthy example in full, rearranging a prose text as verse to point up its antitheses, symmetries, and stage directions.

Do Not Go After Some Rich Woman, But Return to Your Poor Wife

He: Tell me, O highland there to the north,
        resting-place of fogs, where swallows fly,
        what is happening down there in the south?

Then *the highlands answered*—for wanting this man to reject his wife, they flattered him:

Highlands: Come, sir,
              I am beautiful enough for you
              and an honor to our people.
              Do not promote the daughter of poor people.
              In the future when you are rich,
              you will live at ease.

His answer. The husband's words rejecting his wife after seeing the rich woman:

He: She is a sparrow by the side of the road,
          not rejected by me,
          but disowned by her mother.
      Death to that fern-shadow,
      and life to a heart for happiness.
      All that is left is polite speaking.

The wife's reply. The wife's words after hearing this:

She: You surprise me, Mr. No-Rice,
      that "the aftercrop has become the rice"
      and your old love has dropped to second place.
      When I belonged to another,
          you were at pains to seek me;
      when I was not yet yours,
          you paid for me;
      now that I am here,
          you abandon me.
      Now that I love you,
          you make me suffer,
      and when I want to leave,
          you hold me back.
      Still, it is your affair, and [that of] retribution.
      As for me, I must go as all the unloved do.
      If your fate is death, I do not wish it on you,
      but if your fate is love, I give you that.

The husband's reply. The husband answers, no longer trying to conceal his unhappiness.

He: The hawk has flown to Blue-Hill,
      and the bluebird has flown to Leech-Country.
      It was the birds of Colored-Wood that woke you at daybreak;
      at Colored-Wood you did not sleep late in the mornings,
      you arose in the middle of the night.
      You heard them at evening,
      they were still singing at morning;
      at Colored-Wood you did not sleep late in the mornings.

But I am no hawk who has flown to Blue-Hill,
I am no bluebird who has flown to Leech-Country,
for marriage is the heart's choice,
and the place desired becomes the familiar one.

> (Dahle 1877:13–14, trans. Chapus and
> Dandouau 1940:97, and Fox 1990: 224–27,
> no. 206)

At once monodrama and debate, this drama of abandonment and longing could easily be adapted to a number of social interactions. The interplay between the situation depicted and the situation the speaker wants his hearers to think of gives the special delight of *hainteny*.

Performers

Who are the speakers? Mastery of *hainteny* used to be found up and down the Merina social ranks. One day when Paulhan was visiting in Ambato-manga, Shining Rock, a Merina village some fifty kilometers west of Antananarivo, a roofer came to claim his pay for thatching the house of Paulhan's host. The owner offered him half of what he asked; they could not agree. In the evening, they had a *hainteny* contest to settle the dispute. The house owner lost and had to pay the roofer's full fee. The two men agreed perfectly on one thing: a contest in poetic diction was an alternative to direct dispute over money.

Children, too, in 1908–10 knew how to resort to word play in order to press their advantage in dispute. One day near Alasora, about six kilometers south of Antananarivo, Paulhan saw two boys playing a game (*tsiombiomby*) in which they tore the wings off locusts, which represented cattle; these they placed in a hole in the ground representing a cattle pen. When one of the boys stepped away from the game for a moment, the other boy stole his locusts. On his return, the victim showed no anger; instead he sat down opposite the thief and recited a *hainteny*. Apparently they continued to talk in *hainteny* for quite a while, having already grasped the importance of switching styles when one is in a conflict situation.

Though the art of the word on the plateau is no specialist's exclusive property, specialists certainly have existed (Domenichini-Ramiaramanana 1983:343)—monarchs, for example. *Hainteny* and oratory traditionally exist side by side in their repertoire and in that of the Malagasy man of words. That association goes back at least to Andrianjaka, the Merina monarch at the end of the sixteenth century (Delivré 1979). His brother Andriantompokoindrindra (Lord-Paramount-Master) was reputed to be a *tompon'ny teny*, master of the word, as well as a gifted diviner. His skill in speechmaking went along with his fame as a player of *fanorona* (Chauvicourt and Chauvicourt 1972:9). The general belief in Madagascar that political power goes with speechmaking ability must have been well established by his time (Domenichini-Ramiaramanana 1983:412–22).

Oral histories contain vivid scenes of the exchange of *hainteny*. In these scenes, the smaller genre shows its tendency to infiltrate the larger genre of royal oratory. Some *kabary* (orations) are prosaic, lacking rhythm or stylization (Domenichini-Ramiaramanana 1983:381–83), but others, more animated by emotion, make use of parallel propositions and flowering images. Domenichini-Ramiaramanana has analyzed one dramatic scene, which she calls a trial, from the *Tantaran'ny Andriana*. In this scene, the great Andrianampoinimerina exercised his penchant for spectacle. Having set aside his son Rabodolahy (Young-Male-Child) in favor of Radama, who was to succeed him, Andrianampoinimerina sought to rid himself of the possible reproach that he deposed Rabodolahy because he was partial to Radama. His desire to show that all was done in accordance with the strictest respect for laws of the monarchy called forth the most formal, stylized public speech. Passions ran high; in his speeches, Rabodolahy used parallel structures and subgenres like the priamel. "We enter here," Domenichini-Ramiaramanana writes, "into a domain of the greatest rigidity. Here, obedience to purely human feeling would be the behavior of a slave or a serf, whereas a freeman obeys reasons of state and a prince obeys revelations" (1983:406).

Styles of language in Madagascar correlate with class and rank, but the royal bias of Callet's oral histories should not mislead us into thinking that stylized speech has always been limited to royalty. One lower-class orator whom Paulhan knew, Ramanampatsa, was called in as advocate to get a freeman out of paying a healer, whose work had not satisfied him. The orator's status as *andevo* (slave) did not prevent him from being a master of the word. Another person of low rank, a cook in the White Hill (Ambohipotsy) section of Antananarivo, lost a contest in *hainteny* against his wife's lover in an unsuccessful attempt to win her back. As a result, he fell ill. If some of the poems recited that evening were on amatory subjects, as so many *hainteny* are, the contest must have been a delight to those in the audience who had an ear for multiple meanings.

Dialogic though they must be in performance, *hainteny* have a monologic and authoritative effect. The rivalry of the players must end with the victory of one. Since the texts of *hainteny* show many man-woman dialogues, in which propositions, acceptances, refusals, and regrets are a dominant theme, the main power struggle they depict is between women and men. Thus it becomes important to know whether the speakers are always men, and whether a man's speech is always spoken by a male voice. To what extent and in what ways does the situation depicted in a particular poem correspond to the situation the speaker wants his hearers to think of? Though the Merina usually assign formal speech to men (Keenan 1974), women have certainly been known to win in contests. In the part of Antananarivo called Ampandrana (Shrub), Paulhan met a young woman abandoned by her husband. He and his sisters accused her of being a water spirit, an accusation based on the best-known Malagasy legend, which meant that her family was insignificant (Ottino 1981; tales 3.1.21–24 in *Malagasy Tale Index*). She found her husband in Analakely, Littlewood, another part of town, and persuaded him back by means of *hainteny* (Paulhan 1913:11).

Hainteny As Riddles

To define this genre, I must show its complex relations to the riddle and the proverb. Being performed as an evening contest and a prelude to tale-telling, *hainteny* serve as a riddle for adults. The extent to which they rely on the internal structure of riddle can be seen in three examples. The main resemblance is their partially obscured semantic fit, which they achieve by keeping the dramatic situation obscure or unresolved up to the final word of the poem. Often representing the speech of a couple caught at a revealing moment of their relationship, they heighten the surprise of the last word, as a riddle does.

> Tsontsorifako vero
> Folapolahiko fantaka
> Vazo tsy tianao va aho
> No fohazinao mangoam-bodilanitra?
> —Tzy vazo tsy tiana hianao
> Fa ny olona an-tanana tia laza
> Tia tatibolana
> Ny vadinao tia vono

Tia tsongo madinika
Ny ranomasonao no tsy tantiko

> (Domenichini-Ramiaramanana 1968: 232–33,
> trans. Fox 1990: 250–51, no.246)

She: I will whip you with long grasses,
        I will break reeds on your back.
        Am I some mistress you do not love,
          that you wake me at daybreak?
He: You are no mistress I do not love,
        but these village folk like slanders,
          they like gossip.
        Your husband is the one who likes beatings.
        He likes to give you little pinches.
        What I cannot endure is your tears.

Since the key word *vadinao*, which I translate "your husband," has no gender, the first speech could be for the man and the roles could be reversed. There need only be a poser and a responder, and even they may be played by the same speaker. The absence of precise information on who says what in *hainteny* performance indicates that gender roles are not fixed. Most of my analysis will focus, therefore, on the internal dialogism, the representation of two or more voices, that is visible in the printed texts.

Many *hainteny* cast the poser as a male initiating a sexual advance; to complete the riddle-like form, the responder need only answer the proposition.

Ramatoa tokana an'osy
Tsara ririnina
Soa fahavaratra
Mandina raha lohataona
Tsy mba manan-tao-maharatsy aho
Ary tsy mba mandeha main'andro
Fa raha tsy efa lefy ny andro
Tsy mba mivoaka
Ary tsy mba mandro rano an-tsiny
Fa ny ranomasoko ihany no androako

> (Paulhan 1913: 294–95, 1960: 171, trans. Fox
> 1990: 218–19, no. 191)

He: Lady alone on the island,
       you are fine in winter,
       sweet in summer,
       glistening in springtime.
She: I do no work that makes me ugly,
       I do not go out in full sunlight.
       Until the day softens
       I do not go out.
       Nor do I bathe in water from the jug,
       I bathe in the water of my tears.

Like the sequent of a riddle, the last line places everything before it in a new light. Though at first the woman seems rich, vain, and idle, we find out that she is pining. The penultimate line puns on *tsiny*, reproaches: "I don't let myself be touched by blame." Thus her refusal of the man's proposition gives her the victory.

Similar reversal of male dominance occurs in this teasing dialogue.

—Tianao tahaky ny inona ange aho?

—Tiako tahaky ny vary hianao
—Tsy tianao aho izany
   Fa ataonao famonjy fo raha noana

—Tianao tahaky ny inona ange aho?
—Tiako tahaky ny rano hianao?
—Tsy tianao aho izany
   Fa ataonao fitia momba tseroka

—Tianao tahaky ny inona ary aho?
—Tiako tahaky ny lamba hianao
—Tsy tianao aho izany
   Fa raha tonta afindranao
   Ka tsy tsaroanao intsony

—Tianao toy ny inona ange aho?
—Tiako tahaky ny tantely hianao
—Tsy tianao aho izany
   Fa misy faikany aloanao hiany

—Tianao tahaky ny inona ange aho?
—Tiako tahaky ny Andriamanjaka hianao
—Tianao tokoa aho izany
—Mandalo mahamenamaso
  Mijery mahamenatra ahy

—Tianao tokoa aho izany
  Fa tapi-java-nirina aho
  Tapi-java-naleha
—Tiako tahaka an' Ikaky sy Neny hianao
  Velona iray trano
  Maty iray hazo

(Domenichini-Ramiaramanana 1968: 70–73,
trans. Fox 1990:100–103, no. 25)

She: What will you say you love me like?
He: I love you like rice.
She: Then you love me not,
      for you only keep it stored up for the time you are hungry.

She: What will you say you love me like?
He: I love you like water.
She: Then you love me not,
      for your love disappears with dirt.

She: What do you tell me you love me like?
He: I love you like a *lamba* [garment].
She: Then you love me not,
      for when you trade me away,
                you will not keep me in your mind.

She: What do you say you love me as much as?
He: I love you like honey.
She: Then you love me not,
      for the dregs you will spit out.

She: What do you say you love me like?
He: I love you like the queen.
She: Now you truly love me.

He: Her passing inspires respect,
      her glance makes me blush.

She: Now you truly love me.
       There is nothing more for me to want,
       nothing else for me to search for.
He: I love you like father and mother,
      living in the same house,
      dead in the same wood.

After the exchange of metered lines, the closure of the ending is like the closure of a riddle. Much of the complex power of Merina poetic diction resides in that final word *hazo*, wood, which varies the oft-repeated proverb "Those who live in one house should be buried in one tomb" (Bloch 1971:166). In place of *fasana*, tomb, are the several meanings of *hazo*: a forest growing around tombs, hence a forest of taboos and customs; a coffin containing both husband and wife (fantastic though that would be in real life); a wooden funerary pillar symbolizing their perpetual unity after death; the wooden "cold house" or "sacred house" erected by noble families atop their family tombs. That one monologic word points to the dwelling place of the dead, which in its unity solves the dialogic contradictions of life.

Dialogism Contends with Monologism

The dialogue of the riddle is not the only kind available to reciters. Though sometimes they open dialogue by quoting a riddle (Paulhan 1938:180), at other times they embroider on *safidy*, the double riddle discussed in Chapter 2. Riddle, double riddle, and *hainteny* engage each other in intergeneric dialogue.

Alao izay ho anao
Ny vady kely tsy azo ho zavatra va
Fa ny katsabazaha telo fototra?
—Raha izaho no mifidy
Ny katsabazaha telo fototra
No alaiko
Hanina dia mahavoky

Ambolena dia mahafeno saha
Ny vady kely tsy ho azo ho zavatra
Atao aloha tsy mahafa-kenatra
Atao aoriana miherikeri-poana
Entina an-jaika mahamenatra olona
                    (Domenichini-Ramiaramanana 1968 : 284–85,
                    no. 25, trans. Fox 1990 : 292–93, no. 308)

"Which do you choose,
a new wife who can not do things
or three corn plants?"
"If I am to choose,
it's the three corn plants
that I take.
Eat them, they satisfy you,
plant them, they fill a field.
The new wife who can not do things,
if she goes before you, she takes no care for your honor,
if she follows, she looks here, looks there,
take her into polite conversation, she embarrasses everyone."

Safidy form is strictly followed. The two choices are posed, and the respondent must give the correct interpretation of both and choose between them. At the same time, the topic-comment form of *ohabolana* molds the second part of the answer. The intergeneric dialogue has drawn in the proverb. Although the alternation of voices in *hainteny* derives from the riddle, the symmetry, balance, and social control found in proverbs are also heard. The longer form probably was made out of the shorter ones. *Hainteny* add proverbs together, they invert and transform them, and they quote them at length.

To clarify the contributions to *hainteny* by single riddles, double riddles, and proverbs, I distinguish three domains, on the basis of Peter Seitel's study of East African proverbs (1977 : 76). One domain is visible in the "interaction situation" in which the poem is actually performed—the dispute over the fee for a new roof or the attempt to persuade back a husband. A second domain is the one the speaker wants his audience to think of—the situation to which he means the poem to apply, like the superiority of the roofer over the house owner, or the inferior performance of one's opponent in the contest; this Seitel calls the context situation. The third domain is the one I am concentrating on here. Being most available to a reader of the 1836 manuscript or of Dahle's or Paulhan's collections, it is the domain folkloric restatement seeks out. Corresponding to what Seitel calls the proverb situation, it is the set of facts inherent in the text of the *hainteny* itself if I take it literally. The *hainteny* situation is the dramatic scene in which represented characters speak to each other. Once these three domains of *hainteny* are separated, folkloric restatement finds that neither Malagasy history nor ethnography gives us facts as to whether they vary with one another. It is plausible that in the minds of reciters, certain interaction situations evoke recurrent context situations, which they symbolize for their hearers in familiar words. History shows that the more tension there is in the context situation, the more likely the poems performed will be elaborately controlled, embedding their most powerful message in quotations within quotations. This degree of control in artistic language implies a similar degree of control in social life. Reproaches (*tsiny*) would fall on a speaker who mentioned a delicate or dangerous subject too directly. To the extent that *hainteny* use structures of *ohabolana*, they also attempt to exert control both on their hearers and on their own style. There is an abiding tension between riddlelike dialogue and proverblike monologue. There is continual dialogue among genres.

Balance, Symmetry

The kernel structure of the interaction situation is a two-part dialogue. The same kernel structure governs the *hainteny* situation. In the example that follows, a husband has been neglecting his younger wife, in contrast with an Afro-Malagasy convention in which the older wife is usually neglected. The younger makes a vain appeal to the senior wife, through her image of three hearthstones standing for the three members of the household.

> Tsambikim-bato mandeha vato telo
> Babeo aho ry zoky fa sasatra
> Tsambikim-bato mandeha vato telo
> Ny vady eram-ponao eram-poko
> Ny am-pahitra lany
> Ny an-trano tsy misy
> Alehao ny lalana ry zandry.
>
> (Paulhan 1913 : 232–33, 1938 : 141, trans. Fox
> 1990 : 154–55, no. 101)

Second wife: One stone skipped, three stones go together.
                Carry me on your back, elder sister, I am weary.
                One stone skipped, three stones go together.
First wife: Your heart's husband is my heart's husband.
                No more cattle in the ditch,
                nothing in the house.
                Walk the road, little sister.

Clearly, the first wife has asserted her customary authority by answering in appropriate metaphors. Thus the *hainteny* situation depicts a characteristic interaction situation: two speakers symmetrically exchange three-part metaphors, and the second one wins.

In another symmetrical example, the speeches of both characters use the topic-comment structure, which is derived from *ohabolana*. The following *hainteny* is constructed by capping an exchange of two proverbs with a third one. The man warns the woman against his inconstancy, but she wants only him.

Andriamatoa volon-kotona
Mamahatra ambanin'ny rano fa mora tapaka
Ramatoa ravim-bero
Maitso faniry fa mora malazo
Toy ny siny ka tsy manam-po afa-tsy ny rano
Toy ny rano ka tsy manam-po afa-tsy ny siny
                          (Paulhan 1913:96–97, 1938:81, trans. Fox
                          1990:90–91, no. 5)

He: A gentleman is seaweed,
       he crawls under water but is easily cut away.
She: A lady is a grass blade,
       she grows green but she fades fast,
       Like the jar, she thinks only of water,
       Like water, she thinks only of the jar.

Clear as the internal structure is, we wonder about the casting. Nothing in the text denotes the gender of the characters. It was Paulhan who assigned lines 3–6 to the woman. Why not read lines 5–6 as the couple's second exchange, assigning line 5 to the man and line 6 to the woman? Then the verbal parallels will enact their common desire. To construct a poem out of riddles and proverbs thus yields alternative possibilities for performance.

Doubling the Symmetry

Hainteny and *ohabolana* are identical in their use of doubled symmetry, the same means of elaboration as in the *safidy*, or double riddle. Here, after his first rejection, the man boasts, and the woman refuses more vigorously.

> Ravina apetraka
> Apetraho
> Ravina alefitra
> Alefero
> —Saingy izaho mandefitra aminao
> Dia ataonao sabo ho maro manana
> —Ny anarako Andriamiroborobo
> Maro tia
> Maro kiry
> Raha ho tia tsy ampy toa inona
> Raha tsy ho tia tsy ampy toa inona
> —Matesa anie aho ray itsiana
> Fa ny tompony aza tsy tia
> Koa mainka aho nanan-ko ahy
>
>   (Domenichini-Ramiaramanana 1968 : 24—25,
>   no. 7, trans. Fox 1990 : 348—49, no. 376)

He: Leaves to lay down,
      lay them down,
      leaves to fold,
      fold them.
She: Since I have accepted things from you,
      you think I must be there for many men.
He: My name is Prince of Flame,
      I love many,
      I refuse many.
      When I come to love, I resemble nothing else.
      When I do not come to love, I resemble nothing else.

She: Excuse me, you there—
        his mistress doesn't love him;
        much less do I. I have what I need.

Again we wonder about casting. "It could also be assumed" from the manuscript, writes the editor, "that the woman's reply extends as far as the word 'anything'. . . . In that case the woman would be doing the boasting and the man would finally turn away from her" (Domenichini-Ramiaramanana 1968:24). The variability of roles, like the reduplicated structure, confirms the relative equality of women among the Merina, portraying their ability to keep up the dialogic contest.

Such variability is found all through the corpus. It is independent of the reduplication, which is also found in those monologic *hainteny* in which a single speaker answers his own questions. In the next example, a man engages himself in self-praising dialogue.

Inona no manjaka ambanin'ny rano?
Ny mamba no manjaka ambanin'ny rano
Inona no manjaka ambonin'ny rano?
Ny lakana no manjaka ambonin'ny rano
Inona no manjaka ambonin'ny tany?
Ny Andriamanjaka no manjaka ambonin'ny tany
Tsofin-drivotra tsy mba mirona
Taninin'ny andro tsy mba malazo
                    (Paulhan 1913:340−41, 1938:191, trans. Fox
                    1990:320−21, no. 336)

Who is ruler under the water?
    The crocodile is ruler under the water.
Who is ruler on the water?
    The pirogue [canoe] is ruler on the water.
Who is ruler over the earth?
    The king is ruler over the earth.
When the wind blows, he does not bend,
    when the sun burns, he does not wilt.

In performance, this reduplication would probably elicit a second poem in reply, thus reproducing itself on a larger scale.

So it would too in the next example, which shows the Merina love of antithesis—male versus female, rice versus water, raw rice versus cooked rice, irrigated fields versus village.

> Izaho vary any hianao rano
> An-tsoha tsy mifandao
> An-tanana tsy misaraka
> Fa isak'izay mihaona
> Fitia vaovao ihany
>
> > (Paulhan 1913:98–99, trans. Fox
> > 1990:104–5, no. 29)

> I am the rice and you are the water:
> In the fields they don't leave each other,
> In the village they don't separate.
> Each time they meet
> They love each other anew.

Here, lines 1–3 were proverbial, circulating independently as a unit. In the new context, that unit functions like a riddle precedent or topic; the comment (lines 4–5) applies and extends the metaphor. We should not miss the pun in line 3 on the ethnic name Betsimisaraka (the Inseparable Multitude). Whether representing two speakers or one, the *hainteny* is assembled out of existing materials on the models provided by the riddle and the proverb.

The issue of casting arises too in the related genre of *saimbola*, "art of the word" in the dialect of the Sakalava in northwest Madagascar. Texts of *saimbola* are balanced and antithetical, but they do not alternate speakers. They are monologic internally. Nor do Sakalava women play in the poetic duel of their interaction situation. "In *filan' ampela* [woman-chasing, the courting *saimbola*] the man is usually the one speaking. The woman accepts or refuses his propositions," but not by speaking poetically (Hébert 1964:228). The relation of the depicted situation to the interaction situation varies in each artistic community.

Genres in Dialogue

As *hainteny* reproduce the structures of smaller genres, the quasi-dialogic riddle and the quasi-monologic proverb begin to speak to each other and "engage one another actively" (Dorst 1983:414). In their intergeneric dialogue, they act like the speakers in the interaction situation, trying to "regulate differences of a juridical" or argumentative kind (Ferrand's phrase, quoted earlier). One such difference is the opposition between figurative and literal language, which derives from metaphorical riddles. In the riddle "Five men with hats on," the topic is "men"; the answer is "fingers and fingernails" (Grandidier 1908:140). What is opposed is not "the constituent descriptive elements" (Georges and Dundes 1963:114), but the figurative and literal representations of the world. In some *ohabolana*, we saw above, a seemingly chaotic series of unrelated metaphorical lines builds to a climactic, literal last line, which puts everything before it in a new light. This form, based on the same opposition of figurative and literal, is the priamel. It also organizes some *hainteny* in which the literal answer is unspoken. The answer to the following riddlelike piece is "lying, mendacity." I translate Dahle's prose as verse.

Vola ratsy, ka mba mikorintsana; fangady mondro, ka mba mijaradona. Io no ondry bobo fanenjik'alika, tanantanampotsy fitoeran'akoho, i ratsy ao ambavany toy ny zinga lanim-boalavo.

Bad money, but it jingles;
a worn-out spade, but it stands up;
a white sheep chased by dogs,
white seeds for chickens to sit on—
it's as bad in your mouth
as a spoon the rats have chewed.

> (Dahle 1877:35, no. 107, trans. Chapus and Dandouau 1940:117, no. 5, trans Fox 1990:264–65, no. 267)

From the man-made world to the animal world and back again, the piece leads the hearer through a range of metaphors intended "to question at least certain kinds of established order." The priamel, as a more forceful sort of riddle, "make[s] a point of playing with conceptual borderlines and crossing them for the pleasure of showing that things are not quite as stable as they appear" (Köngas Maranda 1971:53). Conceptual borderlines, and genre borderlines too: is this piece a *hainteny*, a riddle, or an *ohabolana*? Dahle's choice was *hainteny*, though he treated it like a riddle when he gave the answer in the title. Since it does not appear in the collections of *ohabolana*, the question becomes, Why is a *hainteny* like a riddle?

One answer is that it expands the riddle form of precedent and sequent by showing speakers taking turns. Sibree translated one example of this expanded riddle as an instance of pathos. I insert quotation marks into his translation to reveal the stylized turn-taking.

> Iza ny olona alohanao?
> Asa iny, fa tsy tratrako.
> Iza iry olona aorianao?
> Asa iny, fa tsy nahatrata ahy.
> Nahoana hianao no dia mijoro?
> Tsy mijoro aho, fa sendra mitsangana.
> Nahoana hianao no dia misento?
> Tsy misento aho, fa manoaka.
> Nahoana hianao no toa veri-saina?
> Tsy veri-saina aho, fa mihevitra.
> Nahoana hianao no toa mitomany?
> Tsy mitomany aho, fa ditsika.
> Nahoana hianano miferin' aina?
> Tsy miferin' aina aho, fa serena.
> Nahoana hianao no lalin' endrika?
>
> Tsy satriko no lalin' endrika, fa maty ny zanako. Dia torana nitomany izy ka nampalahelo ny olona.
>
> HEVERO!
>
> Aza mba manafina ny manjò.
>
> > (Dahle 1877:9–10, trans. Fox 1990:296–97, no. 312, and 400–401, no. 454)

> "Who is that person before thee?"
> > "I know not, for I did not overtake him."
> "Who is yonder person behind thee?"
> > "I know not, for he did not overtake me."
> "Why then are you so erect?"
> > "I am not erect, but chanced to rise."
> "Why then do you sob so?"

"I am not sobbing, but merely yawning."
"Why are you as if beside yourself?"
"I am not beside myself, but am thinking."
"Why are you as if weeping?"
"I am not weeping, but have got dust in my eye."
"Why are you sighing?"
"I am not sighing, but have a cold."
"Why are you woebegone?"
"I do not wish to appear woebegone, but my child is dead!"

[Narrator] Then she bursts into a flood of tears and
makes all the people sorry.
Consider well! Do not hide your calamity.

(Sibree 1889:36)

The woman's repeated denials give the dialogue a crescendo of suspense. Sophocles is famous for a similar use of the same device, stichomythia, in tragedy. The scene is played out through dialogue; a third voice, like Sophocles' chorus, enters at the end to reflect on the meaning of the scene. The pattern which this poem expands, a dialogue followed by comment, is provided by *ohabolana*, as we saw in the last chapter. Thus in the *hainteny* two smaller genres are actively engaging each other.

Conflicting classifications, indeed, characterize the history of the study of this poetry. Dahle prints the pieces as prose, placing them first in his book under the heading *hainteny lavalava*, "longish word-plays." Sibree, translating some of them under the heading of oratory, calls them "Oratorical Flourishes and Ornaments of Speech, which are occasionally expanded into an allegory" (1883:6). Taking in a larger number of pieces, Bakoly Domenichini-Ramiaramanana has devoted hundreds of pages to establishing the possible connection between the poetry and the proverbs (Haring 1985). Her twenty-eight examples of *hainteny* aim at overturning whatever idea of the genre the reader may have formed (1983:90–110). One possible conclusion is the deconstructionist one of undecidability: that we cannot know precisely where proverb leaves off and *hainteny* begins, or where oratory commences to be more than an ornament of speech. A second conclusion might be that Malagasy informants have effectively guarded the secrets of their ancestors' words from Western eyes, which never tire of seeking grids and boundaries. Performance theory suggests a third assumption, that the circumstances determine how a particular set of fixed phrases should be labeled. The 150 years of recorded texts document the continual negotiation of riddle and proverb with each other in their actual occurrence. As Paulhan stated, the *mpikabary* relies on a large stock of fixed phrases that can be adapted to all interaction situations—not merely the exchange of *hainteny*, but riddling, speaking proverbs, and speechmaking too. A literary comparison would be the novel's capacity for incorporating numerous voices and consciousnesses. As the distinguishing feature of the novel, in Bakhtin's view, was its diversity of voices ("heteroglossia"), so the distinguishing feature of Malagasy verbal art is its unceasing dialogue of genres in the heat of performance.

The Malagasy priamel, more than other forms, reveals the *hainteny* to be what John Dorst calls "an arena of generic conflict within which a range of intergeneric accommodations can occur" (1983:416), between monologism and dialogism, between a profusion of bewildering images and what, in the *hainteny* situation, seems to be a literal application of them.

> Ny vorompotsy tsy mahafoy havana (ny omby); ary vorom-pihantonan' ody ny akanga; ary vonton' Alahamady ny ny vintsy. Ary tsara havana ila-tánan-jazavavy, ary tsara ilan-tánan-jazalahy, ka ny havana dia fihamboana; nefa, na izany aza, tsy mba mandray izay tsy atolotra, ary tsy maka izay tsy omena. Ka moa, na dia izany aza, ataonao hangataka va aho no dia arebarebanao ny lambanao?
>
> (Dahle 1877:24, trans. Chapus and Dandouau
> 1940:93 and Fox 1990:340–43, no. 370)

> The egret doesn't leave his friends [cattle],
> and the guineafowl is hung with charms,
> and the kingfisher comes in the middle of [the month] Alahamady.
> And good relations are hands to a girl,
> and good ones are hands to a boy,
> for kinfolk are something to boast of.
>   But, having said that,
> we will not accept what is not offered,
> and we do not take what is not given.
>   So, having said that,
> do you think I would come after you,
> who wear your lamba so loose?

The string of rather clichéd symbols mystifies the hearer like the precedent of a riddle. The egret's friends (*havana*, kinfolk) are the cattle, among whom the bird is always seen; charms, *ody*, were hung on guinea fowl to protect the dooryard; the kingfisher at that season is an unlucky omen. Good relations are good to have, the speaker says, but (with a pair of balanced platitudes) you come too cheap, as you indicate by trailing your shawl (a conventional symbol of availability). This startlingly direct disparagement of the woman solves the riddle of what situation was being depicted: he dismisses her as not good enough for him. Some insight into the rules of *hainteny* construction is available despite mystification. (a) The first set of three images circulates independently in variant forms; one was translated by Sibree, "The whitebird . . . does not leave the oxen, the sandpiper does not forsake the ford, the hawk does not depart from the tree," and on through four more lines (1883:14). Then follows (b) a set of three aphorisms, (c) a transitional phrase, (d) a pair of lines balanced like a riddle, and (c) and (d) again. Thus the poem is an assemblage of smaller units, each of which is associated with riddle or proverb.

Meter in *Hainteny*

Now another player enters the scene of intergeneric dialogue: song. When a reciter utters these monologic-dialogic phrases in an improvised or repeated sequence, he or she has a metrical framework to rely on. Measure, or meter, is a feature of many *hainteny* that are used as song lyrics. Paulhan in 1908–11 collected fifteen poems which Dahle had printed as song lyrics thirty-five years earlier. He heard four of Dahle's *hainteny* sung. Here is one. I rearrange it and mark stressed syllables, to show what its meter might have been.

> Tsirírin'Andríana
> sy áhitra ny Mpanjáka:
> ny ánankiráy sósoka
> ary ny anankiráy dimbin'ántsy
> ka ízy nanao tsy ho tía
> ary izáho afa-po mialóha

> > (Dahle 1877:21, trans. Chapus and Dandouau 1940:108 and Fox 1990:192–93, no. 154)

> Sweet-smelling grass
> and herbs of the sovereign:

the first are replacements [for the dead]
and the others are [only] an aftercrop.
So she acts as if she will not love [me],
and me, I have done with her.

While the speaker's thought moves dialogically back and forth between himself and the woman, dialogue is contained in a monologue. Internal balance and antithesis are as visible as in the shorter *ohabolana*.
Though Paulhan recorded no tunes, he observed metrical regularities in
both *hainteny* and *ohabolana*, confirming their generic connection
(1913:41–48). These observations and his poetic arrangement of texts are
my justifications for rearranging Dahle's texts as verse.

Another poem, printed by Dahle and sung in Paulhan's hearing, is
the following. Malagasy readers find it the most beautiful of all.

Midona ny orana any Ankaratra,
    ka vaky ny tsipelana any Anjafy,
dia mitomanitomany razanaboromanga;
    nefa kosa mihomehy Itsimatahotody.
Eny, fa raha todim-paty, aza manody;
    fa raha todim-pitia kosa, manodiava.

                        (Dahle 1877:2, no. 3, trans. Chapus and
                        Dandouau 1940:112, no. 54, and Fox
                        1990:218–19, no. 192, also 398–99, no. 450)

Rain is striking on Bare-Hill,
    and orchids are blooming on The Branch,
now the bluebird's ancestor cries,
    but also, Fears-No-Retribution laughs.
So be it—if you are punished by dying, you do not deserve that;
    but if you too are punished by loving, that you deserve.

Each of the three couplets is symmetrical and grammatically parallel,
with the same structure found by Kuusi in African proverb-riddles (Kuusi
1974). Internal antithesis of this kind is also a structure in *ohabolana* (proverbs), as in "When angry, you are like a prince, but when quiet, you are a
person" (Houlder 1960:31, no. 397). The same poetic features appear in
nine variant forms of this poem which have been scrutinized by Bakoly
Domenichini-Ramiaramanana (1978).

In the terms of folkloristic performance theory, the figurative language and parallelism signal to a hearer that performance is taking place (Goffman 1974, Bauman 1977). In Madagascar, these and other features link *hainteny*, riddles, proverbs, and oratory. In all, a performer will use a special stance or intonation to signal performance, or pairs of speakers will try to silence and confuse each other. In Paulhan's terms, the abundance of images, the reliance upon verbal music, the parallelism, the balance, and the antithesis in these two examples, as well as in the other two which Paulhan heard sung, link them with poetry everywhere. Paulhan's case is proved. Looking back, we can see his translations of *hainteny* as a manifesto for a new poetry for France and the world. If he did not see the meter, the absence of rhyme was no fault either; indeed it was a hallmark of the poetry of Stéphane Mallarmé and Apollinaire. Moreover, *hainteny* were the poetry of an "illiterate" people, as inspiring to a young *littérateur* as African sculpture to Picasso or Braque. There was even an element of cultural politics: *hainteny* demonstrated that a colonized, oppressed people could compose poetry of high sophistication. In their use of assonance and parallelism, they helped Paulhan and his readers find the style for a new European poetry.

Recent scholarship, by recording a characteristic tune for *hainteny*, has brought the connection between verse and song even closer. Many of the poems have been shown to use stress as regular as four syllables per line, with five to nine unstressed syllables. They also have predictable pauses or rests. So regular are the pitch patterns which reciters conventionally use that they can be transcribed into musical notation (Domenichini-Ramiaramanana 1978: 127–50). When not being sung, *hainteny* were often intoned in a distinct manner, akin to what Paulhan observed when his friends in Antananarivo spoke *ohabolana* (1925: 27–29). This "modulated diction" grew out of an older style of intoning called *vary raraka*, falling rice, which was practiced by possessed persons and some reciters of poetry. Nowadays the falling rice style is used only by a few preachers at peak passages, or by professional reciters deliberately evoking an archaic manner. "Modulated diction," with its shorter breaths, allows us to hear the tetrameter rhythm (Domenichini-Ramiaramanana 1968:l–lvi, 1978: 108–9, 1983: 281). This discovery, which was apparently common knowledge among men of words but never documented until 1978 by Domenichini-Ramiaramanana, is as far-reaching for Malagasy oral literature as Hymes's discovery of measure in Native American narrative.

"Modulated diction" would also be used when a man of words gave voice to a linear series of metaphors which are balanced against each other, like the egret, guineafowl, and kingfisher above. In the following lover's complaint, the ironic names which the man gives to the woman were printed by Dahle in quotation marks, indicating their status as fixed phrases already in circulation. I rearrange Dahle's prose text as verse, making the grammatical divisions correspond to spoken lines and revealing poetic structure.

> Ataoko ity hianao ho "Rasoamahalefitra avy avaratra,
>   ka vavy fotsy tsy mba malazo,—"
>   ka valaka aho.
> Ary ataoko ity hianao ho "Ramora avy atsimo,
>   ka bari-masoko,"—
>   ka trotraka aho.
> Ary ataoko ity hianao ho "Rasoavelo any atsinanana,
>   ka bako lava—"
>   ka taitra aho.
> Ary ataoko ity hianao ho "Ratsitaho avy avaratra,
>   ka bikana,"—
>   ka hendratra aho.
> Kanjo hay! ity olona miteti-pitatra
>   mihoditr' androngo,—
>   ka tofoka aho.

> (Dahle 1877:409–10, trans. Chapus and
> Dandouau 1940:112, Fox 1990:346–47,
> no. 375)

> I believed you would be "Miss SweetPliant of the North,
>   a white lady who would not fade,"
>   but I was disappointed.
> I believed you would be "Miss Kindness of the South,
>   with large eyes,"
>   but I got worn out.
> I believed you would be "Miss Sweetness of the East,
>   tall and slender,"
>   but I was taken unawares.
> I believed you would be "Miss No-Stalk of the North,
>   yet well formed,"
>   but I was cast down.

Alas! the woman is spotted like a warbler
>> and skin like a lizard,
>>>> and I despair.

The discovery of meter, balance, and parallelism in such a prose text finally confirms the poetic status of Merina *hainteny*.

Hainteny and Proverbs

Internally monologic *hainteny* usually draw their material from fixed phrases already circulating in tradition. The mark of the skilled speaker is the ability to select and arrange these familiar phrases in regular proverb patterns like the three-part one visible here. The derivation of this pattern from *ohabolana* and riddles can easily be seen in the shorter examples combining both: "Relations are like bad rope: when pulled tight, it breaks, and when pulled lightly, it unties" (Houlder 1960:14). This informant set the patterns into a sequence familiar from oratory, the points of the compass (though he did not strictly observe it). But the riddle wins out when the compass metaphors are answered by the bitter metaphors at the end.

Intergeneric dialogue is not merely a matter of an outsider's perception. The various genres of *fitenin-drazana* speak to one another in the stock and realizations of the man of words. More than any other genre, the reciter of *hainteny* or the speaker of an oration relies on the *ohabolana* to create new work. His stock includes fixed phrases shorter than a symmetrical proverb, as well as "oratorical flourishes" much longer than a mere aphorism. The existence of this repertoire of fixed phrases, sentences, and linguistic routines in the performances of Malagasy men of words was discovered by Jean Paulhan. At this time, Charles Renel, Paulhan's superior in the school administration, was discovering and collating opening and closing formulas ("Lies! lies!") in Malagasy folk narrative style. Renel also identified numerous recurrent type-scenes and ten recurrent motifs in the tales (Renel 1910:1:xxv–xxvii). Elsewhere, perhaps others were discovering elements of what would later be called oral-formulaic composition in written texts. In Madagascar, Paulhan and Renel had no need to demonstrate that their texts were oral, as Parry and Lord were later obliged to do (Lord 1960, Foley 1980).

This was Paulhan's reasoning. For *hainteny* we may imagine a poetic diction in which two or three hundred metrical phrases and four or five hundred type-verses are permanently fixed in wording. Having learned this stock, the reciter could create new *hainteny* or *ohabolana* in the same form and rhythm by using the same structures. Merina *hainteny* were made out of proverbs by imitation, deletion, expansion, and quotation. We can now add to his list of devices the metrical pattern discussed earlier. So when the longer *hainteny* resemble parts of orations, stringing together phrases from a common stock, it is no accident. As *hainteny* are made out of riddles and proverbs, so *kabary* are made out of *hainteny*.

One of Paulhan's best examples of how *hainteny* are created is a poem that takes two proverbs known separately and makes one answer the other, as if the first were a riddling question and the second the answer. Both proverbs use topic-comment form. One is pure metaphor: "Weaver-finch skimming the waves, not a drop of water on his feet, not a tailfeather moistened." The other refers to the practice of keeping silkworm cocoons in water for a week, after which they were allowed to dry on an earthen wall until they could be detached. "She is as difficult to love as a rotten cocoon: you hardly reach for her before her silk gets tangled" (Domenichini-Ramiaramanana 1970:200, 425). Here, then, is how to make a lyric poem:

> Tsikirity nitety riana, ka tsy volom-body lena, tsy tongotra nifao-drano, tetezam-bolamena: hosy be rano hianao ka saro-tiana toa landy mohaka: tiana, vao misaritaka. (Dahle 1877:3, no. 10, Domenichini-Ramiaramanana 1970:200, no. 1150, trans. Chapus and Dandouau 1940:III, no. 51, Fox 1990:106–107, no. 35)

Weaver-finch skimmed the rapids,
  not a tailfeather moistened,
    not a foot wetted.
Golden bridge,
  you are a flooded ricefield,
    as difficult to love as a softened silkworm,
      loved and immediately tangled.

Were this a *safidy*, tension between the proverbial images would be relieved in external dialogue. A choice would be made between them. Here, only an answering *hainteny* will complete the incomplete half. As to internal dialogue, if the components of the proverb are the two-stressed phrase or the four-stressed line, the component of the poem is the proverb. Many *hainteny* must have been built by such a juxtaposition.

In confirmation of Paulhan's oral-formulaic hypothesis, I would add that the structure of riddles furnishes the man of words with a framework for his poems. Here is another proverb to be elaborated:

Voankazo an' ala
Ny mangidy aloa
Ny mamy atelina

> (Domenichini-Ramiaramanana
> 1970:182, no. 1020)

Fruits from the forest:
   the bitter ones we spit back,
   the sweet ones we swallow.

Once quoted, these familiar words may make the hearer wonder, Why has the speaker quoted this proverb? What does he want me to think of in the present situation? Thus they function as a riddle precedent. By adding to the words, one man of words, an author of the 1835–38 manuscript, gave the answer to the riddle. Two levels of meaning are involved.

Voankazo an' ala ry zandry
Ny mamy atelemo
Ny mangidy aloavy
Raha mahita tiana manova
Fa aza izaho no asiana teny ratsy
—Hono Andriamanitra atsy ambony atsy
Ny teninay sy izoky nifanolana
Izoky nelo-po fa narary
Ary izaho nahitsy fo fa nivavaka
Mahazoa mivavaka hiany anie
Mba hahitako ny soa tsy mba hitako

> (Domenichini-Ramiaramanana 1968: 326–27,
> trans. Fox 1990:252–53, no. 251)

Fruits from the forest, little brother/sister
   swallow the sweet ones,
   spit back the bitter ones.
If you have found a new love, keep on with it,
   but heap no bad words on me.

> Say, o God above:
> my words and my elder brother's/sister's clashed.
> He/she was sick at heart and ill;
> I was upright because I prayed.
> May my right to pray not be set aside,
> may I finally find the goodness I've never found.

Is the "goodness" the speaker has never found a better sexual partner? Is that the kind of praying the Protestant evangelist Ratsimba had in mind the day he told Paulhan that *hainteny* were the work of the devil (Paulhan 1913)? Along with the customary sexual content, the poem, from the days of Ranavalona I, almost certainly alludes to conflict between one's Merina ancestors and the Christians who were being expelled and persecuted at this time.

Still, Paulhan's hypothesis that the larger genres are built out of the smaller has not won universal acceptance. Why could the speaker of a shorter piece not be simply alluding to a well-known longer one? Could not the proverbs about the weaver-finch and cocoon be allusions to the poem? This is the supposition of Flavien Ranaivo, who is the leading poet of written *hainteny* today. As African proverbs allude to folktales which the hearer is expected to recall, Malagasy sayings and proverbs may be derived from *hainteny*. A line from a *hainteny* or oration by some well-known ancestor may be quoted briefly in conversation or as a proverb. Interpreters as well as genres have dialogues among them. To a nonpractitioner, this issue appears a question to be settled through fieldwork rather than a theoretical rule. Malagasy men of words and their audiences have excellent memories. Variants in one genre allude to the other genres. Any set of words that can be heard as a quotation reasserts the unity of ancestral discourse.

Reported Speech

The man of words, summoning up fixed phrases, recombining them on a riddle frame to fit a particular context situation, can encounter a difficulty. Monologue in public, in fact any lengthy speech by one person, presents a serious ethical and artistic problem to the ethics he has been taught. Speaking too long or too well makes a speaker stand out. It puts others into the shade (Keenan and Ochs 1979:143–44). No one should stand out that much, for fear of *tsiny*, reproaches. One *ohabolana* says, *Ny hazo avo halan-drivotra, ary ny manan-karena halan' olona*, The tall tree is battered by the wind, and the rich are hated by other people (Houlder 1960:120). The words of the ancestors, however, are authoritative speech. For their wisdom to be asserted, they must be recited by some spokesman. Conventionally, Merina orators solve this problem by attributing their words to the ancestors instead of to themselves (Andriamanjato 1957:16). Thus they are only quoting. Storytellers also insist that they are only quoting. Their characteristic opening or closing formula for folktales is, "Lies! lies! It isn't I who am the liar, but the ancients who made up this tale" (Renel 1910:lix). The *Tantaran'ny Andriana* quote incessantly too (Domenichini-Ramiaramanana 1983:391–446, Haring 1979:152–54). Quotation has the advantage of removing responsibility for words from the real speaker in the interaction situation to a fictional speaker in the drama being portrayed. *Hainteny* stylize the reporting of speech as one of their most effective devices.

Behind this habit of quotation is what many observers believe to be a terror of isolation. Some monologic *hainteny* cope with this terror by means of quotation, which connects the single speaker with his predecessors. Here is a *hainteny* from Dahle.

> Arosi-lahy tafaraka amy ny tsiriry, ka mitoka-miavaka hiany, na zavo-zavoin'ny beaza, ka isoronan'ny ahibahoaka, fandrao halan' olon' antanana, ary isoronan' ny tsitohintohina, fandrao tohim-pitia samy irery ka raraka. Ka aiza re io no hafenina? Haroso eo aloha, andrao sambo-belon' ny sasany: hatao eo aoriana, andrao tsy mahara-dia; hosakalehina, toa ambin-javatra. Eny, izay avo tokoa no halan-drivotra, ary izay tsy tiana, hono, no matevin' endrika, ary izay halan' olona no be molotra.
>
> (Dahle 1877:22, no. 69, trans. Fox
1990:278–79, no. 293)

A drake stands out among the teals,
   he is separate, he is alone,
   he hides in the crowd.
He edges in among the leaves
   lest he be hated by the villagers,
he edges into the grasses lest,
    being the only one touched by love,
    he be cast out.

O where will he hide?
    In front, he can be captured by others.
    Behind, he cannot follow.
    Under an arm, he will only be superfluous.
Yes, whatever is tall is shaken by the wind,
        and he who is not loved, they say, seems ugly,
            and the one people hate has thick lips.

Riddle and proverb jostle each other. Lines 1–8 state a topic; lines 9–12 comment on it; lines 13–15 comment again by quoting the familiar proverb. They function like the sequent of a riddle. Thus the *hainteny* genre incorporates the riddle instrumentally (Dorst 1983:424). Will the opposition between dialogue and monologue be reconciled? The patterning of monologic *hainteny* according to antithesis, balance, and question and answer, fusing dialogue and monologue, is one means of reconciliation. Another is quotation, the framing of one speaker's words in another's. With constant quotation, reporting of speech, and allusion to familiar words, the dialogue of genres makes *hainteny* elusive. The hundreds of examples constitute an arena in which genres can negotiate with one another. Each performance presents to its hearers a drama, the *hainteny* situation, in which imaginary speakers have dealings with each other. That drama enters into dialogue with the context situation. If the speakers' dialogue is framed into a monologue through stylized quotation, another interaction of genres comes in. In the following example, the drama frames imaginary dialogue inside its *hainteny* situation. The woman is one voice, her absent husband a second, and the village children are a third; there is also an anonymous narrator to contain all the dialogue in monologue.

Hony, rankizy retsiana, ao hiany va Andrianavaradrano? Ary hoy ny ankizy: Ahoanao izy? Asaovy avy, ka asaovy faingana izy, ka ilazao hoe: Ny vadinao, hono, mati-mosary, matin-kainandro. Dia hoy ny ankizy: Tsy ato izy, Rafotsy, fa lasa nankany Imamo, ka rehefa tonga ny fandroana, ary manetsa ny olona, dia tonga izy. Dia hoy ravehivavy: Eny, rankizy retsiana, fa tapak' andro tsy foin-kisarahana, ka nilaozany manontolo taona any aho sy ny zanako, ka veloma hiany.

(Dahle 1877:12–13, trans. Chapus and
Dandouau 1940:95, Fox 1990:178–79,
no. 139)

Woman: Tell me, children, is Sir-North-of-the-Water here?

Narrator:	Then the children answered,
Children:	What do you want with him?
Woman:	Have him come here, have him hurry,
	and say to him,
	"They say your wife is dead of hunger, dead of sunstroke."
Narrator:	The children answered,
Children:	He is not here, lady.
	He has gone toward Imamo.
	And "When it comes time for the [royal] bath,[4]
	and people are thinning out their rice,"
	then he will return.
Narrator:	Then said the wife,
Woman:	I see, children.
	Though I would not want to be separated from him even for half a day,
	he has abandoned me and my children for a whole year. So, farewell.

In this poem, as in many Malagasy prose narratives, the reporting of speech is characteristically full. It is the narrative genre that has entered here to complicate our understanding of *hainteny*. This one frames a question and answer as vivid as, but less playful than, The King and the Peasant's Son (discussed in Chapter 2; tale 1.6.921 in *Malagasy Tale Index*). The woman's questions turn on the vital fortunes of herself and her children. The dangerous, delicate information is conveyed in reported speech. The most dangerous answer of all, the answer to the woman's core question, is given in the innermost quotation.

As Bakhtin delineated such technique in the novel, he might have been describing a *hainteny* contest. The quotation, he said, enters into the theme of the drama framing it; it is only partly assimilated to the syntax and style of the frame, remaining identifiable as "of the ancestors"; the quotation becomes a document of how speech is received; and its integrity is maintained by the convention of verbatim reporting. Formalized speech in Madagascar places the quotation in sharp relief, thus ensuring that intergeneric dialogue will take place.

To attribute delicate and dangerous information to another speaker (not necessarily the ancestors) is a *hainteny* technique that stylizes a Malagasy conversational habit. The Merina seem to Westerners to have a way of rationing information as if it were nearly toxic. Implicitness is a value in formal speaking and in ordinary talk. The more allusive and implicit the conversation, the better. *Teny atsipin'ny mpanahy raisin'ny mpahalala*, A few words tossed out by intelligent people are grasped by those in the know, says a proverb (Domenichini-Ramiaramanana 1970:152). The more destructive a message might be, the more carefully it must be framed (Keenan and Ochs 1979:147−53). The stylization of this framing produces the most elaborate *hainteny*, in which the word *hono*, "he/she/they say(s)," constantly recurs to mark the quotations within quotations.

> Hony, ry olona ato an-tanána, mba nandry teto va Rasoavangaina? Eny, fa nandry teto izy tamy ny herin' ny avy. Ka mba ahoana no resadresany teto? Hoy ny resadresany teto: Toy ny hitsikitsika manito, hono, izy, ka voan' ny dity; ary toa vorona hihy voafandrika, hono, izy, ary toa valala voatango ka very fanahy mbola velona. Ka hianao hiany, hono, no lopiany (tiany), ary izy, hono, no lopanao; ary hianao, hono, hena, ary izy, hono, akalana; ary hianao, hono, ronono, ary izy, hono, voatavo; ary hianao, hono, vary, ary izy, hono, rano; ka an-tsaha tsy misaraka, ary an-tanána tsy mifandao. Fa inona kosa, hono, iny aminareo: zavona va, hono, fa sa ranonorana? Tsy mba zavona tsy ranonorana ireny. fa asa, na Ambanivolo no mandoro tevy, ka ny ety Imerina no toa mitomany,—na izaho no nisao-bady, ka ny tany no toa malahelo. Ka raha tsy zavona ka tsy ranonorana áry ireny, dia aiza ny lambanao ho entiko mampody azy? Ary raha nandre izany Andrianizinizina dia faly ka nisaotra ilay hampody ny vadiny, ka nanao hoe: Raha vola no omenao ahy, dia manam-pahalaniana izany, ary raha lamba no omenao ahy, dia fitafy hiany, fa mbola ho rovitra ireny; fa izany fampodianao ny vadiko izany matavy ka tsy azo didiana.
>
> (Dahle 1877:25, no. 79, trans. Chapus and Dandouau 1940:114 and Fox 1990:184−85, no. 147)

He: Tell me, people of the village,
        did Miss-Fair-Enough-To-Be-Sold stop here?
They: Yes, she stopped here a week ago.
He: And what were her words?

They: Here are her words:
        She is like a hawk broken loose, she says,
           but she is fastened by gum;
        or she is like a trapped bird, she says,
           or like a locust stripped of its wings,
               still alive but with no strength.
        For it is you, she says, whom she loves,
           and it is she, she says, whom you love;
        and you, she says, are the meat
           and she, she says, is the chopping block,
        and you, she says, are the milk
           and she, she says, is the gourd;
        and you, she says, are the rice
           and she, she says, is the water.
        In the ricefield you don't separate,
           and in the village you don't part.
        So, "What is the matter with you," she says.
        "Is it fog," she says, "or rain?"

He: I have no fog, I have no rain.
        I know not whether the forest folk are burning a clearing,
        that Imerina seems to lament,
        or whether it is that I have let my wife go,
        that the earth seems afflicted.

A man: But if you have neither fog nor rain,
        where is your garment,
        that I may wear it to bring her back?

When Undaunted heard that, he was overjoyed
  and thanked the one bringing back his wife, saying,

If you gave me money,
    then it could be spent,
  or if you gave me clothes,
    then they could be worn or could tear;
  but bringing back my wife
    is "fat and not to be sliced."

Several genres are at work here. The poem is an expanded *ohabolana*:
a dilemma (remember the riddle) is resolved by the entrance of authori-

tative speech (a man offers to be the husband's messenger). It cites several proverbial metaphors. It also has a definite narrative shape: what the wife is reported as saying creates a lack, which is promised to be liquidated. Its central character controls too well his powerful feeling, like the bereaved woman who concealed her child's death. Though the onlookers in both poems see the evidences of grief, the character will do almost anything rather than verbalize it. In deference to the sensibilities of an audience that might not welcome more explicit display, just as the hearer begins to confront the husband's grief, the situation is resolved—only in word. In any performance, social forces would multiply the sense of a dialogue of genres.

The Origin of *Hainteny*

> Great poetry is not begotten behind sheltering walls. Its growth is inter-twined with the life of individuals and of groups, with the rise and fall in the destiny of peoples. So it is not surprising that great poems always originate at turns of the tide in the affairs of men, when an old era is dying out and a new era is tuning its first song. That is the moment for the poet to "charm the air to give a sound." Homer and the Greek tragedians lived in periods when the fate of the Greeks trembled in the balance. Dante wrote at the turn of Italian, Shakespeare at that of English history. Goethe's work marks the beginning of national unity for which he created the necessary unified and unifying language. (Morwitz 1943:9)

Is it ever possible to mark the origin of a genre in folklore as exactly as we know the dates of Goethe's birth and death? Storytelling, one example of the difficulty, is as old as language. The kind of story that folklorists today call the "modern urban legend" goes back to ancient Rome (Ellis 1983, Brunvand 1981). Tragedy, the queen of classical genres, was traced by the Cambridge anthropologists to ancient ritual (Harrison 1912). Their successors found connections of other literary forms with other rituals (Phillpotts 1920, Gaster 1950). Today we view these attempts skeptically. Folklorists and literary historians have had little success finding the origins of genres. Seeking the origin of the ballad, British and American scholars confused the medieval origin of this genre of northern European narrative song with the origin of all poetry (Wilgus 1959:3–122). Another example is African American blues. When some folklorists were advocating the doctrine that all myth originated in ritual, Stanley Edgar Hyman became so infatuated that he proposed to seek the roots of the blues in African ritual (1963:291–92).

Despite these discouraging examples, an origin for *hainteny* can be guessed. This genre, being a combination of existing genres, originated at a turn in the tide of Malagasy history. All folklore originates in tension. One clue that tension underlies *hainteny* is that their dialogues so often enact power conflicts. The studies of Bakoly Domenichini-Ramiaraman-ana, somewhat marred by her attempt to reconstruct the origin of specific texts, show that *hainteny* rose into prominence during the emergence of a military conquest state. The genre was probably performed from the end of the sixteenth century (1983:337–446). Thus a contradictory and elusive poetry plays out a contradiction that was very real in Malagasy politics of that time: the struggle between an expanding centralized monarchy and the local chiefs whom that monarchy sought to bring under its sway. Before the sixteenth century, every village in Madagascar was locally ruled or autonomous. Merina villages had their own chiefs (called kings). The royal dynasty was established when a rule of succession was introduced by Queen Rafohy (or Rangita). Thenceforward, for two centuries, the dynasty expanded its control and influence. This tendency reached its apogee in the centralizing, expansionist power of the monarchy of Andrianam-poinimerina. Military force and a strongly hierarchical social structure conquered local and regional princes, who represented a more egalitarian form of government (Brown 1979:120–30, Delivré 1979:134–42).

The struggles of this period are reflected in the symbolism of the poems. One interpretation of the following text sees the bull as symboliz-ing the conquering monarchy. The princes are symbolized by a hippo-potamus, an extinct species in Madagascar.

Raha ombalahibemaso mitrena an-tanety hianao,
  Izaho lalomena mitrena am-parihy;
Raha ombimanga taranaky ny haolo hianao,
  Izaho omby dia taranaky ny omby mahery;
Raha mitrena avy ao andrefana (avaratra) hianao,
  Izaho mitrena avy ao atsinanana (atsimo).
Raha baka mahay manorirana hianao,
  Izaho kirongo tsy azo idirana.
Raha varatra hilatsaka hianao, izaho vatolampy ampy handihizana;

Raha havandra hiraraka hianao, i zaho tanetibe ampy hielezana.
Raha fanala hamotsy hianao, izah o ravin'ampaly tsy
    mataho-kasokasoka.
Raha rambon-danitra hipaoka hianao, izaho vatobe tsy azo
    hontsonina.
Ary raha kanontabe hianjera hianao, izaho akalamanta tsy
    torom-pamaky.
Ny zanaky ny efa mangotraka tsy matahotra izay mangoro-vitsika.

> (Domenichini-Ramiaramanana
> 1983:361−73, trans. Fox 1990:400−401,
> no. 457).

If you are a great bull bellowing on the earth,
    I am a hippopotamus bellowing in the marsh.
If you are a chestnut bull born of wild cattle,
    I am a bull born of mighty cattle.
If you bellow as you come from the west (north),
    I bellow as I come from the east (south).
If you have V-shaped horns that turn aside,
    I have curling horns that are unbeatable.
If you are thunder that is about to fall,
    I am a flat rock for it to dance on.
If you are hail about to drop,
    I am a plain big enough to scatter it.
If you are frost about to whiten everything,
    I am a sandpaper leaf afraid of no rubbing.
If you are a waterspout about to swoop,
    I am a big rock that cannot be shaken.
And if you are a great hammer about to strike,
    I am a chopping block that cannot be split.
The child of what is already boiling
    has no fear of the fire building up.

What is the context situation of this poem? What set of facts would a speaker want a hearer to think of? The text gives little help. The text, found in one published collection and one oral version, must be replaced in the context of the Merina court. *Ombalahibemaso*, the big-eyed bull, may be singular or plural. In one interpretation, it means the king's counselors. In another, it means Andrianampoinimerina alone.

Domenichini-Ramiaramanana suggests that it means both. She speculates that Andrianampoinimerina would have used the metaphor for himself, because the many "bulls" under him lent him their eyes, and with those he was able to extend his power farther than any predecessor. In the plural meanings of a single word she sees traces of the conflicts of the early nineteenth century. Her interpretive method is to read classic Malagasy texts as records of political and social changes. This poem, she believes, should be read as an allegory of violent opposition to the centralizing, expansionist power of the monarchy. In the absence of evidence about any interaction situation for this poem, this interpretation remains no more than a fascinating speculation. It is especially fascinating because the struggle between the central monarch and the local chiefs, like the later struggle between highland and coastal groups, could so well have provided a continuing source of symbolism for the poems.

Another view is more likely. What has been opened here to the reader of Malagasy oral literature is the historical moment when *hainteny* emerged into prominence. The political and cultural stresses arising from the unification of Imerina are reflected, I believe, not so much in the symbolism of *hainteny* as in their relation to their constituent genres. The parallels are striking. For one, both the words and the characteristic interaction situations for *hainteny* invariably enact power struggles. Behind those we may see tamer contests for power in riddling and the assertions of control in proverbs. Riddles and proverbs are pan-Malagasy and are the models for *hainteny*. Riddling, which like *fanorona* starts its players in positions of equal rank, contributes the stylized alternation of speakers to the dialogues of *hainteny*. Such egalitarian dialogism reflects an older, decentralized politics. The invention of the *safidy*, which awarded greater power to the riddle poser, was a move in the direction of *hainteny*. Proverbs speak for stronger authority; they contribute a more monologic flavor. The *hainteny* becomes an arena in which the riddle-like dialogue contends with the authoritative monologue of the *ohabolana*. Into that arena narrative also enters. An insistence on social control in the expressive culture of this period surely responds to the expansion of the Merina monarchy.

Political and social conflict in the highlands seems to have created a new, uniquely flexible, multivoiced genre of verbal art out of an uneasy combination of pre-existing genres. As the expansion of the monarchy resolved the political conflict in favor of social hierarchization, so the *hainteny* resolve their contradictions in favor of monologue. As the expanded monarchy ruled over a wider area, so the *hainteny* expand to take in more genres and more conflicts. In the texts, someone always has the last word. But the rules for composition allow, indeed encourage, a sequent for every precedent. That openness makes the resolution uneasy. In performance, another *setriny*, comeback, is theoretically always possible. Only the verdict of the onlookers, like the consent of the people to a royal *kabary*, brings an end to the session. That verdict is another kind of last word. Again the resolution may be uneasy. There could be another session, another round. The dialectic between monologue and dialogue never really ends.

If *hainteny* as a genre did not in fact originate in the efforts of Malagasy men of words to record political struggles, their texts certainly seem to be evidence that Malagasy men of words devised an artistic method to overcome the contradiction between conflicting forces. Genres can be viewed critically and dialectically as "positive means of ideological production" (Dorst 1983:425). Then the *hainteny* is the genre that produced a new ideology for a new political-social order among the Merina. The thoroughly dialogic and antagonistic form of *hainteny* simultaneously deconstructs and glorifies the riddle and proverb genres, while it reminds us about the inevitability of narrative (Jameson 1981:86). If the principal action in a riddle is "to question at least certain kinds of established order," a principal action of *hainteny* is to question the boundary between riddle and *ohabolana*. If the riddle "make[s] a point of playing with conceptual borderlines and crossing them for the pleasure of showing that things are not quite as stable as they appear," then the *hainteny* make a point of playing with generic borderlines (Köngäs Maranda 1971:53).

The origin of *hainteny* may never be known. Nor can anyone name or exhaust the multiple meanings that arise from intergeneric dialogue and verbal allusion in Madagascar. Gabriel Ferrand, who understood Madagascar deeply and was well able to play the *hainteny* duel, evidently knew this inexhaustibility. Even from him the game guarded its secret. "During one of my stays in Madagascar," he writes,

> I was debating in *hainteny* with some southeastern Malagasy [not Merina], and I opened the debate with the proverb "Forest water is clean and blue." It went on rather a long time; then suddenly, at the end of my argument, I chanced to throw out this: "The dog barks and the moon glitters." My adversary remained open-mouthed and those present declared me the winner. Translated into French, this improvised debate would seem to have no head or tail, but the Malagasy recognized an esoteric continuity in arguments that

had no logic *à la française* and that seemed to them supremely appropriate to this oratorical context. (Ferrand 1914:156)

Ferrand never knew why what he said brought him victory. With such instinctive penetration of the Malagasy art of the word, he, echoing Paulhan, had the wisdom to quote the ultimate Malagasy tribute to the art of the word: *Hovalahy mahay kabary ka tsy misy tsy vitany*, When a *hova* [freeman] knows how to do formal speaking, there's nothing he can't carry to completion (Paulhan 1913:74, Ferrand 1914:154).

5. Marriage: Petition and Delivery

God has been aloof, if not dead, to Malagasy religion for centuries, although he does appear in *ohabolana* (proverbs). *Andriamanitra tsy an' ny irery*, God does not belong to one person only: *Ny iray fahifahin' olombelona, fa ny iray fahifahin' Andriamanitra*, One is blessed by man and the other is blessed by God (Houlder 1960:2). The blessing of God is ceremonially invoked when people marry. But blessing and judgment, in many Malagasy life crises, belong more to a visible community than to a distant divinity. What happens when God removes himself from human activity, as happens in some Malagasy myths (tales 2.1.03, 2.1.11–13 in *Malagasy Tale Index*)? He is replaced by a symbolic discourse. It was Friedrich Nietzsche, of all people, who delineated this phenomenon. What Europeans had instead of God, said Nietzsche, was "a mobile army of metaphors, metonyms and anthropomorphisms—in short, a sum of human relations, which have been enhanced, transposed, and embellished poetically and rhetorically, and which after long use seem firm, canonical, and obligatory to a people" (quoted in Taylor 1986:219). These words of Nietzsche's describe the Malagasy conception of truth. This conception, that truth is the verbal enhancement, transposition, and embellishment of human relations, pervades Malagasy *ohabolana*. It explains the temptation proverbs offer to persons like Houlder, Mondain, or Dama-Ntsoha, who have systematized Malagasy philosophy. The verbal symbolizing of human relations reaches its peak in the Malagasy art of oratory. Acknowledged by performers and audiences as firm, canonical, and obligatory, this art in actual performance is highly variable. In oratory, an army of metaphors and ancestral sayings is mobilized for a contest, knowledge is constructed and transmitted, and a life crisis is surmounted.

Formal oratory, *kabary*, the Malagasy form of a widespread African practice (Finnegan 1970:444–56), is the showiest and most authoritative form of verbal art in Madagascar. Oratory expands and dramatizes the characteristic tension between the two tendencies we observed in *hainteny* poetry. It acknowledges separateness, fragmentation, and conflict as it asserts integration, unity, and resolution. Like other genres, it pertains to a certain stage of living. Riddling is a game of childhood; proverbs are uttered by older persons to younger; *hainteny* poems are exchanged in a contest by adults; marriage and funeral orations, a game played to mark a life crisis, call for formal oratory.

Variable Definition of Oratory

Changes in the meaning of the word *kabary* through history demonstrate again the variability of Malagasy culture, where performance is always emergent despite assertions of stability, and concepts are fluid despite assertions of solidity. As the society of the highlands became more hierarchical, the definition of *kabary* changed. According to the shifting needs of speakers under changing social and political structures, the word *kabary* has meant several things. (1) One meaning, probably dating from before the Merina monarchy but still current, is the general category of formal speaking by adults, including riddling, proverb-speaking, and contesting in *hainteny* poems. Among the Merina, formal speaking is especially practiced by men (Keenan 1974). Within that general conception, *kabary* could also mean (2) the formal debate between heads of families at the time of a proposed marriage, during which the eligibility of each prospective partner is established and the conditions of marriage are publicly asserted; this debate will be discussed below. It can also mean (3) any ceremonial oration, such as the funeral speech discussed in the next chapter.

A fourth meaning for *kabary* made more sense to European observers who knew centralized governments. This was (4) a pseudo-dialogue in which a king announces plans or hands down orders to his people. This dialogue may have been genuinely reciprocal, at an earlier stage of the Elevated People's history, before the monarchy began to assert itself (Delivré 1974); or its egalitarian stage may be a fiction. Texts of royal ordinances show dialogic if not egalitarian elements. By the end of the sixteenth century, during the reign of Ralambo, *kabary* was established as a king's formal, authoritative speech. It required no more than a formal reply from the assembled people. But the earlier, dialogic character of the genre was still present. If the king wanted a building constructed, firewood brought from the forest, runaway rebels judged, or troops recruited, he had to speak and get an answer. After seeking advice from courtiers, judges, and chiefs in their hierarchical order, the king would address the people: "I solicit your consent, o you 'under the sky' [*ambaniandro*]. Here are the terms in which I do so. . . . Now how shall you and I come to agreement?" If the people accepted the king's determination, all was well. If they disagreed and the king accepted their determination, he would thank them and follow their opinion—or so said the oral historians of 1872–76, always solicitous of the reputation of monarchs (Callet 1974:1:540–46). Though dominated by the king, *kabary* at this point was as dialogic as the contest in *hainteny*; it would end its debate with a winner. But in time, the growing strength of the monarchy came to be asserted through authoritative speech. The king assumed, by means of formal speaking, more power to disregard a contrary opinion of his people, and to make a unilateral decision. His dialogue with his people, however equal it may once have been, began to lose its dialogism when the king took greater authority than in earlier generations.[1]

Since speaking is always related to power, *kabary* always made history and was made by history. As highland society became more hierarchical and vertically integrated, historians gave a fifth meaning to the word: (5) a monologic oration by the sovereign (Delivré 1974:61). It was within the same movement toward a more hierarchical society that *hainteny* began to combine dialogue and monologue. Thus these two closely related genres became arenas of intergeneric dialogue. Multiple voices and reported speech entered the poems. The two-sided debate and the monologic oration jostled each other in oral performance. They continue to do so in the dictated and written texts historians have so reverently preserved. The oral historians themselves, indeed, fell upon oratory as an essential rhetorical device. To fix the monarch's decisions in memory, they cast his or her edicts in the first and second person as *kabary* to the people. Reported speech thus maintained its central importance throughout the literate stages of Merina history.

A dialectic between literal and figurative language also colors the history of this genre. Domenichini-Ramiaramanana distinguishes historical *kabary* that are not especially rhythmic or flowery from others that are animated by emotion. These make use of parallelism and simile (1983:381–83). Generally, she says, the council meetings of Andrianampoinimerina were formal and metaphoric rather than functional and literal. Similarly, in the marriage debate, the real marriage arrangements have been made offstage in literal language. What takes place onstage is the symbolism of a drama including a plot, principal and supporting roles, fixed dialogue, narrative, and lyric.

The definition still seems fluid. For many Malagasy today, *kabary* means an authoritative speech; for others, like the Betsileo, who cultivate rice just south of the Merina on Madagascar's central plateau, the very idea implies dialogue. In their system of folklore genres, a true *kabary*, marking an event of public importance, separates the speaker from the audience, in both his posture and his role. In all highland oratory, it seems, the speaker's address to the audience has something of dialogue in it. More important, Betsileo *kabary* must have two orators, who answer each other as if two groups were debating (Michel-Andrianarahinjaka 1986:274).

For other Malagasy, especially in the highlands, *kabary* is characterized by variability. Performances of the marriage debate vary, under the pressure of the opposed forces of individual enhancement and adherence to tradition. So do the rules which speakers are expected to follow. "Rules of *kabary* performance . . . are a frequent point of departure for long discussions by local elders, particularly during the ceremonial season, when *kabary* are given several times a week in different villages" (Keenan 1975:94). Disagreements in these evaluative discussions reflect different conceptions of the rules, and more broadly reflect the inherent variability of Malagasy culture. Even the ideal lacks unity: Keenan's informants asserted that seven, twelve, and three parts were essential to the marriage request, that proverbs were critical to it, and that proverbs had no place in it (Keenan 1975:98). Some, under European influence, preferred a straightforward, literal discussion of the arrangements; others insisted on the elaborate formality of performance and metaphor.

The Marriage Debate

Traces of older dialogism can be found. In Madagascar, oratory around marriages and funerals is a debate, performed in two voices. Structured like a gigantic riddling session, the marriage debate is a two-sided drama. In words and actions, the drama attempts to realize an ideal harmony and integration between conflicting parties. That harmony exists mainly in the discourse that creates. The opposed interests of the parties to a marriage can be denied, wished away, or whitewashed, but not forgotten or reconciled. Their inevitable anxieties over losing a daughter and rearranging land rights (Bloch 1978) can be allayed only by the power of the word. Language in this genre, therefore, has to be as powerful as possible, to master the struggle over differential power and inequality. The orators attempt to harmonize disparate genres as a means of winning over each other. In the marriage debate, a complex event involving religious observance and feasting, men of words integrate several verbal genres—

proverbs, riddles, poems. In all these taken separately, language shows its power; the larger integration of them must be more powerful still.

With its many genres, scenes, and motives, oratory also has crucial social functions. In African marriage ceremonies, for comparison, it is bridewealth which must legalize "the conventions and patterns of behavior and the reciprocal obligations which are raised between the kinship groups concerned and must be observed if the union is to be successful" (Howell 1954:70–71). But Africa is not Madagascar, where it is by the art of the word that Malagasy custom legalizes conventions and obligations. That art is ineluctably dialogic.

The Merina marriage debate belongs to a genre whose complexity and originality arise from its dialectic between tradition and situation (Hymes 1975). Merina tradition declares that the families being united should be thought of as equal; at the same time it puts the groom's family in inferior status and directs their representative to try to sweep all before him, while it allows the bride's spokesman to fight him at every step, attempting to control the contest. Situation, the social facts conditioning a particular ceremony at a single place and time, may even bring about a failure of the ceremony (Keenan 1975). In common with all African oral poetry, moreover, oratory depends centrally upon familiar and novel patterning of images furnished by the smaller genres. "The metaphorical movement found in the proverb [and the riddle and poem] . . . supplies the structure necessary to carry a complex theme" (Scheub 1985:4–10).

This struggle makes the event difficult to classify. *Kabary*, an arena for interfamily and interclan conflict, is also an arena for conflict among folklore genres. Consider the contestants, one spokesman for the groom's family ("petitioner") and another for the bride's family ("deliverer"): they act like contestants in *hainteny*. If an utterance is attributed to the ancestors, is spoken by a person of authority to subordinates, and sums up and passes judgment on the altered situation of the families, it is behaving like an *ohabolana* (proverb). Indeed, the debaters quote innumerable recognized proverbs at each other. The debate is also a gigantic riddle. Its turn-taking and the gross units of its drama both derive from riddling. It is a formidable representation of how to carry on a serious, formal interrogation (Roberts and Forman 1972:184). The debate is also a poetic duel in which debaters exchange measured, fixed phrases and stanzas in an attempt to best each other. As to its meaning, investigators such as Bloch, Keenan, and Andriamanjato bear witness to conflicts over interpretation. There are even conflicts over whether to hold it. Some Merina cut it short, and others want to omit it altogether (Bloch 1978:31). In other cases, members of the bride's family acted as their own advocates instead of employing a spokesman (Bloch 1971:185–86).

Nowadays the debate will often have lost one of its contestants. The solo performer, spokesman for the groom's family, may be a professional speaker instead of a relative. The convergence of Malagasy and European cultures, as well as the influence of print, has tended to transform *kabary* from an improvisatory art into a recitation (Andriantsilaniarivo 1947:3–4). Still, even a hired man of words is perceived as powerful, especially if he possesses variable techniques, strategies, and tactics of negotiation. The petitioner in Imerina today may perform no more than a few sections of the oration as prescribed—an apology for speaking (*miala-tsiny*), an excuse, an array of proverbs—and then proceed to ask for the young woman. Even these few sections are really a dialogue of contestation.

> As the speech proceeds, the girl's family continually interrupt the speechmaker, challenging him to give proof of his assertions, objecting to what he says, and making offensive remarks about the groom and his family. The speechmaker, for his part, must listen and approve all this without losing his temper and must even thank the interrupters for their remarks. (Bloch 1971:185–86)

Heckling the speechmaker, the bride's family is carrying on the traditional function of the deliverer. It is her family who constitutes his real antagonist because it speaks for the conflicting interests of the parties. *Koa ny akoho no maty, eran' ny mpivady; ary ny fanambadiana no raikitra, eran' ny vaventy*, For if a chicken dies, the couple allowed it, and if a marriage is agreed upon, the elders allowed it (Rasamuel 1973:13).

Contest as Context for Marriage

Marriage involves both verbal and economic conflict. Contests in vituperation and invective have been held, for the sake of honor and prestige, throughout human history. In Africa and the Near East, as well as among African Americans, verbal dueling is a special activity of males (Mayer 1951, Dundes et al. 1972, Abrahams 1970). The Malagasy form of verbal dueling is the poetic duel, the *hainteny* contest. In Anglo-Saxon England, old Norway, and ancient Greece among other places, contests were people's method of choosing a bride or bridegroom (Huizinga 1955:83). Marriage in Madagascar is also contestatory. Families have often found it appropriate to make a show of opposing by force the departure of a daughter to join another family. Like the temporary setbacks in folktales, the show of force retards but does not stop the groom's movement toward acquiring a wife (Poirier 1964). Some Merina marriages have seemed so conflict-ridden that the aim was to humiliate the groom's family (Bloch 1978). In the marriage debate, these two contests converge. The family conflict is played out as a verbal duel, modeled on the preexisting contest in *hainteny* (unless, of course, the larger genre engendered the smaller one, a question to wonder about; Paulhan 1913:30). Dispute gives the performance its charm. Its effect on the vital fortunes of two families and the community gives it its seriousness.

Traditionally, ethnographers such as Raymond Decary tell us, this contest was a public performance at a fixed place and time, played in public on an appointed day by two spokesmen. When the day comes, one writes, numbers of people would arrive and jostle one another to get good seats. Inside the house was a mass of people pressed together "like beans in a pot," who took over the doors and windows. Those outside also listen attentively. Sometimes, in order to satisfy the crowd's curiosity, the meeting would take place in the open air (Rasamuel 1928:6). What a Western observer would call the real negotiations had already taken place: the two families had investigated each other's lineages and agreed to contract the marriage. Was there ever a time when the public performance governed the union (Molet 1979:2:234−35)? It seems doubtful. The families would also have agreed on the sequence and content of the drama, though the spokesmen might try to change the rules later. The role of chance was quickly settled: trial marriage, which sometimes led to pregnancy, was one means of determining astrological compatibility, and a diviner's reading of the *vintana*, destiny, of the couple was another. The bridegroom's family would designate three, five, or seven members to call on the young woman's family. The odd number would be symbolically completed by the addition of the bride on the wedding day.[2] With the setting of a date, the separation part of the ritual commenced. Thenceforward the couple were supposed not to see each other until the bride-to-be would emerge from the wings during the performance. On the appointed day, the young man and an odd number of *mpaka*, takers, would make their way to the bride's dwelling for the marriage *kabary*, a debate which in former times went on for several hours. The *mpangataka*, petitioner, would claim the young woman in the name of the groom (who remained silent); the *mpanatitra*, deliverer, would debate with him, exchanging poetic insults. The silent bride was not to appear until near the end of the drama, which was climaxed by handing over the *vodiondry*—nominally a sheep's right leg with the tail, actually a small sum of money symbolizing it (Decary 1951:36–37). Both sides win, for as the proverb says, a male crab is exchanged for a female crab.

As in the contest in *hainteny*, only two voices were heard in the central debate. Near the end, the eldest male in the bride's family was expected to give the blessing.

> Ka dia hitsodrano amin' ny anaran' ny be sy ny maro aho. E! 'zay Andriamanitra nahamanitra antsika mianakavy, 'zay Zanahary nahary tongotra aman-tànana, hitahy anareo mivady andro man' alina anie, ka mba hifankasitraka sy hifanaraka am-panahy hianareo mivady!
>
> (Rasamuel 1973:42, trans. Colançon 1928:40)

In the name of all present:
may God, who has perfumed our families,
creating our feet and hands,
bless the newlywed couple day and night,
so that you shall love each other
and cordially agree.

Rasamuel's Marriage Oration

To demonstrate the features and functions of the debate, I shall go back three generations and analyze one lengthy text, found in an orators' handbook that is still in print (Rasamuel 1973). It is not the only *kabary* to have been published by any means. Malagasy publishers have always found a market for handbooks of speeches to be made on formal occasions, reinforcing and stabilizing oral tradition with literate texts. Many texts printed by collectors are fragmentary (Andriantsilaniarivo and Abraham 1946, Fontoynont 1941, Dubois 1938:684–88, 690–91). The authenticity of the lengthy text by Maurice Rasamuel is rooted in its author-transcriber's motivation to preserve the sayings of the ancestors. An Anglican minister and teacher, Rasamuel was an experienced man of words who favored cultural conservation. He wrote, "It is all very well to devote oneself to poetry or knowing a foreign language, but it would be a great loss to the Malagasy language and people if the beautiful expressions that the ancestors formulated and bequeathed to their descendants were forgotten and fell into disuse" (1928:491, 1973:62).

Rasamuel believed in literacy. In his eyes, thirty years after the French conquest, oral improvisation was already a lost art. He deplored the disappearance of these old words of the ancestors. They saw performers making cuts in the old texts (presumably family manuscripts) and selecting only certain passages for performance. That tendency to reduction was already evident from the brevity of the excerpts from orations in Dahle's collection fifty years before. But they hoped that print, the most potent form of authoritative speech, would remedy this tendency. It could replace improvisation with memorization. Thus Malagasy culture would be preserved against European influences.

Some readers might call Rasamuel's marriage debate a work of Malagasy literature rather than folklore because it is an idealized, prescriptive compilation (Bloch 1978:25). Certainly, Rasamuel's version is no field-collected transcription. It is a monologic version of what is inescapably dialogic and conflictful. A printed script to be followed by actors, it even has stage directions. For example, at the beginning of the drama, Rasamuel creates an atmosphere of disquiet as the audience gathers. He shows us conversation beginning with conventional greeting formulas (Bloch 1971:185–86), then dropping off. Becoming impatient, people look at each other as if to say, "We should really get started." The two speakers separate themselves. A moment of silence follows.

> Petitioner: Gentlemen, the youth of the day is the morning, the old age is the evening, time cannot be stopped. We all have to go home. Yet there is something for us to speak about. What shall we do? Are we all gathered, or is someone still missing from this meeting whom we must await before taking up our business? For here it is as with gatherings during rainy season, better for them to take place in the morning.
> Deliverer: All gathered, sir. No one is missing. You can take up the subject.
> Petitioner, *with false modesty*: Mr. X, Mrs. Y, please begin speaking.
> Mr. X or Mrs. Y: You begin. We shall be grateful if you do. (Rasamuel 1928:3–4, 1973:8)

The introduction effects a transition between ordinary talk (*resaka*) and formal oratory (*kabary*). Foreshadowing the extensive quoting that will be heard throughout, this segment has ended with the quotation of a proverb, this one in topic-comment form:

Lanonam-pahavaratra
  Ny maraina ihany no izy
                (Domenichini-Ramiaramanana 1970 : 33,
            no. 1892)

Public songs in rainy season
  should be held in the morning

    With its stage directions and strategies, this idealized text offers fuller information than many a fieldwork document. In discussing it, I quote the Malagasy text where it resembles the poetry of *hainteny* or quotes *ohabolana* (proverbs); elsewhere I only translate or summarize.

Synopsis

The four large divisions and the fourteen riddlelike turns of the marriage request debate can be seen from the following synopsis. The linear movement of Rasamuel's libretto carries the speakers and hearers forward toward the acceptance of the proposal, the delivery of the young woman, the discussion of obligations, and the report home, all by means of turn-taking with repeated alternations of balance and imbalance.

SCENES	CHARACTERS
Prologue (*tari-dresaka*)	Petitioner (*mpangataka*)
(Turn 1, Exordium)	
Genealogy (*manontany resaka*)	Petitioner asks, deliverer answers
Apologies (*fialan-tsiny*)	Petitioner
Salutations (*arahaba ny fanirian-tsoa*)	Petitioner
(Turn 2, Proposal)	
Proposal (*hataka*)	Petitioner
Consent (*fanomezana*)	Deliverer
(Turn 3, Response)	Petitioner
Thanks (*fisaorana*)	
Entrance of the bride	Bride (mute)

(Turns 4–6, Reciprocal
    Obligations)
(Turn 4)
Obligations of the son-in-law   Deliverer poses, petitioner answers
    (*loloham-binanto*)
(Turn 5)
Details about the wife (*dinidinika*   Petitioner poses, deliverer answers
    momba ny zazavavy)
(Turn 6)
Recommendations concerning   Deliverer poses, petitioner answers
    affection due the future wife;
    remarks about wife-battering
    (*hafatrafatra ny amin'nyhitia-*
    vana ny zazavavy sy vahavahan-
    teny ny amin'ny famonoana)
(Turns 7–9, Property)
(Turn 7)
Dividing joint property into three   Deliverer demands, petitioner
    parts (*ny fahatelon-tanana*)   answers
(Turn 8)
Debts (*ny amin'ny trosa*)   Deliverer demands, petitioner
                                              answers

(Turn 9)
Children old enough to inherit   Deliverer demands, petitioner
    (*ny zaza ampy mihira*)   answers
(Turn 10)
The wife's clothes (*ny fitafian*   Deliverer demands, petitioner
    jazavavy)   answers, deliverer retorts
(Turn 11, Bridewealth)
The sheep's rump (*ny vodiondry*)   Petitioner offers, deliverer accepts
(Reconciliation, unification)
Symbolic meal   All participants
(Turn 12)
Blessing (*tsodrano*)   Petitioner, giver of the blessing
                                              (*mpitsodrano*), deliverer

(Turn 13)
Recommendations (*hafatra*)   Deliverer, petitioner
Return home   All "takers" from groom's
                                              family

(Turn 14)
Report to groom's family   Head of family asks, petitioner re-
    (*fanontaniana*)   plies, head of family acknowledges
Banquet   All present

To discuss delicate, dangerous matters without incurring *tsiny*, the speakers alternate so that no one person has all the responsibility.

Intergeneric Play as Strategy

The two antagonists serve the audience as models for the formal asking and answering of questions, as in riddling, and models of mastery over tradition, as in *hainteny* contests. Since knowledge of the right fixed phrases will secure a wife for the groom, hearers could be reminded of a folktale in which the verbal skill of a man of words is rewarded, like The King and the Peasant's Son. In particular, the alternative strategies available to speakers are visible in Rasamuel's text, when, for example, they need to regain the advantage. Published texts of *hainteny* poems, in which reciters also need to gain the advantage for their contest, have told us nothing of the strategies. The internal structure of the poems, however, suggests the strategy governing their external sequencing. *Hainteny* reciters seem to have in mind an expansible pattern of question and answer, or precedent and sequent. The riddle is its smallest manifestation. We could think of this speaking pattern as a skeleton or scaffolding, which they fill in according to the models and rules they have learned, their mood and goals of the moment, and the reactions of their audience.

In the marriage debate, as Rasamuel's text shows, men of words fill in the riddle pattern with the hundreds of *ohabolana* and *hainteny* they have learned. They add others which they produce by varying the old ones or creating new ones on the old models. This principle, called the *maqam* after the term in Arabic oral performance, yields certain passages that are stereotyped and other passages in which the performer has great freedom (Lloyd 1967:66–69). Orators of the European Renaissance followed the same principle. "Their choice of form did not shackle originality, nor was it incidental to the expression of their ideas . . . the humanist oration could be a stultifying and imitative stringing together of expected clichés, but it could also become an elegant, imaginative, and serious argument" (Gray

1967:511). The excellence of Malagasy men of words is judged by how well they carry out the *maqam* principle. They are expected to quote *ohabolana* and *hainteny*. Rasamuel marked many of the *ohabolana* with quotation marks.

The Apologies (Turn 1)

In Turn 1, Rasamuel directs his petitioner to avert *tsiny* by means of full and florid comparisons. I translate about half the section.

> Koa ny akoho raha hanatody miala faditr' ahitra; ny akoholahy raha haneno miala kopakopaka; ny ombalahy raha hitrena miala saron-tandroka: izaho kosa hiteny eto anatrehanareo ka miala tsiny sy miala saloy fito. Ialàko ny tsiny, fa ny tsiny tahaka ny hady lalina ka itataova-mahafanina, ianjera-mahafaty; tahaka ny afo, ka izay mambomba azy no may; lála-malama ka izay mandia azy no lavo; poizina ka izay mil-elaka azy no simba. . . .
>
> Ialàko ny tsiny, fa ny tsiny tsy mandrahona hivalozana, tsy mivongo-vongo tahaka ny rahona . . . fa tahaka ny rivotra an-kadilàlana: tsin-jovin-tsy hita ka mipoaka vao mahataitra, ary avy nisoko toa ranom-panala ka an-koditra vao mahangoly.
> (Rasamuel 1928:9–10, 1973:10)

As the chicken, before laying, throws away some of the grass,
as the cock, before crowing, flaps his wings,
as the bull, before bellowing, cleans the ends of his horns,
so I, before speaking here among you,
apologize seven times and salute seven times.

Next comes a sequence of quoted *ohabolana*.

I avoid reproaches,
for reproaches are like a deep trench,
he who comes too close and hangs over it falls to the bottom;
like fire, he who carries it under his shirt gets burned;
like a slippery road, he who walks on it falls;
they are poison, he who tastes it is injured.
I avoid reproaches,

because they don't threaten, so that one might ask for grace,
they do not fade away like the clouds . . .

They are like the wind in a narrow pass:
    one looks but doesn't see it,
    then it blows and surprises,
it arrives furtively, like white frost,
    and chills as soon as it touches.

The man of words must be able to summon up numerous traditional, reassuringly fixed comparisons like these.

The Debate as a Riddling Session

Like a riddling session, the Merina marriage debate tests the memory and skill of two men of words. Genealogical recitation is one test of memory. Early in the negotiations, the petitioner inquires about the ancestry of the young woman: "Allow me first to ask this question: who are Miss ——'s ancestors?" He keys performance when he disclaims responsibility for such a direct question, by citing two proverbs. "For as the proverbs say, 'Better ask foolishly and risk mockery than act [without being informed] and be reprimanded.' 'One may not apologize *after* passing in front of the person.' What then is the young lady's lineage?" Though this information is already known to the groom's family through informal consultation, it must now be publicly stated in formal dialogue. The correct answer requires the deliverer, representing the bride's family, to recite accurately the names of her paternal and maternal forebears. He thus assures both families that none of the groom's ancestors are among them, which would make the marriage incestuous, and that the marriage will unite groups of comparable rank.[3] Later, when he makes his formal request for the young woman, the petitioner will have to repeat all the names verbatim, thus giving another correct answer. To omit a name then would be to give the deliverer an opening. He can reproach the petitioner with the omission, proclaim the person omitted as the woman's most important ancestor, and reject the petition. The more skillful player will be declared the winner. Rasamuel's text thus provides for emergent performance.

    This emphasis on verbatim repetition of genealogy contrasts with the large number of *fitenenana*, sayings, associated with marriage, which deny the central fact that two unrelated parties are to be united. The families are "Still water with no high or low"; they are "dug with one root, gathered in one basket"; they are "living in the same house, dead in the same tomb" (Randriamandimby 1973, Domenichini-Ramiaramanana 1970:583, no. 3369, 85, no. 458).

Among other Merina in the past, the same riddlelike capacity for right answering has sometimes been expected of the young couple themselves. The groom would have to repeat the genealogy of his young lady exactly, being sure to give an exact account of social rank. Before the young woman accepted, she herself would have to reciprocate. Literacy makes its mark on genealogical recitation, too. "Nowadays," said an observer in 1977, "the two orators exchange lists containing the complete genealogy of the two families" (Aly 1977:118n).

As in riddling, then, the genealogy involves accurate recall, recitation, turn-taking, and right answers. The most important influence of riddling, however, is that both genres transpose marriage into the verbal realm. One folklorist points out that riddles are, on their small scale, "a miniature structural model for marriage in that marriage relates two unrelated principals" (Dundes 1980:24–26). The marriage *kabary*, pitting two representatives of unrelated principals against each other in a contest of wit and memory which one must win, and ending in a reconciliation, is a gigantic structural model of marriage. Both speakers throughout use language to overcome the social contradiction of marriage.

Despite this strong influence, the relation between debaters (in Rasamuel's text, and doubtless in the emergent performances of today) is more complex than the superior-inferior relation of riddle players. Their sequences of utterance and even their transitions are prescribed, and both are constantly maneuvering for advantage. Moreover, the debate is a more theatrical occasion than is a riddling session. After the genealogy, the petitioner makes his apologies, beginning with the denial that this stylized verbal duel is anything but ordinary talk. "Yes, ladies and gentlemen, this is not a public speech but a conversation, a chat under the same roof." The public, formal nature of the occasion emerges through the speaker's disclaimer of performance. After the apologies, he will acknowledge the presence of all the ranks of society in his audience.

Proverbial Comparisons in the Excuses

The apologies section which I quoted above recurs so often in Malagasy speechmaking that it has attracted much comment. Observers of Merina culture point to the threat of reproach that hangs over the marriage ceremony. The orator's attempt to avert reproach is a stylized deflecting of the anxiety of the occasion (Andriamanjato 1957:1–18, Rajaona 1963). The speaker is threatened with innumerable reproaches for taking a turn at speaking, speaking before the elders speak, making an error in recitation, or allowing the deliverer to take advantage of him in debate. Violating these *fady*, taboos, was believed in former times to have heavy consequences. One could die young (Callet 1974:1:543). To counteract it from the outset, the antagonists make extensive use of simile and metaphor. Recurrent similes assert connections among the assembled ranks of society, their visible world of winds, waters, and cattle, and the invisible world of spirits and the dead. These similes are quoted from, or are the origin of, proverbs and proverbial comparisons or *hainteny*.

The kind of excuse which a speaker could employ was recorded by Callet (1974:1:542–47):

> The spoon is an extension of the hand, and the hand stays near the mouth. That is how I shall speak. For I am like a spade worn out in its owner's hands: even if it strikes stones, it cannot refuse to serve him. . . . Since I speak before all these persons, I follow the footsteps of my predecessors, who began by averting the omens of *tsiny*. For *tsiny* are like a waterfall. (543)

Similar excuses, invariably stringing together proverbial comparisons, have been recorded from the Merina, the Betsileo, and the Tanala (Forest People) (Dahle 1877, Paulhan 1913:358–61, Rasamuel 1950, 1973). Among the Tanala, some two hundred kilometers south of the plateau, even the king himself, probably through a spokesman, had to apologize while reflecting the social hierarchy.

> Not because of status or rank do I arise;
>   I must speak a truth and proclaim justice.
> Words of weight are like stones that cannot be carried.
> Juniors are watched over by elders,
> elders by parents,
> parents by persons of rank,
> persons of rank by officers:
> that is why excuses must be made.
>   (Olsen 1929:39–40)

Traditional and reassuring though the excuses are, they create a disequilibrium. Like the precedent of a riddle, they call for balance to be restored. This is the role of the salutations. The excuses have addressed the audience indirectly by means of the authoritative speech of the ancestors; the salutations address them directly. The excuses have removed taint from the speaker; the salutations confer a positive blessing upon the assembly. The same succession of disequilibrium/equilibrium, familiar from riddles and folktales, will occur again in the *kabary* on a larger scale. Turn 1, comprising the excuses and salutations, functions as the precedent for Turn 2, the proposal and consent.

The Salutations (Turn 2)

Turn 2 verbalizes the social order. The petitioner salutes all the living members of the audience, putting into formal words the hierarchy of Merina authority. Under the nineteenth-century monarchy, as the *Tantara* show, he began with the queen. Under the colony, he began with the Governor-General. Since independence, he addresses the President of the Republic (Rasamuel 1973:10–11). But the traditional formulas remain much the same: he compares the President to a mountain, a hill, a promontory, a ridgepole, a waterlily, a fig-tree, a man of silver. He will not neglect the officers and civil servants, addressing them as "morning stars, wives of the sun, husbands of the moon." The army he salutes in panegyric:

> fa ireny no lehilahy voafidy sy noranitana ho tandroky ny Fanjakana: ireny no tandroka aron' ny vozona, lefona maranitra sy ampinga matevina aron' ny vady aman-janaka. . . .
> (Rasamuel 1928:11, 1973:11–12)

> sharpened to be the nation's horns,
> the protective horns of the neck,
> the pointed spears and thick shields
> protecting women and children.

He salutes the people:

> Isika vahoaka rehetra kosa, izay vodi-ahitra arivo; angady lava lela hahamainty molaly ny tany; valala tsy mandady harona, kofehy manara-panjaitra; amboara ifatorana, ala ikirizana, vato fandiavana, kitro ifaharana, manda itokiana, lamba itafiana.
> (Rasamuel 1928:12, 1973:12)

ourselves, like thousands of grass blades,
long iron spades, who make the soil produce,
grasshoppers who cannot get out of the basket,
thread following the needle,
amboara [tree] to cling to,
forest to be resisted,
rock to tread on,
hoofs to last,
walls to trust,
clothes to wear.

He ends his salutations with a prayer for peace, numerous offspring,
long life, and prosperity: "May we see the year return a thousand times."
By emphasizing the stability of this hierarchical order of society, the
speaker reminds his audience that the imminent change from this marriage
will not threaten the status quo. He also reassures them that these two
families are adhering to custom, to offset whatever movement they are
making toward social advantage or economic gain.

The Proposal, a Riddle Precedent

After these reassurances, which help to cushion the impending alterations
of relation and role, the petitioner has arrived at the moment of greatest
risk. Now panegyric must be most potent. First he names the hierarchy of
the groom's ancestors—another reassurance from tradition—and connects
them to the natural environment.

> Izany no tendrombohitra niteraka ny vodivona, vodivona niteraka ny
> lohasaha, lohasaha niteraka ny loharano, loharano niteraka ny ony, ka
> nitranganay mianakavy.
> (Rasamuel 1928 : 12, 1973 : 12)

> They are the mountains that gave birth to the hills,
> the hills that gave birth to the valleys,
> the valleys that gave birth to the springs,
> the springs that made the stream
> our family came from.

Metaphors from plant, animal, and social worlds assert the unity of
the families.

Tsy mba vahy mandady amin' ny hazo tsy fantatra, na hena tsy fan-tatra anarana hampieritreritra, fa ny vorona mpiara-manidina, ny akanga mpiaramanjohy, ny fody mpiara-mitsindroka, ny toho iray rano, ny omby iray kijana, ny saonjo iray fototra, ka hadina iray fo-totra, raofina iray harona, velona iray trano, maty iray fasana, hazo iray no vaky, tondro iray no nisimaka, olona nifanongoa loha sy nifan-apa-tsinay, niombon-dray niombon-dreny. Koa tahaka ny molo-bi-lany izao isika izao, ka tsy hafa fa iray manodidina, fandrin-drano ka tsy misy avo sy iva, any tahaka an' Ilailava mandry amorom-patana izahay, koa zovy fa tsy Izoky ihany, ary zovy fa tsy Izandry ihany.
(Rasamuel 1928: 12–13, 1973: 12–13)

We are no creeper grasping an unknown tree,
no meat of unknown origin, eaten fearfully,
but birds flying together,
guineafowl nursing together,
fody-birds pecking together,
fish swimming in the same water,
cattle grazing together,
Herbs of a single root,
 and dug from a single root,
 gathered in a single basket,
living in a single house,
 dead in a single tomb,
a single trunk that is split,
 a single finger that is divided.
Persons who heaped one head on another,
 sprung from the same father and the same mother.
We are like the rim of a single pot
 not different, but one piece all the way round.
We are still water with no high nor low,
 as in the tall pot by the hearth,
no different from the firstborn,
 no different from the lastborn.

At this point of greatest risk, the speaker has employed the largest possible number of proverbial comparisons to deny the separation of the two families. He depersonalizes them and denies any innovation, to intro-duce the bride's genealogy: *saingy efa fomba àry ny mifampitonona amin' ny raharaha toy izao, ka dia mitonona izahay,* Only to speak according to custom do we carry this out and name over our origins. Modern European poets like W. H. Auden and William Butler Yeats have often felt the need of a system whereby to objectivize and depersonalize their metaphors. The Malagasy man of words has the advantage of being able not only to refer to such a system but to submerge his entire performance in it. The "rim of a single pot" and "dead in a single tomb" are extremely familiar sayings, as are others in this sequence (Houlder 1960:1, nos. 9, 10, Domenichini-Ramiaramanana 1970:566, no. 3258). Accurate quotation of the bride's genealogy comes next. Then comes the actual proposal.

Tonga nandondona izahay, ka efa novohanareo varavarana: tonga nitsidika ka efa nampandrosoinareo, noraisinareo amim-panajana. Ary izao dia miloa-bava indray hangataka ka mba omao. Avy miantsakana, avy miandavana, mangataka ny ho fara, mangataka ny ho dimby, mangataka ny ho vohitra, ny ho tokan-trano, mangataka ny ho zazavavy hotezaina, hitsongo volo fotsy, hipetrahana amorompatana, hamelona raha reraka, hanavotra raha very, hanafy raha rovi-damba, hanome hanina raha noana; hitsabo raha marary, handevina raha maty. Ka mangataka an-dRamatoa Ra . . . , tompoko, ho vadin' Andriamatoa Ra . . . é.

(Rasamuel 1928:13–14, 1973:13–14)

We came to knock at your door;
    please open to us.
We arrived for a chat;
    bid us come in.
We open our mouths to ask;
    please give to us.
We come wide open, we come fully extended.
We ask for children to come,
we ask for offspring to come,
we ask for the village to come,
    for the household to come,
We ask for a girl to stand upright,
            to braid white hair,
            to shelter at her hearth,
            to nourish in weakness,
            to redeem in loss,
            to dress when clothes are ragged,
            to fill when there is hunger;

> to care in sickness,
> to enshroud in death.
> So we ask for Miss ——, gentlemen, to be the wife of Mr. ——.

As in riddling or a *hainteny* contest, the effort to submerge one's discourse in the inherited wisdom of the ancestors exerts the maximum of control over the most delicate and dangerous message. To reduce the multiplicity of human voices to two and to mold all messages into balance and antithesis creates monologism out of dialogue.

At this most vulnerable moment, the performance might vary from one occasion to another. Three pitfalls await the petitioner. One is an inexact quotation. To avoid heckling or, what would be far graver, a refusal of his demand, he must repeat the woman's genealogy without a flaw; if he is caught omitting even one name, he will lose a point and have to effect re-entry into the debate with an apology. Second, he must give the bride's and groom's names correctly or risk hearing, "We have several daughters here" or "You have several boys in your family, and we do not know which is the one." The third pitfall is an incorrect addressee. The kinsmen, who are the guardians and honor of the family, must receive the proposal, not the absent bride.

The Consent, Sequent of the Riddle (Turns 2–3)

As in the other contests, again the spotlight oscillates. In all published *kabary*, the use of parallelism within and between speeches asserts the contractual nature of the debate. Parallelism links the delivery to the proposal that elicited it. Now the deliverer, star of the drama, the man of words who represents the bride's family, takes the stage. Following the prescribed order, the deliverer must make his apologies for speaking before his elders by embroidering on an *ohabolana*. He quotes it:

> Ny hitsikitsika no tompon' ny dihy
> ny vivy no tompon' ny rano
>
> (Domenichini-Ramiaramanana 1970:191,
> no. 1074)

> The kestrel-hawk is lord of the dance,
> the grebe is lord of the water.

Then he sets human beings over bird species: *ary ny ray aman-dreny no tompon' ny teny*, But it is parents who are lords of the word.

The deliverer's reply almost perfectly balances the proposal. Summarizing: he averts *tsiny*, the reproaches which "have been thrown into the water and carried off by the river" by the petitioner. He omits repeating the salutations, "for I follow what the cattle trod and what the spade readied. I shall not glaze what is already polished, I shall not sift what is already clean." He parallels what the petitioner has said, demonstrating his capacity for recall, repeating his words without irony, and acknowledging the request. He makes the delivery: *Omenay malalaka, menay madiodio, omenay mangarangarana*, We give her freely, we give her cleanly, we give her clearly.

If the speakers are well matched, the consent just spoken as a reply will elicit another reply. The parallels make a background for a new assertion the deliverer will soon make, that the woman's family, by losing a daughter, is being impoverished. But the petitioner must thank the deliverer in *hainteny* style.

Eny, tsy dia rano isika ka hiady fidinana; tsy rivotra ka hiady fiakarana, tsy toho ka hiady rano, ary tsy valala ka hiady fandriana.

We are not like water that quarrels as it descends,
not wind that quarrels with the mountain,
not fish that quarrel over water,
not locusts that quarrel over a resting-place.

Entering silently, the bride symbolizes her delivery by taking a place next to the groom at the north of the hearth. The two sides have reached a temporary equilibrium.

Key Change (Turns 4–10)

With Turn 4, the tone of the marriage debate becomes more authoritative and monologic. Once the woman is present, less space is left for ambiguous language and plural meaning. On the continuum between *resaka*, the ordinary talk of women, and *kabary*, formal speaking by men, the language moves toward the explicitness of *resaka* (Keenan 1974). This explicitness in Turns 4–10 "is experienced as authoritarian, whereas implicitness, allusion, and indirectness [were] essential to traditional, reciprocal, consensual modes of resolving issues" such as the more egalitarian *hainteny* contest (Hymes 1980:42). Yet the debate continues to be a performance, keyed (Bauman 1977) by extensive quotation, special formulas, and repeated appeals to tradition. In an atmosphere of diminished risk, the *kabary* will attempt, ever more explicitly, to create in words a reconciliation between these opposed parties. The dialectic between informal and formal speaking and between figurative and literal language continues as the two opponents constantly quote allusive, obscure *hainteny* at each other.

Lengthy as this debate is, with its details of obligation and property, no one in Madagascar finds long-windedness a fault. Malagasy orators are highly valued for their eloquence. For similar reasons, "no contemporary member of the culture criticized an Indian temple, a Moorish Palace, a Gothic Cathedral, or a Spanish Baroque Church as 'over-ornate.' The concept did not exist" (Gombrich 1979:17). The dialogue of genres is itself persuasive. Both speakers attempt, almost symmetrically, to convey their injunctions with such a profusion of simile, metaphor, and *ohabolana* that they sweep aside all possible objections and reservations. If the petitioner could speak authoritatively enough, he would forestall dialogue, blocking his opponent like a *fanorona* player. In actuality, dialogue always continues. Thus the question and answer pattern, which in riddles, *safidy*, *ohabolana*, and *hainteny* gives ever-increasing amounts of power to a single speaker, finds in the marriage debate its fullest, most authoritative assertion by including all the other genres.

The continuing dialogue of genres shifts the power relations of the adversaries in Turns 4–10. According to Rasamuel's text, the debate contrasts with riddling or a *hainteny* contest in awarding greater power to one contestant from the outset. Though the petitioner was the first to speak, the deliverer has power to decide how many details will be discussed and to direct the whole debate. Indeed, he can refuse to yield up the young woman. Like a good *fanorona* player, he prepares his position, launches offensives, and sets traps for his adversary (Chauvicourt and Chauvicourt 1972:8). The prescriptive Rasamuel takes the side of dialogism against excessive monologism. If the petitioner fails to adhere to traditional fixed phrases, adopts an arrogant, pretentious manner, or threatens violently, the deliverer can easily riposte by interpreting one of his metaphors literally. As he limits the range of debating possibilities in his printed text, Rasamuel reaffirms the traditional view of retribution against such an offender: the petitioner's attempt to sweep all before him will only fall back on himself. Of course, if the petitioner is caught out, he can release himself with a fixed-phrase apology: "Even when eating rice, a certain amount always falls. You are our father, you are our mother; don't notice the mistaken words, don't hold the words that escaped me."

The deliverer begins to take control by means of a classic *ohabolana* as he addresses the groom's family. *Eny, tompoko, omenay anareo Ramatoa Ranona, kanefa na dia omena aza: "foza vavy natakalo foza lahy." ka izy ho anareo, fa Andriamatoa Ranona kosa ho anay* (Rasamuel 1928:16, 1973:19), Yes, gentlemen, we are giving you Miss So-and-so, yet as it is said, "A female crab is exchanged for a male crab." She will be yours, but Mr. So-and-so will be ours. His list of the obligations of the son-in-law creates a new disequilibrium (Turn 4). The young man will have to take care of the aged, children, and women; he will work in house and field; he will put forth all his efforts, providing clothes and help, lending money, conforming to another proverb. *Hianao no ho andrinay sy tanjakay, amin' ny zavatra rehetra,* You will be our pillar and our strength on all occasions, *fa "ny iterahan-ko dimby, ary ny anambadian-ko namana"* for "childbearing is having descendants, and marrying is having a companion" (Rasamuel 1928:17, 1973:19, see Domenichini-Ramiaramanana 1970:85, no. 451).

Again by means of proverbial comparisons, he warns the new son-in-law against violating these obligations.

Raha tsy hanefa loloha, fa hanao voromahery mipaoka ka mahazo dia tsy hitodika, hanao toy ny tsiriry vorona ka hanifi-drano dia lasa, indrindra ka hanao fitondran-tsy mitovy amin' ny havam-bady: tsy azonay omena ny zanakay mihitsy ny toy izany.

(Rasamuel 1928:17, 1973:20)

If he does not act as we have said,
but plays the sparrowhawk,
    swooping down on its prey and not turning back,
or plays the teal,
    flapping its wings in the water and then taking flight,
especially if he holds himself above his wife's family,
    we could not give our daughter in marriage.

Explicitness is insisted on in a series of six further similes about the son-in-law's future behavior. These create disequilibrium. The authoritarian, monologic context situation leads, in the immediate interaction situation (the debate itself), to dialogue. As the proposal demanded a consent, so the similes demand an answer. To restore equilibrium and finish the turn, the petitioner must answer point by point, denying that burdens fall only on the son-in-law. He introduces his rebuttal with *ohabolana*.

> Raha ho any an' ala manantena hahita hazo. Raha ho any Namehana manantena hahita voasary. Ary raha hanambady dia manantena hahita loloha.
>
> (Rasamuel 1928:18, 1973:22)

> When in the forest, one expects to find trees,
> >when at Namehana, one expects to find lemon-trees,
> >>and when one marries, one expects to find burdens.

Part of the rebuttal confers the power of the word on the son-in-law, in an imaginary reported exchange of *ohabolana*.

> Ary efa nidinika tamin' Andriamatoa araka ireo efa voalazanareo ireo izahay, ka nampiseho azy fa tsy raikitra raha "Ny tanin' Andrian-tian-konenana, nefa ny hetran' Andrian-tsy haloa," ny zanak'olona tian-kovadina, kanefa ny loloha tsy ho entina. Nanome toky anefa izy, fa tsy "raha malaza ho lahy tsy handry an' efitra; raha saro-tahotry ny masony, tsy ho tia vidy ny lohany" ary tsy hanambady raha tsy vonona ny hitondra loloha."
>
> (Rasamuel 1928:18–19, 1973:22)

> We have conversed with the future husband and have pointed out:
> "To live on the sovereign's land,
> >it's bad not to pay the sovereign's tax,"
> to marry someone's daughter,
> >it's bad not to carry the burdens.
> He has told us to count on him:
> "One doesn't lie down in the desert
> >unless one is known as a man,
> >one doesn't buy an ox head
> >if one is afraid of its eyes,
> >and one does not marry
> >if one is not ready to bear the burdens."

The command of traditional speech that the spokesman attributes to the bridegroom by pseudo-quotation asserts his manly status and responsibility. More persuasive similes, which I omit, again assert the unification of the two families. Quotation, balance, antithesis, and parallelism all enact interdependence. The petitioner's reply about the son-in-law's duties also includes twenty lines of injunctions to the bride's family, two similes, and several more *ohabolana*, as well as an allusion to the most popular of all *hainteny*, "Rain falls on Ankaratra" (see chapter 4).

Details About the Wife (Turn 5)

By answering the deliverer so fulsomely, the petitioner hopes to have restored the equilibrium and regained the winner's position. He must first obey the rule in Malagasy formal speaking to introduce disagreement by agreement. In his response, concluding Turn 5, the deliverer seems to give ground, acknowledging his opponent's words and pleading the woman's youth and inexperience by metaphor: "She has not yet kept house. Up to now she has been a finger raised toward her mother, a spade handle leaning against a pillar, something small resting against something big." Then he puts upon the groom's family the responsibility for teaching their new daughter a lesson, if need be, or informing or scolding her if necessary. In his superauthoritative statement, the appropriate rhetoric is the topic-comment form used for many *ohabolana*.

> Koa ataovy "androngo miditr' ala," ka hianareo efa mahita ny làlana no aoka hitarika; hianareo mahalala no aoka hanoro.
> (Rasamuel 1928 : 22, 1973 : 27)

> Then act like "the lizard entering the forest."
> You who know the way shall guide her;
> You who have experience shall instruct her.

Turning to the classic *hainteny* form of priamel, he arranges his metaphors in climactic order.

> Fa izay monina am-bava ala mahita ny hazo mahitsy ho kapaina; izay monina amoron-drano mahita ny marivo hirobohana; izay monina amoron-kady mahita ny tevana hiviliana; ary izay efa nitondra tokan-trano mahalala ny mety hatao.
> (Rasamuel 1928 : 22, 1973 : 27)

For "he who lives at the forest's edge
knows which straight trees to cut;
he who lives on the riverbank
knows which ford to cross;
he who lives near the ditch
knows which holes to avoid."
And he who has carried household goods
recognizes what should be done.

To regain superior power, the petitioner will assert complete agreement and equality between the parties. *Tsy misy tapaka hotohizana izany voalazanareo izany, tompoko, na lesoka hotovonana,* Nothing in what you have said is broken that must be repaired, gentlemen, nothing flattened that must be raised. He acknowledges the interdependence of the families. *Fa hifampitazana tahaka ny vorona mitaingina an-kazo vokoka izahay sy hianareo, ka hianareo hijery ny ataonay, izahay kosa hitazana ny ataonareo, ka sady no adidinay no ho adidinareo ny fanoroana azy,* You and we shall act like birds on a bent branch: you will watch over our acts, we shall watch over yours, and both our parties shall be responsible for the girl's education. He quotes more imaginary speech when he points to the bad reputation that would result from her misbehaving.

> Ho avy ny ataona' ny olona hoe: "Eisy! nitera-poana izay ray aman-dreniny: Biby fa tsy olona! Koa tolo-kanin-dry Ranona moa, ka aiza no tsy hanahaka azy! Mitoetra amin' olona adala, ka adala mianakavy! Ny omby jamba, ny tevan-dalina, ny mpandroaka adala, ka any an-kady avokoa iza mianakavy!"
> (Rasamuel 1928:23, 1973:28)

> People will say, "Oh, her parents begot her in vain. She is an animal, not a human being. She was raised by Soandso, why doesn't she take after him? She lives with fools and acts like a fool. The ox is blind, the ditch is deep, the oxherd is a fool, let 'em all fall into the ditch!"

With the end of Turn 5, the marriage debate reaches a pause. In his transition, the deliverer uses the topic-comment form of a proverb and labels this stylized performance as casual talk. *"Ny resaka moa tahaka ny oram-pahavaratra, ka 'indraindray' andrasan-ko ritra vao manondra-drano,"* Conversation is like summer rain: one says "it's over," then the streams rise (Rasamuel 1928:24, 1973:29).

In each of the fourteen turns of the contest, some temporary balance is achieved, risk is diminished, and closure is attempted, against the recurrent tendency to fragmentation and failure. The movement of the whole day toward balance and closure appears with deceptive clarity in Rasamuel's orderly, controlled scenario. Even he admitted that in performance, disagreement can endanger the outcome. If both families, however, are determined to effect a marriage that must produce descendants for them, the tone changes, the *kabary* begins to be trivialized, and the seriousness of debate turns into a game (Keenan 1975, Bauman 1977:40–42). Thus a variability between order and disorder affects the tone of the event. A similar variability, says Jacques Faublée, characterizes narrative performances among the Bara (1947:14).

In what remains to be said—recommendations about affection due to the wife, remarks about battering, agreements about property and debts, and other reciprocal exchanges—the same dialectic between dialogism-equality and monologism-dominance will govern the debate. Both speakers will assert the interdependence of the parties; at the same time, each will separate himself from the other, claim greater authority, and try to have the last word. To seize the advantage now, the deliverer expounds a new opposition. At the moment the daughter is leaving, "we feel how extremely dear she is to us." To deny the breach, he enjoins the groom's family, "Do not change any of the customs according to which we brought her up." The innuendo that the other family may be of lower rank will not have been lost on a skillful petitioner.

The Technique of the Orator

The official, monologic task of the two debaters is the same task that Samuel Taylor Coleridge assigned to the poetic imagination. The artist's faculty brings about "the balance or reconciliation of opposite or discordant qualities: of sameness, with difference; of the general [community property], with the concrete [the performer's goals and preferences]; . . . the sense of novelty and freshness, with old and familiar objects" (Coleridge 1951:269). Their unofficial, dialogic effort, of course, is to win the contest. Marriage among the Merina is conflictful and reconciling at the same time. The *kabary*, like holiday celebrations elsewhere, is "a stylized rendering of some of the central expressive practices and moral concerns of the group" (Abrahams 1983:98), notably the dialogue of genres. The principal technique available to the *mpikabary*, to manage these two tasks and overcome the contradictions of the situation, is the selection and arrangement of fixed phrases. The other tool, especially in the later, more explicit turns, is literal injunction. Lengthy instructions to the couple, mostly negative, follow and oppose the figurative language of metaphor in these turns, just as literal and figurative language oppose each other in riddling and *ohabolana*.

The orators quote proverbial comparisons, *ohabolana*, and *hainteny*. They may also create or insert new sentences modeled on the familiar patterns. Thus Rasamuel's *kabary* text, like the many variants and excerpts published by others, confirms and enlarges Paulhan's hypothesis. Equipped with two or three hundred metrical phrases and four or five hundred poems, Merina men of words compose-and-perform their debate as if it were a huge contest in *hainteny*. They use existing verses as models for the creation of new ones, in the familiar tetrameter pattern. They cast their new verses into the patterns of the proverb—symmetrical, doubled-symmetrical, order-of-climax, or topic-comment. In addition to quoting, they imitate proverbs and poems, half-quoting them allusively, developing or shortening them, surrounding them with differently metered phrases so that their parallelisms will stand out. Thus the performers create, in each performance, a new text that sounds old. Though their tireless quoting of fixed phrases can be seen as a form of rhetorical misdirection to take advantage of one's opponent (Bloch 1971), the quotations reassure the audience that "we have changed nothing in the customs of the ancestors." Rasamuel, one such man of words, recorded but one full version; many more have been composed and performed.

This kind of composition is not confined to Madagascar. Composition of an individual poetic or musical performance by assembling or varying smaller fixed units is a method that many peoples have invented independently. Homeric and medieval studies have been revolutionized by the theory that the texts we read today were composed and performed orally by men of words relying on fixed phrases that they disposed in traditional meters (Lord 1960, Foley 1980, 1988). Greek, Serbian, African American, and other poetic traditions award varying freedoms to the performer to depart from old material or keep to what is prescribed. The issue is central to an understanding of artistic creativity. The folklorist in Madagascar knows, however, what the classicist must seek to prove, that performance events are the context for this kind of composition-and-performance. In Madagascar, oratorical creativity takes place in a setting of contestation and a spirit of conflict.

Legal Details (Turns 6–10)

However polite or amusing, a proposal of marriage in the highlands of the Merina is a call to battle. Debating contest, poetic duel, and law case, the marriage debate, for all its theatricality, is also an *agon*. In Turn 6, the deliverer applies pressure to the groom: "Love her, do not mistreat her." If the two fail to get along, battering is ruled out, in a powerful string of balanced phrases:

> Fa lehilahy sy vehivavy. Sao manongo-bolo, sao mandringi-tsofina, sao mahapotsi-maso, sao mahafa-nify, sao maharava tarehy, sao manakendakenda, sao maha tapa-pe sy maha tapa-tsandry, sao mahafoladamosina sy maharava taolam-balo, sao mahavaky hoditra sy mahavaky rà, sao mahalatsa-boa, sao mitaritarika mamely diamanga sy mandabodaboka totohondry, ary mandangilangy hazo . . . tsy mba ataonay vitavita foana.
> (Rasamuel 1928:25, 1973:30)

> For one is a man, the other a woman.
> If you pull her hair, pull her ears, whiten her eyes,
> if you break her teeth, disfigure her, choke her,
> if you break her arms or break her legs,
> if you break her back or dislocate her eight bones,
> if you tear her skin or make her blood flow,
> if you strike her kidneys,
> if you drag her to the ground,
> or strike her with your fist,
> or hit her with a wooden stick . . .
> all these we would not accept.

Such behavior creates disequilibrium. The petitioner supports his monologic listing of symmetrical phrases, familiar to the *hainteny* audience, by summoning up the authority of the two families. If conflict, symbolized by dialogue, arises between the couple, the families who have witnessed this contract will intervene to have a monologic last word. *Fa "ny akoho no maty, eran' ny mpivady," ary ny "fanambadiana no raikitra eran' ny vaventy,"* For if the chicken is dead, the couple agreed on it, and if the marriage took place, the elders agreed on it. So close are the two families, says the deliverer, that they must remain impartial, forswearing the behavior of the proverbial *tsingala*, a water insect who can kill one ox by piercing its bowels from within or show partiality to another by avoiding being swallowed. *Tsy hanao tsingala mahalala ombin' ny tena*, No one of us will act like the *tsingala*, who knows his own ox.

In his response, the petitioner again tries to regain the advantage by acidly denying that the groom's family needs lessons in correct behavior.

> "Zanak' omby tsy ampianarin-domano" izahay, "sotrobe tsy ampi-anari-mitantana," ary ray aman-dreny tsy ampianari-mitondra.
>
> (Rasamuel 1928:27, 1973:31)

> We are "no calf needing to be taught to swim,
> no big spoon needing to be taught how to serve,"
> no father and mother needing to be taught how to manage.

As to the deliverer's innuendo about rank, "it is not to make Miss So-and-so a servant or a worker or to make her miserable that we come to take her. It is to make her mistress of village and house, honor of the name and family, child and descendant." Now, as a new genre enters the *kabary*, the petitioner shows his talent as a storyteller. With no transition, the petitioner introduces two satirical parables. In the first, he depicts an unfed, hardworking husband whose wife refuses to feed him, saying, "'If you're hungry, make your own meal.' . . . The man could not hold back. His heart overfull of with anger, he struck her." In the second story, a forbearing husband returns from work to find his wife absent, the kittens starving, the chicks drowned, the ox bellowing, the pigs ravaging the neighbors' houses, and the neighbors claiming damages. When the wife returns and contemptuously answers him, "May I not go where everyone goes?," he strikes her. Both these forbearing husbands raise a hand only when the wife talks back. As the silent bride listens, the spokesman for her new husband's family generalizes. Unruly women "jump up and down, pull their husband's hair, and scratch them like cats. . . . After all, no husband strikes his wife without reason, or merely out of malice." The petitioner climaxes his rebuttal with a *hainteny* that devalues the bride and her family:

> Mihantsy amboa hanaikitra azy izy; setroky ny kitay alainy; main' ny afo natsangany; ary akohovavy maneno ka lozain' ny ataony.
>
> (Rasamuel 1928:30, 1973:34)

She incites the dog so that he bites,
she is smoked by the grass she has gathered
or burnt by the fire she has lit;
and like a crowing hen, she receives the evil of her actions.

Some hearers might remember the popular tale of the animal languages. A man threatened by his wife with desertion is shown by a cock
how to discipline her (tale 4.670 in *Malagasy Tale Index*). The petitioner
ends Turn 6 conceding, "It is very bad to beat one's wife. . . . If it is a
question of curing a cold and an infusion is enough, no chicken is needed.
If the matter can be resolved by a few, many should not intervene. This is
a word to the wise; those who understand must receive it. Like an ox's
hump given to a strong man: the mouth chews and the heart reflects."

To the extent that the petitioner (or his opponent) seeks victory, he
pushes the *kabary* toward the monologism of the *ohabolana*. The need for
control explains the sudden appearance of two satirical parables, the elas-
ticity of *kabary*, and its stylistic elaboration. As in *hainteny*, the more delicate the topic, the more elaborate the style.

The deliverer's next challenge raises the delicate and dangerous theme
of the conditions regulating joint property if the marriage should be dis-
solved. The division of property, the debts each partner incurs, and the
reversion of children to the bride's family will probably provoke no controversy, but they must be stated. Equally uncontroversial are the *tao-
zavatra*, the "made things" each brings into the marriage, which will be
divided as originally held. To introduce these agreements, the deliverer
quotes twelve old-fashioned clichés about marriage: "Marriage is not a
knot but a slip knot. Separation by death is painful, but in life it means
little. If destiny wills, one remains a husband; if not, he will leave. Marriage is a market open for sale to all comers; when something is not pleas-
ing, one exchanges it, for Madagascar has no lack of beauties and beautiful
things; even an old basket finds a suitable buyer." Here for the first time
quotation is used ironically. "Marriage today," he replies to himself, "is
quite different. It is a final, unconditional sale." *Mpikabary* acquire their
reputation for piling on similes from monologic strings like the deliverer's
diatribe against divorce by a bad husband.

Tsy mba azo atao "robodranon-dRamiangaly ka raha marivo irobo-
hana, fa raha lalina ihemorana." Tsy mba azo atao "andram-boankazo
an' ala: ka raha mamy atelina, fa raha mangidy aloa." Tsy mba azo

atao tahaka ny varavarana ka azo idirana sy azo ivoahana. Tsy mba azo atao tahaka ny entana ka raha zakazaka dia lolohavina, fa raha tsy zakazaka dia apetraka. Ary tsy mba azo atao tahaka ny lamba, ka itafiana raha vao, fa soloana raha tonta. Tsy mba azo atao toy izany ny fanambadiana ankehitriny, enti-maty toy ny tarehy: lamban' akoho ka faty no isarahana: ary tahon-katsaka ladinim-boavahy ka aina no fetra.

(Rasamuel 1928:32, 1973:35).

One cannot act "like Ramiangaly crossing the river:
  if it is high, he crosses,
  and if it is low, he turns back."
One cannot act "like someone tasting the fruits of the forest:
  if they are sweet, he swallows,
    if they are bitter, he throws them away."
One cannot act like a door,
  which can go in or can go out.
One cannot act like a parcel,
  to carry on the head if you like,
    or put down if you don't like.
Nor act like a garment,
  to wear when it is new
    but replace when it is threadbare.

He answers his own negatives in more similes.

One cannot treat marriage today in that manner.
Like the face, one carries it until death:
  like the chicken's feathers,
    left behind only when she dies:
for the limit of life is what binds the marriage.

For all that, the possibility of divorce, with its consequent division of property, is conceded. In that case, "following the custom of the ancestors, two parts will be taken by the husband, one by the wife." This proportion, prescribed in myths (tale 1.2.81 in *Malagasy Tale Index*), is voiced by the deliverer to forestall a demand by his opponent. That concession should win Turn 7 for him. The petitioner agrees that divorce is unthinkable because the couple are uniting freely. Full disclosure of the joint estate is necessary. "Nothing will be hidden, from the good needle down to the one with a broken eye, in country or town."

Who Wins?

As the debaters urge each other toward that climactic moment in Turn 11 when the petitioner will offer and the deliverer will accept the *vodiondry*, the "sheep's rump," the pace of their exchange quickens. The bouts of quoting come more rapidly as the deliverer calls for brevity in a metafolkloric comparison, "We shall act like Ikirijavola pulling up yams: he digs in his spade only where the yams are." To explain why debts contracted by the husband will not fall on the wife, and vice versa, he puts forth a series of symmetrical *ohabolana*.

> Vahavahaina eto aminareo izany dieny ankehitriny, sao "ny kary no mihinana akoho, ka ny saka no voatapa-drambo"; sao "Ifaravavy Ramainty no mitetika anana, ka Raivo Rangita no ho tapatànana"; sao "ny Tanindrana no mamono mamba, ka ny Betsileo no miravaka ny nifiny"; ary sao ny ratsy no mampidi-trosa, ka ny tsara no mandimby ananana.
>
> (Rasamuel 1928 : 33–34, 1973 : 37).

This we declare to you now and henceforward,
  for fear that "the wildcat devour the chicken,
    and the domestic cat have its tail cut off";
  for fear that "the black girl cut the vegetables,
    and Raivo have her hand cut";
  for fear that "coastal people kill the crocodile,
    and the Betsileo adorn themselves with the teeth";
  and for fear that the bad partner contract debts
    and the good one sacrifice property to pay them.

To respond and conclude Turn 8, the petitioner agrees that husband and wife are individually responsible for their own debts, and then tries to outdo his opponent in quoting *ohabolana*. "If the unhoped-for happens and minds change, what [the deliverer] has said must be followed. *Androngo an' asa ka samy miaro ny rambony tsy ho tapaka*, Lizards under the spade: each one keeps his tail from being cut off."

In the interaction situation of marriage negotiations, who seems to be winning at this point? The groom's family has been promised the young woman; "the gain by the wife-takers implies their superiority over the wife-givers" (Bloch 1978:24). Rasamuel's libretto for the day prescribes several symbolic compensations, however. Chief among these is the reversion of the children to the bride's parents, to compensate their loss of a woman and her children. As the deliverer puts it, "A girl given in marriage no longer belongs to her parents. Living, she will no longer remain in their house; dead, she will not be buried in their tomb." By custom, the children *ampy mihira*—those big enough to "perform the various parts in singing" (Richardson 1885:35), since all life requires the integrated performance of parts—will revert to the bride's parents, replacing her in the family (Bloch 1978:24). To conclude Turn 9, the petitioner agrees, but citing a riddle: "They will inherit in both lines, like a goat with a big beard bearing traits of both his parents." This reference to the riddle "What looks like a man, an ox, and a dog at the same time? — A goat" (tale 1.4.70 in *Malagasy Tale Index*) again shows the petitioner's skill at citation.

Other symbolic compensations to the bride's family must also be detailed in literal language (Turn 10). In former times, clothes for the bride and parents, money to reimburse the cost of toys bought when the bride was a child, gifts to those who carried her on their backs, and sweets all came along with the "sheep's rump" as recompense for the care of raising the bride. In today's cash economy, the *vodiondry* is usually a small sum of money. Another symbolic compensation is the ritual submission that must be displayed by the groom: being inferior in status, he is not allowed to buy a wife but only to ask for one. The discourse, however, does not acknowledge differential status. Only indirectly does the deliverer ask for compensation for the expenses of her upbringing. "Her mother drank cold water unwillingly," he says.

> At the delivery, she leaned alone against the wall. . . . She bent her back carrying this child; her knees wearied of holding her, her arms wearied of carrying her, her eyes wearied of watching over her. . . . When she was sick, there is no telling how much was spent to take care of her. . . . Everywhere anyone went, they brought her dainties in their hands, pockets, or corners of their *lamba*. . . . You, on the other hand, are receiving her all readied.

Maintaining symmetry against the inequality of the outcome, the petitioner acknowledges yet reduces the claim: "Whoever has raised children has these same troubles; we too had similar worries in bringing up this young man." Then he offers "clothes for the girl, an ordinary *lamba*, an ordinary dress, simple shoes. . . . We deliver these to you to even our account."

Ideally, therefore, both sides should win. Actually, from all accounts, symmetry and inequality continue to conflict. How much, for instance, is the bridewealth really worth, and in what languages of exchange is it understandable? When the "sheep's rump" is handed over, the language of gesture supplements the figurative and literal languages heard up till then. The amount of the *vodiondry* would preserve symmetry if it corresponded to the price of the banquet to be held at the bride's family's house. Bargaining over it, however, is bad form. To those under European influence, like Rasamuel, the whole presentation began long ago to seem outlandish, and only justifiable in the archaic language he directs the petitioner to use.

> Ny ondrilahy be hofaka, ny omby matavy rangaranga tandroka, izany no tokony ho entina ho anareo. Kanefa tsy ananana izany sady tsy azo: ka ny rano fotsy tsy azo ho vary; ny tanimena tsy mba mirehitra; ny valala tsy an-tànana tsy atolo-jaza; ny tanimena tsy azo omena fa izay kely azo novimbinina kosa dia nentina.
> (Rasamuel 1928:38, 1973:41)

> A ram with large tail,
>   or a fat ox with long horns,
> that is what we should have brought you.
> But we do not have that and could not get it.
> For clear water cannot turn into rice,
>   red earth cannot burn,
>   a locust not in the hand cannot be given to a child,
>   red earth cannot be given,
> so we have brought the little we do have.

The deliverer accepts the "sheep's rump," a symbolic food, in few words. Once it is handed over, all the "takers" from the groom's family are given other symbolic food, *tolotra*, small pieces of beef or duck threaded on strings. If food is a language, then *tolotra* is a metalinguistic message that ritually unifies the takers with the givers, bringing an end to Turn II. After the speaking of the blessing (quoted above), the debate finishes. If the negotiations have been as successful as Maurice Rasamuel designed them to be, both sides have won. If not, the symbol system has not been impaired.

Reporting the Agreement (Turn 14)

Question and answer have another task. Now that the long discussions have been completed, they must be reported to the many who were not present, in particular the groom's family. The dialogue of the ceremony, which has been contained in the monologism of agreement, now becomes a message to be reported. The bride's spokesman cites a symmetrical proverb, *Ambarambarao amin-janany holazalazainy amin-drainy; ary ambarambarao amin-drainy holazalazainy amin-janany,* Let the children know so that they will inform their father, let the father know so that he will inform his children. The petitioner promises that his party will "eat the fruits of remembering" and report accurately. Reported speech, we recall, was a crucial device in those *hainteny* which handle the most delicate and dangerous matters. The marriage request and other Malagasy *kabary* provide precise documentation for the Bakhtinian exposition of reported speech in literature by Volosinov and Bakhtin. "It is the function of society to select and make grammatical . . . just those factors in the active and evaluative reception of utterances that are socially vital and constant," in both linguistic form and theme (Volosinov 1973:117). Again and again, the folk have invented and stylized their central expressive practices and moral concerns in ways which Bakhtin foresaw.

The same coincidence occurs again in Turn 14 of the *kabary* drama, when all the "takers" have returned home to report on the success of their mission. "The received utterance," Volosinov writes, "is framed within a context of factual commentary. . . . [A] reply (*Gegenrede*) is prepared" (Volosinov 1973:118). So it happens in Imerina. The scene is the house of the groom's family, presumably not far away. Still occasionally observed in 1928 was the old custom of having the bride walk round the house three or seven times to attach her to it. Once everyone is seated, a new question and answer sequence takes place. A senior member of the groom's family questions the takers, who say they can only summarize, for "so many things were involved that they can't be spun out in detail." Rasamuel gives the petitioner a form for the summary: "When we asked for Miss So-and-so to be our son's wife and companion, they gave her to us with a good blessing." The report, in the position of a precedent, is answered by its sequent when the head of the family acknowledges the success of the mission. Then a banquet is given to all by the groom. Those who have brought the wife are given gifts parallel to those given earlier to the groom's party.

Multiple Descriptions

The marriage *kabary* depends on the same norms of indirection and non-confrontation as other Merina ways of speaking, especially by men. I have been describing it primarily as a stylized way of speaking. Functionalist anthropology, with a different emphasis, would describe *kabary* by pointing to what it does for society. Like other prestige ceremonies—an infant's first haircut or circumcision—the Merina marriage debate creates in words a solidarity not created by redistributing material and personal resources. Both families gain prestige through the proliferation of *fitenin-drazana*, sayings of the ancestors. By their *mahay-teny*, power over words, both spokesmen have helped to raise the social status of the family who employs them. More than a mere surrogate for the son-in-law (Bloch 1978:30), the petitioner confers on the family the power associated with winning a dialogic contest. As European observers in British Columbia at first failed to understand the potlatch ceremony of the Kwakiutl, who destroyed blankets and canoes for prestige, so at first they found Malagasy orators to be wasting words. But, I repeat, no one within the culture finds Malagasy men of words to be verbose. It was Sibree, not any of his converts, who took segments of dialogue to be oratorical flourishes for a monologuist. The obscure history of *kabary*, revealed only in Alain Delivré's painstaking analysis of oral histories (1974), has concealed the fundamentally dialogic nature of the form. Yet all its components—the apologies, salutations, statements of obligation, recommendations of proper behavior, and thanks, with their disagreements, complications, and innuendoes—are needed to accomplish fully by means of language the complex tasks of deflecting anxiety, involving the whole group, and transferring the bride (Dez 1973).

In an aesthetic description, the marriage *kabary* should be viewed as a work of art, a response in the medium of words to the problems posed by social logic. Given the special day, time, and audience for its performance, the debate cannot be experienced as ordinary talk (*resaka*) or as a novel improvisation by the speakers. Like the ritual symbols studied by Victor Turner (1969, 1974), its pattern of question and answer condenses the array of disparate meanings and relationships of Merina culture. To return to Nietzsche's idea: human relations are enhanced, transposed, and embellished in the debate, but most of all they are streamlined. Those disparate, conflicting messages are stylized by the debate into an alternation of question and answer. So it was in Greek tragedy, where at the moments of heightened intensity, characters stylize the multiple questions in human consciousness and the multiple voices of human conversation into a strict alternation of metrically identical lines. A contrast between the dialogic *kabary* and this Greek device, called *stichomythia*, is that in Sophocles, for example, such alternating lines have a strong forward movement which leads to a definite answer. Tiresias and Oedipus exchange hexameters in order to identify who is responsible for the curse on Thebes. The Malagasy *kabary*, by contrast, emphasizes the contestatory nature of such dialogue. While the speakers follow the same forms and repeat each other's words, they are seeking to stop each other. By their constant assertions that nothing has been changed in the customs of the ancestors, moreover, the two speakers symbolically purge the social order of disorder and restore its integrity (Wolf 1966 : 98). So tragedy, Aristotle said, was a kind of civic therapy (Aristotle 1970, Goodman 1954). I would say the same of the marriage debate. By their interdependence, the two *mpikabary* symbolize the interdependence of the two families and of all Merina people.

A symbolic description of the marriage *kabary* would connect it to myth, in that it enables people to think acceptably about their universe. Contradictions abound in the life of the Merina, between the opposed interests of the families and their new connection, between dominance and submission, between stability and change. Since 1896, if not before, another contradiction has been strongly present.

> For the older generation, the deepest and most unavoidable conflict remains that between what is *razana* ("of the ancestor") and that which is *vazaha* ("of the stranger"), which means anything even remotely associated with Europe. One is considered good and trustworthy; the other, disturbing and doubtful. . . . One way of reconciling claims by two incompatible sets of values is by continuing the custom of burial in the family tomb. Another is to cooperate with *foko* [clan] members for important events, such as circumcision and marriage, and to give hospitality and financial help. (Nelson et al. 1973 : 94).

The Merina, like all Malagasy, have a long history of coping with incompatible claims. Like all folklore, the marriage *kabary* reconciles people to the existence of such incompatibility by expressing it in figurative and artistic language. When Rasamuel and other folklorists have preserved *kabary* in print, they have striven to help their countrymen know themselves better and repel the forces of cultural invasion with their mobile army of metaphors.

6. Funeral Oratory: Living and Dead

Every folkloric event is heard as a mosaic of quotations—recurrent phrases, images, rhythms. Formulaic openings and closings are cited verbatim in folktales (Renel 1910:lvii–lxiv). The trickster repeats the behavior he exhibited last time; the youngest son is again successful. The *Motif-Index of Folk Literature* is a dictionary of familiar quotations. Plagiarism is at the back of all folklore except the first text. That one has vanished.[1] Regarded as performance instead of as text production, every folkloric event is constituted by a mosaic of complex relationships to other events (Tadié 1987:220–26). Every folklore performance comes into existence—biographically, psychologically, theoretically—by the absorbing and transforming of another performance, which defines its aesthetic shape and its functions.

Thus the theoretical basis for folkloric creativity, in Madagascar and elsewhere, is a creative adherence to style most evident in parody. A classic Western example is the parody Homeric epic *Batrachomyomachia* (ca. 500 B.C., but with many later interpolations). This, says Bakhtin, is "an image of Homeric style. It is precisely style that is the true hero of the work" (1981:51). For European literature, the directional signals in homages, imitations, or parodies have been analyzed with great thoroughness and subtlety by Gérard Genette (1982). All of Malagasy verbal art is, in Genette's term, literature of the second degree. No *hainteny*, no *ohabolana* can be heard as an independent entity. Every performance works to activate two or more other performances at the same time. By signaling his hearer that he is parodying or imitating a predecessor, the *mpikabary* produces the activation of the present and the past performances.

The history of Malagasy genres must examine the relations between them, as the critic of *Batrachomyomachia* looks at frogs and mice taking the place of heroes and warriors (Ben-Porat 1976). My analyses and texts of riddles, poems, proverbs, and orations in earlier chapters show that the *mpikabary*, man of words, fills his performances with what Zvi Ben-Porat names "directional signals" to the discourse of his craft. In the artistry of *kabary* (in its general meaning of formalized dialogue), directional signals function to produce superior performances. When performances are more complex, engaging, and multileveled than *resaka* (ordinary talk) or medio-cre speeches, they are valued by Malagasy audiences as superior. To name the relation between homages, imitations, or parodies and their models, I coined the word *interperformance*, meaning that relation of inclusion which connects *kabary* events to the various types of discourse which en-gender them (Haring 1988).

This neologism transposes a category from literary criticism into folk-lore. *Intertextuality* is Julia Kristeva's term for the relation between literary texts explicated at length by Bakhtin. All discourse, according to Bakhtin, and most emphatically the discourse of art, orients itself to other dis-course. Everyday talk, law, religion, the human sciences, rhetorical genres all take part in the continuing conversation of mankind (Bakhtin 1981). As intertextuality is to literary texts, so interperformance is to folklore perfor-mance: the relation of a performance of a riddle, *hainteny* poem, *ohabolana* (proverb), or oration to other performances. For Malagasy folklore, an especially fruitful application of interperformance is intergeneric dialogue, in which "genres engage one another in varying degrees of integration and exchange" (Dorst 1983:416). Like folk performers everywhere, Malagasy *mpikabary* make use of five important directional signals: allusion, quota-tion, framing, metafolklore, and variation. To demonstrate interperform-ance in Malagasy *kabary*, I shall cite a string of riddles from an unexpected context.

Let me ask you some questions. Do you know:
[1]   What is the mountain with the good streams?
[2]   What is the big broken jar?
[3]   Who has lost a big knife with an ivory handle?
[4]   What do you feel everywhere but never see?
[5]   What is poured out but never exhausted?
[6]   What is the whim one later regrets?
[7]   What is it that is caressed but not loved?
[8]   What is half buried but never rotten?
[9]   What is completely ruined?
[10]   Who is driven crazy by losing just one thing?
[11]   What are the scraps one gives to old people?
[12]   What is the greatest punishment for a leper?
[13]   What is the big mat that dogs love?

To right and left are people of wit,
   people like sealing wax,
   who can make a canoe go on dry land,
         light a fire under water,
      and fight a hedgehog barehanded without getting hurt.
Yet none of them can answer the questions I just asked but me.

The mountain with good streams is the king.
The big broken jar is a wife and mother who has died, for she is like
a treasure chest.
He who has lost his beautiful knife with the ivory
handle is one who has lost his son, for his help has vanished.
What is felt everywhere but not seen is the wind.
What is poured out without being exhausted is laughter.
The whim you later regret is scratching yourself.
What is caressed but not loved is laughter.
What is half buried but never rotten is he who has children.
The ruined one is the one who is childless.
Those who are driven crazy by losing just one thing are the poor.
The scraps given to old people are the fire.
The leper's punishment is coming out in broad daylight.
The mat that dogs love is the grass.

These thirteen riddles constitute the first of three sets, totaling fifty-three items, which appear in a funeral oration of the Merina. The text was transcribed and translated in 1908 by Gustave Mondain, a great *malgach-isant* of early colonial days. He saw nothing specially wonderful in it; to him the whole oration was a string of unrelated images. Perhaps those uninteresting riddles were meant to drive away the thought of death. For him it was a bit of history. For me, it is a distillation of the Malagasy art of the word.

Having observed the conflict between dialogue and monologue in other Malagasy folklore, what can we see in Mondain's text? For one thing, no free dialogue is allowed in the interaction situation. The oration is as monologic as a proverb. The *mpikabary* silences the audience; not even the most powerful persons before him possess his power over words. For another, some of the riddles unite the interaction situation of a funeral with the context situation. References to bereavement appear in the sixth, eighth, ninth, and tenth riddles. The twelfth alludes to the theme of hiding one's sorrow, treated in the *hainteny* of the bereaved woman trying to hide her sorrow, quoted above. The first three riddles, metaphorical and non-oppositional, echo his earlier salutations to the dignitaries present, by saluting the king, the bereaved wife, and the father. The fourth riddle quotes the common metaphor for *tsiny*, reproaches, which, like the wind, are everywhere felt and nowhere seen. Though the others are obscure to us today, they have literal, metaphorical, and oppositional structures in common with the riddles analyzed in Chapter 2.

Any Western reader would be as surprised as Mondain to find fifty-three riddles, so reminiscent of childhood play, spoken at a funeral. How could a children's game help to deflect the anxieties of bereavement? "Mirth cannot move a soul in agony," as Berowne says in *Love's Labour's Lost* (5. 2. 847). Yet Mondain's Merina were not the only Malagasy who entertained each other in this way at funerals. Peoples such as the Tsimihety (Those Who Do Not Cut Their Hair),[2] would exchange bawdy metered couplets, called *baheza*, during death observances. Two men would face each other, beating time on a dish full of water and mocking each other; the audience would answer by repeating the first phrase of each couplet (Mattei 1938). The Tanala stage a wrestling match the night before a burial (Beaujard 1983:430−34). Outside Madagascar, many other peoples have performed contests or games that would seem similarly inappropriate in bourgeois Europe or North America (Abrahams 1983, O Súilleabháin 1942:223−24). A close parallel occurs on the Caribbean island of St. Vincent, reported by Roger D. Abrahams. There riddles are performed during wakes much as they are in Madagascar, as a response to the threat posed by death. In both islands, the death ceremony readjusts social boundaries. Most important, riddling at a Madagascar funeral, as in St. Vincent, explores power relationships by awarding authority to a person not normally vested with it. In Imerina, that person is the *mpika-bary*, who "contend[s] wittily with the problem of community confusion" and astonishes the audience with his *mahay-teny*, power over language (Abrahams 1972).

To find any two-sided game in Imerina makes us suspect that more than child's play is involved. The question-and-answer pattern, modeled on the smallest scale in the riddle, has shaped the formal utterances and observances associated with other crises of Merina life like puberty. The same pattern is at work here, in a long formal speech that aims at giving pleasure as well as allaying anxiety. The funeral oration is just as much a dialogue as the marriage request debate. By analyzing the internal structure of this one text, I can answer the riddle of what those riddles are doing there and illustrate interperformance. The answer will be that the fifty-three riddles, framed within the oration, which in turn is framed within the ceremony, are using language to meet the greatest possible challenge. Words will defend the living against "the horror and shock of abeyance of life" (Jacobs 1964:182) by denying that there has been any breach and by alluding to and quoting as much artistic language as possible. Merina artistic language here will deny death.

The Funeral As a Context for Speaking

"The conspicuous burial of the dead," one observer has written, "is the ultimate activity of Malagasy systems of religion, economics, and social prestige" (Huntington, quoted in Kottak 1980:211). Burials and *famadihana*, "bone-turnings"—ceremonies in which the dead are removed from their tombs, given new shrouds, and joyously reinstalled, sometimes in new tombs—have been extensively discussed in Malagasy ethnographic literature, as have the impressive stone tombs and funerary art (Callet 1974, Decary 1951, Dubois 1938, Faublée 1946, Grandidier 1908–28, Urbain-Faublée 1963). Recent field researches, especially the influential work of Maurice Bloch, show that burial has lost little of its importance under European impact (Bloch 1971, Kottak 1980, Beaujard 1983, Huntington 1987). Although many Malagasy maintain a belief in a soul that departs from the body at death but remains nearby for the funeral and some time afterward (Kottak 1980:219–20), their death rituals smooth over the breach, asserting death to be no more than a "transition between earthly existence and life beyond."

The "simplicity and philosophical fatalism" (Decary 1951:249) which an older generation saw in their acceptance of death, however, is not well borne out by the descriptions observers have given us of funerals and funerary orations. Many tensions and stresses are associated with burial. Merina persons whose economic needs and mobility have taken them far away from home experience anguish if they cannot be buried in the family tomb (Bloch 1971). Their physical separation increases their emotional attachment to the ancestral tomb. Another tension is the desire to make certain that burial is permanent. Tanala, like most other Malagasy, have a strong attachment to the tomb, but they also know that the dead do not want to stay in it. Hence they take pains to transport the deceased to his tomb so circuitously that he cannot find his way back again (Beaujard 1983:465).

That death is a separation, while life has been a unity, is clearly stated in Malagasy myths narrating how death came into the world. In many such myths, two or three creators share the task of creating mankind, one making the physical body and the other imparting life to it (tales 1.1.11–39 in *Malagasy Tale Index*). After death, each takes back his contribution. In a Betsimisaraka tale collected in 1907–10, a black god fashions animal figures but does not know how to vivify them. The white god animates the figures, stipulating that after death, the souls he has imparted will return to him. The black god agrees. That is why the bodies of human beings remain in the earth, which belongs to the black god, while their souls go to the heaven of the white god. In a Betsileo tale, three creators are jointly responsible, one fashioning the flesh into shape, the second contributing blood and bones, and the third giving the breath of life. Men are enjoined not to separate them in their prayers, but today they violate the prohibition. That is the origin of death (Dubois 1938:1331–32).

Two principles of Malagasy ethos are seen in these many myths of the origin of death. One is that all tasks of any importance must not be undertaken by any person alone, but must be shared among a group, especially in bereavement. The Tanala say, *Amponga vaky tsy misaraka antambo*, Broken drums do not part in grief (Beaujard 1983:413). Funeral responsibilities, for example, are to be shared among whole villages. "A dozen men might easily contribute their effort to construct a coffin for the deceased," one pair of observers writes. "We once saw six different men participate in turn and sometimes jointly in the sawing of a *single* board for a coffin!" (Keenan and Ochs 1979:143). Even the spirits leaving the body of the dead man or woman are conceived by Betsileo as dual (Kottak 1980:212). The other principle taught by the myths is that the unity of life is temporary. Death returns us all to a separated condition. It is that separated condition, denied by an ethnic name like The Inseparable Multitude (Betsimisaraka), to which the funeral oration must accustom the survivors.

A Dialogue with the Dead

A Malagasy funeral addresses itself to the deceased, who is undergoing a change of status, as well as to the bereaved. Dying does not take a Merina man out of the social system, but it does change his class (Andriamanjato

1957:30–38). "Betsileo do not think of death, which permeates their lives, as termination, but as an inevitable rite in passage along an indefinite path linking past and future" (Kottak 1980:219). A funeral oration, like a marriage request, is shaped by the question-and-answer pattern. Like the marriage debate, it alludes to the shorter forms of riddle, proverb, and poem by means of allusion, quotation, framing, and variation. By citing the shorter forms, the orator enacts a dialectic between the genres, between dialogism and monologism, between question-and-answer and decree, between egalitarian polyphony and hierarchical, authoritative speech. Thus, for a few minutes at least, he will create a unity out of elements always disparate—the newly deceased, the previously dead, and the living. Then, consistent with other genres of folklore, he will speak a monologic last word to give a sense of closure to this ceremony and help effect a transition from the world of the living to the world of the dead.

Devices of interperformance have been a frequent feature of funeral oratory in Madagascar. Among the Betsileo of the mid-nineteenth century, who were under Merina domination, a funeral orator would make an explicit connection between a life crisis and formalized dialogue:

To have something to warp is to have something to weave;
to have a death is to have to speak.
When an ox is dead, he is carved with a knife;
when a man is dead, he is carved with the mouth.

It also framed reported speech into the oration: "We called to our kinsmen and neighbors, 'Come to our aid, for we are struck deep.'" Speech was framed within speech as well: "At the governor's dwelling, we said to him, . . . 'We have been sent here to say, "Take one pebble away from the sum, for R—— is no more." Here at your dwelling, we ask to build a tomb and shed our tears'" (Dubois 1938:684–88).

With comparative study, Mondain's 1908 oration thus becomes less obscure. When he published the text, Mondain sought to capture in it one moment of the Merina past—not, like Rasamuel, to write an etiquette book for cultural revivalists. Folklorists have long known what literary critics more recently discovered, that even a unique text like this, recording one performance, is situated at the junction of several texts which it re-reads, accents, condenses, displaces, or deepens (Tadié 1987:220–21). Mondain's funeral oration quotes, accents, shortens, varies, and deepens the inherited words of earlier orators. Those transformations are what I mean by interperformance. To be "folk," it is sometimes said, a saying or poem would have to be accepted by a particular community (Jakobson and Bogatyrev 1971:91). We have enough variant forms of Merina oratory to believe Mondain when he tells us that his oration has already undergone community censorship and received acceptance: the oration "has been said and said again many times over the tombs of persons in southern Imerina; it has been heard by thousands of auditors who applauded its hidden subtleties" (Mondain 1908:99).

Despite the prevalent monologism of the oration, every section of it is dialogic, depending for its meaning on acknowledging the audience and even another speaker. There are three prefatory sections and one long body. As in the marriage *kabary*, dialogue begins by acknowledging the audience and apologizing for speaking. As conventions of oratory, the salutations and apologies allude to other speeches the audience will have heard. The orator salutes the king (local chief) by quoting four flattering similes in topic-comment form.

> Hianao no toy ny dimpotra, toy ny voromanga, ka na zavozavoin' ny be aza mitoka-miavaka ihany.
> Hianao no toy ny tatamo tsara farihy, izay mahita anao ho finaritra, izay manamorona eo akaikinao mody aina.
> Hianao ny toy ny hazo be rahaka, izay eloanao maitso, ary izay tandindominao mandina.
> Hianao no toy ny korintsambolamena nirina, raha miondrika ravaky ny ory, ary raha mitraka voninahitry ny tany.
> (Mondain 1908:99–100)

You are like the *dimpotra* [bird of ill omen],
  or like the bluebird:
you stand out even when almost hidden by the crowd.
You are like the great waterlily in a pond:
  who sees you is delighted,
You are like the tree of huge shade:
  those whom you shade grow,
  those whom you shelter shine with well-being.
You are like the color of gold:
  when you incline yourself,
    you are the jewel of the afflicted,
  when you stand straight, you are the glory of the earth.

Similar salutations greet the chief in four similes for his power and resources.

Along with allusion and quotation, a crucial device of interperformance to ensure excellence is what Alan Dundes has called "metafolklore . . . folkloristic statements about folklore" (Dundes 1966). This device occurs when a performer includes in his dialogue a covert message to another performer, without an explicit signal. Malagasy folklore, including the texts analyzed in earlier chapters, is doubtless full of these covert messages, unseen by me. Metafolklore also occurs when one performer's words speak about, or to, another performer's words, or about the genre in which he is performing. That occurs in Mondain's text when the orator assimilates his own genre to another, thus stating through their connection that he is playing a two-sided game.

> Ny kabary àry toy ny fanorona: notsipazako eroa an-daka kelynofoinako etsy am-poibeny, telo lahy no foinan' ny irery, ka hamono sa hanahala?
>
> (Mondain 1908 : 101)

Orations are like *fanorona*:
  I draw my pieces back a few squares
  and surround my opponent in the middle of the board.
If one of my pieces captures three,
  then am I beaten or matched?

Though Mondain's manuscript does not name a second speaker, it implies an adversary. The *mpikabary* refutes an unidentified preceding speaker, thus revealing that the funeral oration is one side of a debate. *Miady Iàlana foana toy izany*, All your ideas seem to fight each other, the speaker says. His invective to an unheard adversary incudes several *ohabolana*, with their usual function of stopping a rejoinder. *Tahaka ny sisy hazon'Andriamalaza: tsara endrika fa haroka aty; tahaka ny vary ambolena aoriana na misy voa aza voa ilany, koa sady tsy mahay no maharenina*, Your ideas are like the trees at Andriamalaza: they look good but they are hollow; or like rice planted late, a few grains but all on one side.

The Orator's Power and Risk

Through his use of quotation, allusion, and metafolklore, the orator reasserts traditionalism. Reassurance is especially appropriate at a time of distress, when threatening reality must be controlled by language about language. "No speaking all at once," he says. "No arguments. We are like a fountain: the first do not leave with an unfilled jug, and the last do not carry away half." By repeating time-honored words, the *mpikabary* is not carrying out a frozen ritual. He is creating a new artistic product "which is immediately understandable because of the oral nature of his presentation and the limitations which this places upon his audience. He must present pieces that can be understood almost as a reflex action" (Abrahams 1967 : 9). To rely on "practiced means of communication, with which the audience will be familiar," enables the Malagasy orator, as it enables the African storyteller, the Italian Renaissance poet, or the British novelist to create. Most great art, says the British critic Raymond Williams, has been created in these conditions (Williams 1966 : 32).

Yet power carries a risk. After the salutations, all this boasting has caused the speaker to stand out and risk *tsiny*, separated from the crowd as the dead person has been separated from the living. His apology for speaking takes a sarcastic tone about adversaries. He must disclaim this separated position. In contrast to the contradictions he attributes to unheard previous speakers and the insincerity he says is betrayed by their dress, the speaker's own clothing is homespun, and his speech genuinely belongs to him, *Izao kabariko izao*.

This disclaimer of performance signals that the body of the formal oration will now begin. A new kind of dialogue and a new kind of quotation enter in. The speaker becomes the voice of the dead man. As a direct answer reveals the meaning of a riddle, and as literal language, in many *hainteny*, answers metaphor, so the voice of the dead in the funeral speech is reported by his living spokesman. Such quotation will effect the transition of the deceased to his new status. The dead man bids farewell to earth and its inhabitants.

> Koa finareta, hono, veloma iry làlambe mianatsimo! finareta iry là-lambe miankandrefana! finareta iry làlambe mianavaratra! finareta iry làlambe miantsinanana na fa Ranona tsy ho any intsony.
> (Mondain 1908 : 103)

> "I greet you," he says, "and farewell o roads to the south!
> Farewell o roads to the west!
> Farewell o roads to the north!
> Farewell o roads to the east!
> Ranona will go there no more."

Farewells follow to his door, village, fields, friends, relatives, wife, children, threshold, place by the hearth, bed, and dwellings. In this use of reported speech, Mondain's funeral *kabary* resembles those long, subdued *hainteny* in which an intermediary must give the message of rejection or regret. The dead man's farewells occupy the place of the precedent of a riddle; they require an answer from the voice of the living. After the quoted farewells, the *mpikabary* shifts into the role of the messenger and survivor. Does he shift pitch and intonation? Unequivocal metaphors answer the voice just heard.

> fa toy ny voro-manga noseranin-dambo lahy Ranona ka lasa, tsy hi-tampody fa handry; tsy antenaina hiverina intsony fa honina. Sira latsaka an-drano izy ka tsy hiverina intsony.
> (Mondain 1908 : 103)

The dead man is gone

like the bluebird passing by the boar.
He shall not be seen again, for he will sleep.
He shall not find his way back, for he will be away.
He is salt dropped in water, he shall not return.

As in the marriage debate, the actual proposal was surrounded by attempts to avert *tsiny*, so here the admission that the deceased is really gone has been carefully prepared. Further difficult truths follow: the wife, children, and prince of the place will see him no more, "for he has left us today, and there one stays much longer than here." The crowd, says the speaker, has gathered with them to weep "with the doors that saw him pass, with his wife and children."

Three Sets of Riddles

The admission that the dead man is really dead has been the most difficult moment, combining literal and figurative language. This emotional peak is followed by the puzzling recitation of three sets of riddles,[3] beginning with those quoted above. Memory of the riddling game of childhood connects the happy past with the present bereavement and future loss. Since riddles involve yoking together seemingly unrelated facts, perhaps they are being used to resolve the contradiction between presence and absence, past and present, life and death. Metaphor in Malagasy thought, according to one of Madagascar's deep thinkers, is not merely rhetoric to convince persons unable to understand reason. It *is* reason, because comparison integrates a particular truth into a universal order. "Comparison, for the Malagasy, is not simply a means to make an abstract thought concrete, or to make it more tangible or palpable. More than that, it is an integral part of the notion of moral and philosophical truth" (Rajaona 1959). All funerals call the assembled persons to contemplate the universal order. Merina funerals use allusion, quotation, and metafolklore to voice that call.

Quotation of riddles and allusion to divination are the means. After the first set of riddles, pseudo-dialogue continues with fifteen more. Monologue frames the dialogue: the speaker states a riddle-like metaphor and then explains it himself. References to divination in items 14, 16, 19, 20, 23, 25, 26, and 27 remind the audience that all creatures, beginning with those of highest rank, are members of the universal order. The sequence echoes the earlier salutations.

[14] Tale ny papango, vorona ela indrindra.
[15] Omaly ny vorompotsy, voron-tsy mahafoy omby.
[16] Bilady ny tataro, vorona manatody an-tany.
[17] Fianahana ny hindry, vorompitomany anaka.
[18] Abily ny akoho, tsy afaka an-trano. (Mondain 1908:106)

[14] The hawk is called chief [term for the first column of signs in divination]; that is the longest-lived bird.
[15] The white bird is called ox[4]; that bird never leaves the cattle.
[16] The goatsucker is called "left on the ground"; that bird lays its eggs on the ground.
[17] The buzzard is called "kinsman"; that bird that weeps for its children.
[18] The chicken is called "slave"; it never leaves the house.

After these images of domestic order, the inevitable threat which an uncontrollable universe poses to what is most dear comes in.

[19] Betsimisahy ny vanga, voro-mpandeha alina.
[20] Asorotany ny tahia, vorompihihan' Andriana.
[21] Haja ny angaka, voron-tia rano.
[22] Fahavalo ny goaika, vorompihinam-paty.

[23]   Fahasivy ny vorondolo, voro-mpihaza alina. (Mondain
       1908:106–7)

[19]   The shrike is called "many fearful ones"; that bird steals by
       night.
[20]   The little duck is called "fourth month"; that bird is eaten by
       nobles.
[21]   The big wild duck is called "honor"; that bird likes water.
[22]   The crow is called "enemy"; that bird eats the dead.
[23]   The owl is called "ninth" [unlucky]; it hunts by night.

Divination helps allay the threat of an unpredictable future.

[24]   Safary ny tsintsina, vorom-panatody an-dàlana.
[25]   Kily ny fody, voro-mahay trano.
[26]   Haka ny vorondreo, vorompaneno ambony.
[27]   Ombiasa ny kankafotra, voro-mahalala taona.
[28]   Saily ny fandiafasika, voro-miemonemona. (Mondain
       1908:107)

[24]   The sparrow is called "traveler"; it lays its eggs along the
       road.
[25]   The *fody* is called "tamarind" [seeds used in divining]; it has
       power to build houses.
[26]   The roller-bird is called "perfect"; it sings from high above.
[27]   The cuckoo is called "sorcerer"; it sees the future.
[28]   The sandpiper is called *saily* [medicinal plant?]; it perches so
       high.

Persons, plants used for discovering the truth through divination,
plants that heal and restore endangered life—all are placed in ordered systems. Symbolizing such an ordered system, in any region of Madagascar,
is divination, which has been remolded from Arabic sources into a
uniquely Malagasy practice (Decary 1970, Vérin and Rajaonarimanana
1991). The orator is directed by Mondain's script to connect the astrological system of divination to classifications of Malagasy birds (Mondain
1908:112). The universal order is acknowledged.

Cattle Riddles

According to the interperformance approach, this funeral oration is a tissue of references to things known to the audience. All the riddles so far have played upon the prominence of death in the minds of the hearers, connecting it to the larger cosmic order. The cattle symbolism in the last set of riddles makes the same connection by developing a single complex image. The riddles are metaphors for the various parts of the slaughtered ox which will be given out for the funeral feast. In this section, as in the first set of riddles, the questions come first, followed by a boast by the speaker to retain the floor, and finally the answers. I omit the Malagasy text.

> Now do you know what these are?
> [29]   Two trees standing together.
> [30]   Two fighters who don't agree.
> [31]   Two bullets face to face.
> [32]   What is in first place but will not eat.
> [33]   The stones that are exposed.
> [34]   Those who inspect what they get.
> [35]   The good bellows made by God.
> [36]   The bridge to carry loads.
> [37]   The one that suffers when pressed down.
> [38]   What presses down when it stands up.
> [39]   The great ones who lean on others.
> [40]   The big mass that stops the rest.
> [41]   The lord's red cane.
> [42]   What pushes out as it goes in.
> [43]   The great one who walks behind.
> [44]   The little one trying to enter.
> [45]   The one who admires silken threads.
> [46]   What fools take for rags.
> [47]   What even old people can chew.
> [48]   A red silk *lamba* that is badly dyed.
> [49]   The old lady's pretty shuttle.
> [50]   A coin of good weight.
> [51]   Gold pieces lined up.
> [52]   The bent old man.
> [53]   What makes one look sick.

Before giving the answers, the speaker emphasizes his *mahay-teny*, power over words. "Whoever you are . . . I am as strong as the Europeans. If they mount on a chair, I jump to the chopping-block. Think on this. Be warned. See if we are not equal." Then he lists the twenty-five answers: "The two trees standing up are his horns; the two who are quarreling are his ears; the two bullets face to face are his eyes." All the parts of the slaughtered ox are named: mouth, teeth, jaws, nostrils, neck, chest, hump, shoulders, hide, penis, flank, thigh, rump, tail, stomach, liver, lungs, spleen, heart, kidneys, "jelly," and intestines.

This riddle sequence framed into the oration is an independent piece, indeed a Merina favorite whether recited or sung (Dahle 1877:416–17). The framed quotation of known material, which is the means of composing *hainteny* and *kabary*, is an essential device in interperformance. Paulhan noticed it in translating *hainteny* (1913:322–23; cf. Domenichini-Ramiaramanana 1970:342, no. 1940, Houlder 1960:82, no. 1014; Paulhan 1913:82–83, Houlder 1960:15, no. 178, 32, no. 402).

What is the symbolism of this riddle sequence? Especially in ceremonials, metaphor integrates a particular truth into a universal order. Versions of this sequence sung in circumcision ceremonies give us the clue. They connected the ox to be eaten with the central character of the interaction situation, the boy being circumcised. They also anticipated the feast by allotting the various parts to their various uses: "Its horns to the maker of spoons, its teeth to the plaiters of straw, its ears for medicine for a rash, its hump to make fat" (trans. Sibree 1880:273–74). Here in the funeral oration, the ox again symbolizes the central actor—the dead man. This equivalence is confirmed by a Tanala practice. Before slaughtering the ox for a funeral, young men beat it with sticks, throw stones at it, and set their dogs on it, all with the explicit purpose of putting the ox through the same sufferings undergone by the dead man (Beaujard 1983:424). Thus when the meat is distributed and eaten, the dead man will be reassimilated into society.

What, then, is the place of those riddles in the funeral ceremony? Formally, they are a climax to the oration, after the salutations, apologies, belittling of previous speakers, and admission of the fact of death. Psychologically, their consoling message is that the living and the dead are all parts of a larger order. That order is not to be directly comprehended; it can only be understood through metaphor. Also, the riddles evoke the games of childhood, as well as the *hainteny* contest of adult life. Mondain may have been right to think they were meant to be funny. Perhaps these riddles ventilate "anxious and guilty feelings by placing together things which do not really fit" (Jacobs 1964:248). Socially, furthermore, these monologic riddles enforce the lesson that dialogue, with its tolerance of alternative voices and points of view, is to be contained and controlled by monologue and that one person must have authority. Most forcefully, I think, the riddles assert life against death. In the atmosphere of disquiet and grief engendered by separation and fragmentation, the funeral oration creates a unity and an integration that can exist only in the poetic discourse of performance. The unity is a unity of voice, a monologism of quoted sayings. Like much other folklore in Madagascar (and everywhere else, for that matter), the formalized dialogue of the riddle in the *kabary* expresses incompatible claims in its symbolic language and, by expressing them, ends them.

The event is not over. The fifty-three riddles, taken as a unit, form a precedent that requires a sequent. The ox metaphors especially create a disequilibrium, which will be answered nonverbally when the meat is distributed. That feast will be the next action of the ceremony. Then after the feasting, authoritative speech resumes, with its usual antithesis and balance. In his transition to the last section, the speaker quotes from himself, referring to riddles 16 and 49. *Koa dia hasiako fiantefana hoatry ny vorona, ary hasiako fiefana tahaka ny tenona. Aleveno è ny maty, ha hariva ny andro.* "I shall act like the bird, letting my word be laid upon the ground; like the shuttle, I shall put an end to my work. Bury the dead then, for night is coming." Insisting on order and correct observance as the funeral ends, the *mpikabary* prescribes the correct relation between kinds and colors of cattle to be sacrificed in future rituals and favorable astrological conditions. *Alahamady, omby mena. Adaoro, taboro fehi-loha, mara loha, Adizaoza taboro malefaka, mipentimpentina.* "In Alahamady [month], a red ox. In Adaoro [month], a bull whose head has different-colored spots. In Adizaoza [month], a young spotted bull," and on through the year. The balanced phrases assert order, but the oration ends on a pessimistic note. Each month that brings its own sacrifice brings also its own ailment. *Alahamady, mari-koditra. Adaoro, aretin' an-doha. Adizaoza, hatina.* "In Alahamady, a chill. In Adaoro, headache. In Adizaoza, the itch," and nine more. Astrological indications of this kind have counterparts all over Madagascar (Rusillon 1929:79–87, Faublée 1946:105–15, Cotte 1946:89–102, Decary 1970, Bloch 1968, Beaujard 1983). After the speaker says "Good night and goodbye," all that remains is to distribute the leftovers among the parting guests.

Mondain's funeral oration should be evaluated more highly than he did. It is more complex, engaging, and multileveled than many another *kabary*. Its complexity would not emerge without prior knowledge of the riddle, *hainteny*, and proverb genres it incorporates. With knowledge of these, it can be seen to take in a large range of human experience. A broader study of Malagasy speechmaking in the field, oriented to the ways in which varying occasions elicit variable performances, would, I believe, show *kabary* to occupy the place in Malagasy oral communication that Bakhtin claimed for the novel in Europe (Bakhtin 1981; Williams 1966:278).

Allusion, quotation, and metafolklore are not the only devices of interperformance. The most prominent device is the most familiar to folklorists: variation, which involves several aesthetic choices. Many variations in *hainteny* occur within the process of transmission from one performer to another. Others result from the demands of situation. Textual variation, as studied by Domenichini-Ramiaramanana (1968:20–21, 106–9, 148–49) is a subset of interperformance.

Conclusion

What contribution does the study of Malagasy folklore through print make to related disciplines? Folklore "proceeds from a particular conception of the world or from an original way of approaching problems," as has been said of anthropology by Claude Lévi-Strauss (1967:344). My conception of the world, as a folklorist, is an arena of interacting forces, which tend to reduce and overpower dominated cultures. The "original way of approaching problems" that characterizes folklore was identified by Arnold van Gennep, who began his career by analyzing totem and taboo in Madagascar. What distinguishes folklore is not its facts, theory, or system, but the angle from which it observes facts. From that angle, all the multitudinous details and variant forms in time and space become not aberrant, not obstacles to the work, but normal. As a result, a major study like Henry Glassie's *Passing the Time in Ballymenone* demonstrates definitively how a folklorist can produce a detailed examination of the representation of the world through the eyes of a distinct group. "What we call folklore (or art or communication)," Glassie writes, "is the central fact of what we call culture" (1982:xiv). The general problem of entering the world of the other, of coming to terms with a foreign culture, is shared by folklore with anthropology, history, and literary criticism. To all these frames of reference, the study of Malagasy folklore has something to say.

With anthropology, first, folklore shares a deeply ingrained ambivalence about whether "states of society and culture [are] already formed, and understood as such, by social actors" (Marcus and Fischer 1986:78). Folklorists such as Glassie assume that their data are best presented in the words and formulations of the people they are observing. The anthropologist James Clifford has traced the influence of such thinking in anthropology (1988:21–54). Some anthropologists and folklorists believe, however, that their data convey information about states of society and culture which are not understood by their participants. As Lévi-Strauss has put it,

> the reality of the object [the social sciences] are studying is not wholly limited to the level of the subject apprehending it. These appearances are underlaid by other appearances of no greater value, and so on, layer by layer, as we look for the ultimate essence of nature which at each level escapes us, and will probably remain forever unattainable. These levels of appearance are not mutually exclusive or contradictory. (1981:638)

This ambivalence lends itself to system building, in three steps. First, divide the phenomena—social groupings, marriage rules—into manageable units so that they do not rise up and contradict you. Second, by including data from other topics in your materials, suggest repeatedly that there is a system whether the people know it or not. Finally, disclaim contradictions ("At various moments, the system can appear to be any of the three") while retaining a commitment to a monolithic model called "the" system. Doubtless I am guilty of this sort of system building in the foregoing pages. Conversely, as Robert Lowie pointed out, a culture like Madagascar might be "shreds and patches historically and yet still have unity from the point of view of those within it." What the Malagasy perceive as unity is "an *a*-historical phenomenon of some sort" (Leaf 1979:213), namely tradition.

One component of that unity, not articulated by any Malagasy so far as I know, is the question-and-answer pattern I have delineated. It is a generative principle whereby Malagasy people generate the symbolic forms which are our means of understanding them. Being outsiders, "we can never apprehend another people's or another period's imagination neatly, as though it were our own . . . but we do so not by looking *behind* the interfering glosses that connect us to it but *through* them" (Geertz 1983:44). The question-and-answer pattern, however, is no such interfering gloss: it is rather a principle operating in the behavior of speakers. Future research could confirm or disconfirm the degree to which speakers can describe it abstractly.

Can this ambivalence about views of culture be resolved, or is it destined to continue as a dialectic? Neither the outsider's nor the insider's perspective deserves automatic privilege. Yet the study of folklore, which situates the observer on the boundary between outsider and insider, encourages a search for mediations. One cultural critic who has offered a mediation between the particulars of living and the forces behind them is Raymond Williams. His "structure of feeling" attempts to articulate "richly described experiences of everyday life [in novels, for instance] with larger systems and the subtle expressions of ideology." Williams clearly wishes to deal with questions of value. As Williams's work is described by anthropologists, "experience, the personal, and feeling all refer to a domain of life that, while indeed structured, is also inherently social, in which dominant and emergent trends in global systems of political economy are complexly registered in language, emotions, and the imagination" (Marcus and Fischer 1986:78). When one reads Williams's *Long Revolution* (1961), the concept of "structure of feeling" seems theoretically fuzzy. He clarifies it in his splendid account of Britain in the 1840s, but harder data seem necessary. The ethnography of communication and the performance-based theory of folklore, which insist upon accurate observation of speakers and language in context, but which allow us to consider questions of value at the same time as questions of hard fact, combine into a framework. When one reads the oral literature of Madagascar in that framework, and observes the constant interaction of dialogue and monologue, a structure of feeling emerges quite clearly. It is a structure that, I believe, has given and continues to give Malagasy people a reality and sanity sorely needed in the face of foreign exploitation. It is a special case of culture giving to people, as Ralph Linton said, ready-made answers to their problems.

Study of Malagasy folklore also contributes data to history. All folklore study does this, of course; in Madagascar the need for a folk-based history is all the greater because folklore is omitted by historians such as Deschamps and Brown. Some historians, of course, must continue the rediscovery of the Malagasy past (in the journal *Etudes Océan Indien,* for example). Others confront the question of how to pursue the means whereby oppressed groups maintain resistance to being overpowered. "I think we still have a lot to learn," writes feminist historian Linda Gordon earnestly but tentatively, "about the mediations by which groups of people, including subordinate groups, create what you might call a culture, something that's deeper than style but not as deep as fundamental power structure" (quoted in DuBois 1984:229). The need which Gordon acknowledges for more information is filled by folklore. The dialogic genres studied in this book are the kind of mediation Gordon looks for: a principle of style which lies between surface behavior and the enduring power structure. Another such mediation familiar to folklorists is the interaction between informant and outsider in which the investigator becomes a special audience for a performance (Haring 1972).

As to literature, though folklore has begun to profit from the sophistication of literary theory, influence in the other direction has hardly commenced. Hymes has pointed out the importance of folklore for work in sociolinguistics (Hymes 1974:125–34); I point out the importance of folklore to literary theory. For instance, the intertextuality which presents itself to literary theory as a discovery is, even to the most conservative folklorist, an old empirical question. When Harold Bloom says, "Any poem is an inter-poem, and any reading of a poem is an inter-reading" (1986:332), the folklorist says, "Of course." No one doubts that texts of folktales, songs, or poems must be studied in the context of their other versions and variants. I have provided a basis for intertextual study of Malagasy narrative in my *Malagasy Tale Index*, and in the pages above I have applied similar reasoning to other folklore genres, as well as suggesting the notion of interperformance. Theorists could afford to look to folklore, with its attention to recurrent structures, for solutions to questions about the intertextual relations of universes of discourse (Stewart 1979:48–49).

As a more telling contribution to contemporary literary theory, folklore gives an empirically based answer to Jacques Derrida's view of language. It invites the philosopher to look again at the realities of language and at least to imagine, if not replace, verbal art in its context of occurrence. Derrida's vision in *Of Grammatology* attributes to writing a power of bursting through semantic horizons in the absence of a sender, a receiver, or a context of production. That power is meaningless without them. Malagasy or any folklore does, however, amply support Derrida's attack on the doubling representation of the critic, who always lets something escape. Folklore texts always hide something of their assumptions, laws, or rules. The presentation of Malagasy folklore in the foregoing pages hides the uncollected texts, the folkloric events that do not conform to the dialogic pattern, the background and training of men of words, the critical evaluations of audiences, and much more. If deconstruction means the uncovering of that inadequacy, folklore has been uncovering that inadequacy for generations. Folklorists today such as Hymes or Tedlock, who strive for a more accurate representation on a printed English page of an American Indian performance, well know that something always escapes. What escapes from some folklore texts is documented (Fine 1984). In Madagascar, the Norwegian Lutheran Dahle explicitly proclaimed his duty to expurgate his texts (1877:vii–viii). Philippe Sollers's point that "the text belongs to all, to no one" (quoted in Tadié 1987:221) is what Paulhan found to be true of *ohabolana*. Variation confirms that a text is never finished, but Merina testimony states that it is and must be a finished product.

Is folkloric representation a fraud or a chimera? The field of the folklorist, Derrida might say, is unknowable not only at this empirical level, but also theoretically. If this distinction between the theoretical and the empirical means anything, it points to Derrida's attack on the dominance of metaphysics over Western thought. Folklore must concede his point. The history of folklore pays ample tribute to the "impossible dream of plenitude," and many a folklorist has privileged speech over writing. Dialogic genres in Malagasy verbal art show to me a specific cultural pattern that forms part of the Malagasy representation of the world. To identify that pattern is, I concede, "a systematic tracking down of a truth that is hidden but may be found" (Spivak 1976:xix; Bauman 1977, 1982). Much folklore proceeds on this principle. With sustained study of a distinct, self-conscious cultural group like the Malagasy or Dogon, and through interaction among oneself, one's informants, and published sources, an anthropologist can arrive at, or be given, a detailed examination of how the group represents the world. This prolonged interaction produced the exposition of Dogon mythology and religion in Marcel Griaule's *Conversations with Ogotemmêli* (1965). It remained for a second generation to invent "ethnolinguistics," which scrutinizes how the same people use language artistically to support and extend their representation of the world (Calame-Griaule 1986).[5] Folklore does tend to assert the real existence of cultural patterns without denying "that culture has no substance; it is composed of forms and nothing more. But in the view of almost all modern philosophers, idealists as well as positivists, this is equally true of everything else" (Bagby 1953:541). There is no reason to single out "culture" as especially illusory or to stigmatize "representation" as singularly fraudulent.

Finally, Malagasy folklore contributes to folklore theory in three realms: oral-formulaic study, philosophic base, and historical justification. When Jean Paulhan set forth his anticipation of the Parry-Lord theory of oral composition, he cared nothing for the Homeric Question, nor had he any need to establish the orality of the texts. He attempted rather to understand another topic in oral formulaic studies, namely the training of the performer (Paulhan 1925, Lord 1960:13–29). Future work will require that oral-formulaic composition be examined within the confines of cultural relativism. The Malagasy material in particular shows the force of Malagasy cultural emphases. The technique of assembling new pieces out of older, smaller ones serves the peculiarly Malagasy notion of genre as sliding, variable, and responsive to various circumstances.

A philosophical base that commends itself to folklore theory is the social constructionist approach, which takes rise in Thomas Kuhn's assertion that knowledge "is intrinsically the common property of a group or else nothing at all" (Kuhn 1970:210). This assertion is literally true in Madagascar. The *fitenin-drazana*, sayings of the ancestors, are experienced and proclaimed as a strong component of group knowledge. The dialogic pattern I have found in Malagasy folklore, if not a fraud or a fiction, is the common property of a group. Eminent folklorists have held that the existence of folklore depends entirely upon such group acceptance (Jakobson and Bogatyrev 1971). Against this theoretical background, the study of "artistic communication in small groups" (Ben-Amos 1971) facilitates conceiving the production and reception of written literature and philosophy as taking place also in small groups. It comes as no novelty, to a folklorist or an anthropologist who has devoted much attention to how group acceptance comes into being, to be told by Richard Rorty that "we understand knowledge when we understand the social justification of belief, and thus have no need to view it as accuracy of representation" (1979:170). Indeed, Rorty is nicely describing what Bauman and other folklorists have shown and transposing it onto the discourse of philosophers. Folklorists have much to say in the growing conversation about social constructionist theory in psychology, philosophy, literary criticism, sociology, and education (Bruffee 1986).

What justifies the study of Malagasy folklore? The "elastic unity" of my approach, like the approach of the social anthropologist as described by Rodney Needham, may come largely from what I choose to study and the assemblage of evidence and principles that I find useful, rather than from some prior circumscription of the limits of folkloristics (Needham 1981:14–15). At a moment when anthropology, history, and critical theory all are trying to understand the implications of their own history, folklore too is conceiving and re-conceiving its object of study, its methods, and the relationship between them. To call such re-conceiving the only true theorizing, as some theorists seem to do, is to condemn folklore to perpetual recursion on its own history and method, as if writing the history of its own scientific practice would relieve folklore of its obligations. But the obligations do not go away when we ignore them. As part of a program of research and pedagogy, folklore in Madagascar must justify itself by giving back to an exploited people, in twentieth-century terms, the cultural patrimony which, they believe, was stolen from them in the nineteenth. To acknowledge this obligation is not "missionary optimism" (Bouillon 1981:306–10); after all, no one has to grant any power to Western modes of analysis, and no one has to read a folklore book. At the same time, folklore can demonstrate, as I believe I have demonstrated, that cultural patrimonies are less easily stolen than some Malagasy, or some other exploited people, imagine. The honor awarded to Dahle's collection and other printed texts of Malagasy verbal art are a recognition that enlarging the audience for traditional culture was a good thing. The reports of contemporary ethnographers (Huntington 1987, Beaujard 1983) show the vitality and continuity of a culture that exemplifies Bakhtin's conception: the sum of the "discourses which preserve collective memory—commonplaces and stereotypes as much as exceptional words. Each subject must situate him/herself in relation to these discourses" (Todorov 1981:8).

Notes

Notes to Chapter One

1. Names of ethnic groups in Madagascar are given in the translations by Aidan W. Southall, *Encyclopedia Britannica*, 15th ed. (1985), 21, 168.

2. A comprehensive general account of Madagascar from the point of view of its development needs today is Heseltine 1971. The standard English-language history is Brown 1979, the standard French one Deschamps 1972. The best introductions for the American reader are Kent 1962, 1970, and 1979. For the reader of French, the best introductions are Pierre Vérin, *Madagascar* (Paris: Karthala, 1990), and *Malgache, qui es-tu?*, the collection of essays published by the Musée d'Ethnographie de Neuchâtel (1973). Basic for the French reader are the oral histories of the highland Merina collected by R. P. Callet under the title Histories of the Kings of Madagascar, *Tantara ny Andriana eto Madagascar* (Antananarivo, 1908), referred to in modern Malagasy as *Tantaran'ny Andriana* and translated as *Histoire des Rois* by G.-S. Chapus and E. Ratsimba (Antananarivo, 1974). The precise and deep historical research of contemporary French-speaking scholars today can be sampled in Raison-Jourde 1983 and Delivré 1974.

3. All translations not otherwise identified are mine.

4. Law, indeed, provides corroboration of the continuing vitality of Malagasy tradition. The introduction of written laws, in imitation of Europe, drove out neither oral law nor the power of the royal word. Rather, written law solidified the stratification of society (Domenichini 1973).

5. The great monument of psychologizing the Malagasy was not a work of folklore, but an essay attempting to explain the bloody rebellion of 1947, O. Mannoni's *Psychologie de la colonisation* (translated as *Prospero and Caliban*, 1950). This essay analyzes the dependency on which colonialism rests, while revealing more European than Malagasy psychology. It should be required reading for Westerners journeying to former colonies.

6. The history of Malagasy linguistics is traced by today's leading authority in Dez 1978.

7. With his recognition of cultural diversity, Catat would have made a first-class folklorist. His anti-Merina prejudice made him so sympathetic to the southern tribes that he would have done excellent folklore fieldwork there. His *Voyage à Madagascar* makes crisp reading.

8. Few *malgachisants* dared to question Grandidier's authority. Ferrand's critique was linguistic. A seventeenth-century Dutch traveler named Houtman had produced a word list from his contacts with people around the Bay of Antongil,

in the northeast. According to Ferrand, Houtman faithfully reproduced phonetic habits of the local people, the northern Betsimisaraka. Re-editing his lexicon, Grandidier, who had not the smallest knowledge of Malayo-Polynesian comparative linguistics, "corrected" the lexicon by means of Merina spellings. To a local speaker, Ferrand said, these would be pure barbarisms.

9. To describe themselves, these people have a complex system of not fewer than eight groups, which (like other Malagasy systems of classification) tend to overlap and lack fixed boundaries.

10. The language and people are called Merina (pronounced *mairn'*), their region Imerina (*eemairn'*).

11. Roger D. Abrahams's phrase for West Indian performers aptly translates the Malagasy word.

12. Since *fanorona* used to be forbidden in the rainy season, its eating metaphor contains a distant echo of the Southeast Asian use of eating to mean clearing new ground for cultivation (Condominas 1977).

13. After the account in Callet 1974, dictated in the 1860s, the first detailed description by a foreigner is Montgomery 1886. I cite Alfred Grandidier's *Ethnographie de Madagascar* as quoted in Chauvicourt and Chauvicourt 1972, 1984.

Note to Chapter Two

1. Found in many Betsileo tales, this figure often plays the role of king or chief in traditional society (Michel-Andrianarahinjaka 1986 : 300).

Notes to Chapter Three

1. Examples of folk similes (proverbial comparisons) include Dahle-Sims 1971 : 244, nos. 159–63; Houlder 1960, nos. 886, 1375, 1387, 1393. Clemes 1877 : 428–29.

2. The last two examples are from Fontoynont and Raomandahy 1938 : 207 and 1939 : 32. Previous examples are from Houlder 1960: nos. 169, 409, 807, 1064, 1332, 1397, 1987. Houlder's collection, about twice as numerous as its predecessor (1871) by Cousins and Parrett, had to wait twelve years before Sibree began to serialize it in the *Antananarivo Annual*. By the time it was finally published in book form in 1916, a French translation had to be added. My references are to the 1960 reprint by Imprimerie Luthérienne, a standard folklore book in Madagascar today. Examples of folk similes (proverbial comparisons) include Dahle-Sims 1971 : 244, nos. 159–63; Houlder 1960, nos. 886, 1375, 1387, 1393; Clemes 1877 : 428–29.

3. The saying, *Maimay hivady ka dodona hisaraka*, is no. 1813 in Houlder 1960.

4. Later historians such as Deschamps and Kent, with better evidence, have agreed that the ancestors of the Malagasy lived for a time on the African coast.

5. In former times, the full moon was the occasion for amorous play and wife-swapping, practices welcomed by wives or husbands who were not getting on.

6. Examples not quoted include Houlder 1960: nos. 38, 59, 85, 89, 93, 178, 400, 402, 494; Fontoynont and Raomandahy 1938:206, nos. 39, 45. My favorite example: *Raha asa zama no atao, satriko ny telo-polo lahy an-trano; fa raha ny ama-lom-boasina, tsy manan-kavana afa-tsy ny maty*, When there's hard work to do, I'm glad to have thirty men in the house; but if there's salted eel [to eat], I have no relatives except the dead (Clemes 1877:428).

7. Used for ordeals (Decary 1951:196–202).

8. Other examples include Clemes 1877:428–29.

9. Other examples include Houlder 1960: nos. 544, 560.

10. According to Taylor, "the Priamel . . . enjoyed remarkable literary vogue in Germany during the fifteenth century and a little later. The exact nature of this literary form is difficult to define: it consisted in an accumulation of assertions, usually unrelated in appearance, which are often united at the end by a single remark binding them together in an epigram" (1931:179).

11. Examples of this topic-comment structure include Dahle 1877:40, nos. 7, 12; 42, no. 33; 44, no. 69; 45, no. 87; 47, no. 135; Houlder 1960: nos. 1337, 1348, 1372, 1373, 1381, 1384, 1398, 1475, 1483, 1495, 1501, 1510, 1511, 1518, 1519, 1530–31, 1465, 1487, 1564, 1603, 1634, 1718, 1732, 1740; Clemes 1877:430; Fontoynont and Raomandahy 1939:31, no. 3.

Notes to Chapter Four

1. Malagasy texts throughout are presented verbatim, representing different orthographies, some of which are now regarded as archaic.

2. The final simile gave Paulhan the idea for a monograph that asserted that meals and eating in Imerina were surrounded by the secrecy and shame with which Europeans treat sex (1970).

3. A few texts had been printed earlier, in an English-language periodical that had no circulation in Madagascar (Baker 1832).

4. Spring, the beginning of the year (Razafimino 1924, Molet 1956, Bloch 1989).

Notes to Chapter Five

1. This distinction was also understood in Tikopia, as Firth reported (1975:35).

2. In joyful ceremonies like marriage, circumcision, and *fatidra*, blood brotherhood, where wishes are being fulfilled, odd numbers patterned the scenario. In a funeral, which symbolized the completeness of life on earth, even num-

bers were used. The hair of the deceased was braided in six or eight strands, and he or she was wrapped in two, four, or six mats (Decary 1954).

3. This recitation of genealogy is likely to be a tendentious assertion of a family's title to landholdings by virtue of the family's history. Alliance by marriage will aid a family to reside in a desired territory; appropriate genealogy will justify its title (Delivré 1974:104–6, Randriamandimby 1973). Myth and legend recitations serve the same purpose in other settings.

Notes to Chapter Six

1. I plagiarize Jean Giraudoux.

2. "While other Malagasy peoples were always obliged to shave their heads at the death of a chief, or the supreme sovereign, and to keep them shaven for a year, this tribe has always refused to do so" (Sibree 1924:210 n.).

3. Mondain numbered them separately; I number them consecutively for clarity.

4. The manuscript reads *omaly*, yesterday, probably a copyist's error for *omby*, ox (Mondain 1908:106).

5. Ethnolinguistics, in the United States, would probably be practiced under the name of folklore.

Sources Consulted

Aarne, Antti, and Stith Thompson. *The Types of the Folktale*. 2nd rev. FF Communications no. 1984. Helsinki: Suomalainen Tiedeakatemia, 1961.

Abinal, R. P., and Victorin Malzac. *Dictionnaire français-malgache*. Tananarive, 1888.

———. *Dictionnaire malgache-français*. 1893. Reprint. Paris: Éditions Maritimes et d'Outre-Mer, 1963.

Abrahams, Roger D., with George Foss. *Anglo-American Folksong Style*. Englewood Cliffs, N.J.: Prentice-Hall, 1967.

———. *Between the Living and the Dead*. FF Communications no. 225. Helsinki: Suomalainen Tiedeakatemia, 1980.

———. *Deep Down in the Jungle . . . Negro Narrative Folklore from the Streets of Philadelphia*. Chicago: Aldine, 1970.

———. "Introductory Remarks to a Rhetorical Theory of Folklore." *Journal of American Folklore* 81 (1968): 143–58.

———. "The Literary Study of the Riddle." *Texas Studies in Literature and Language* 14 (1972): 177–97.

———. *The Man-of-Words in the West Indies*. Baltimore: Johns Hopkins University Press, 1983.

———. "Proverbs and Proverbial Expressions." In *Folklore and Folklife*, edited by Richard M. Dorson, pp. 117–27. Chicago: University of Chicago Press, 1972.

Abrahams, Roger D., and Alan Dundes. "Riddles." In *Folklore and Folklife*, edited by Richard M. Dorson, pp. 129–43. Chicago: University of Chicago Press, 1972.

Abrahamsson, H. *The Origin of Death: Studies in African Mythology*. Uppsala: Alqvist and Wiksell, 1951.

Ailloud, P. *Grammaire malgache-hova*. Tananarive, 1873.

Albert, Ethel M. "Culture Patterning of Speech Behavior in Burundi." In *Directions in Sociolinguistics*, edited by John J. Gumperz and Dell Hymes, pp. 72–105. New York: Holt, Rinehart and Winston, 1972.

Aly, Jacques M. "Etude ethno-linguistique de quelques dialectes malgaches." Dissertation, University of Paris VII, 1977.

Andriamanjato, Richard. *Le tsiny et le tody dans la pensée malgache*. Paris: Collection Présence Africaine, 1957.

Andriantsilaniarivo, E. "La langue malgache." *Madagascar*, special number of *Cahiers Charles de Foucauld*, 5th ser., 20 (1950): 211–22.

———. "Le théâtre malgache." *Revue de Madagascar* n.s. 1 (April–July 1947): 3–13.

Andriantsilaniarivo, E., and Elie-Charles Abraham. "La littérature malgache." *Revue de Madagascar* (July 1946): 16–25.

Archer, Robert. *Madagascar depuis 1972: la marche d'une revolution*. Paris: L'Harmattan, 1976.

Aristotle. *Poetics*. Translated by Gerald F. Else. Ann Arbor: University of Michigan Press, 1970.

Asad, Talal. *Anthropology and the Colonial Encounter*. London: Ithaca Press, 1973.

Austerlitz, Robert. *Ob-Ugric Metrics*. FF Communications no. 174. Helsinki: Academia Scientarum Fennica, 1958.

Ayache, Simon. "Beyond Oral Tradition and into Written History: The Work of Raombana (1809–1855)." In *Madagascar in History*, edited by Raymond K. Kent, pp. 197–227. Albany, Calif.: Foundation for Malagasy Studies, 1979.

Bagby, Philip. "Culture and the Causes of Culture." *American Anthropologist* 55 (1953): 535–54.

Baker, Edward. "On the Poetry of Madagascar." *Antananarivo Annual* 3, part 2, 1886: 167–77. Reprinted from *Journal of the Bengal Asiatic Society* (1832): 86–96.

Bakhtin, M. M. *The Dialogic Imagination*. Translated by Caryl Emerson and Michael Holquist. Austin: University of Texas Press, 1981.

———. *Problems of Dostoevsky's Poetics*. Translated by Caryl Emerson. Minneapolis: University of Minnesota Press, 1984.

———. *Rabelais and His World*. Translated by Hélène Iswolsky. Cambridge, Mass.: MIT Press, 1968.

Barakat, Robert A. *A Contextual Study of Arabic Proverbs*. FF Communications no. 226. Helsinki: Suomalainen Tiedeakatemia, 1980.

Barley, Nigel F. "Structural Aspects of the Anglo-Saxon Riddle." *Semiotica* 10 (1974): 143–75.

Barth, Fredrik, ed. *Ethnic Groups and Boundaries: The Social Organization of Culture Difference*. Boston: Little, Brown, 1969.

Bascom, William. *African Dilemma Tales*. The Hague: Mouton, 1975.

———. "Folklore Research in Africa." *Journal of American Folklore* 77 (1964): 12–31.

———. "Four Functions of Folklore" (1954). In *The Study of Folklore*, edited by Alan Dundes, pp. 279–98. Englewood Cliffs, N.J.: Prentice-Hall, 1965.

Bauman, Richard. "Conceptions of Folklore in the Development of Literary Semiotics." *Semiotica* 39, nos. 1–2 (1982): 1–20.

———. *Verbal Art as Performance*. Prospect Heights, Ill.: Waveland Press, 1977.

Beaujard, Philippe. *Princes et paysans: les tanala de l'Ikongo. Un espace social du sud-est de Madagascar*. Paris: L'Harmattan, 1983.

Ben-Amos, Dan. "Toward a Definition of Folklore in Context." *Journal of American Folklore* 84 (1971): 3–15.

Ben-Porat, Zvi. "The Poetics of Literary Allusion." *PTL* 1 (1976): 105–28.

Bernabé, Jean. "Contribution à une approche glottocritique de l'espace littéraire antillais." *La Linguistique* 18, no. 1 (1982): 85–109.

Bersani, Jacques, ed. *Jean Paulhan le souterrain*. Paris: Union General d'Editions, 1976.

Berthier, Hugues. *Notes et impressions sur les moeurs et coutumes du peuple malgache.* Tananarive: Imprimerie Officielle, 1933.

Bickerton, Derek. "The Nature of a Creole Continuum." *Language* 49 (1973): 640–69.

Birkeli, Emile. "Folklore sakalava recueilli dans la région de Morondava." *Bulletin de l'Académie Malgache*, n.s. 6 (1922–23): 185–423.

Blacking, John. "The Social Value of Venda Riddles." *African Studies* 20 (1961): 1–32.

Bloch, Maurice. "Decision-Making in Councils Among the Merina." In *Councils in Action*, edited by Audrey Richards and Adam Kuper. Cambridge Papers in Social Anthropology. Cambridge: Cambridge University Press, 1971.

———. "Marriage Among Equals: An Analysis of the Marriage Ceremony of the Merina of Madagascar." *Man*, n.s. 13 (1978): 21–33. Reprinted in *Ritual, History and Power: Selected Papers in Anthropology*, pp. 89–105. London: Athlone Press, 1989.

———. *Placing the Dead: Tombs, Ancestral Villages, and Kinship Organization in Madagascar*. London: Seminar Press, 1971.

———. "The Ritual of the Royal Bath in Madagascar: The Dissolution of Death, Birth and Fertility into Authority." In *Ritual, History and Power: Selected Papers in Anthropology*, pp. 187–211. London: Athlone Press, 1989.

Bloom, Harold. "Poetry, Revisionism, Repression." In *Critical Theory Since 1965*, edited by Hazard Adams and Leroy Searle, pp. 330–43. Tallahassee: Florida State University Press, 1986.

Bødker, Laurits, et al. *The Nordic Riddle: Terminology and Bibliography*. Copenhagen: Rosenkilde and Bagger, 1964.

Boudou, Adrien. *Les jésuites à Madagascar au XIXe siècle*. 2 vols. Paris: G. Beauchesne, 1940.

Boudry, Robert. *Jean-Joseph Rabearivelo et la mort*. Paris: Présence Africaine, 1958.

Bouillon, Antoine. *Madagascar, le colonisé et son "âme."* Paris: L'Harmattan, 1981.

Bronner, Simon J. *American Folklore Studies: An Intellectual History*. Lawrence: University Press of Kansas, 1986.

Brown, Mervyn. *Madagascar Rediscovered*. Hamden, Conn.: Archon Books, 1979.

Bruffee, Kenneth A. "Social Construction, Language, and the Authority of Knowledge: A Bibliographical Essay." *College English* 48, 8 (December 1986): 773–90.

Bruniquel, Adolphe. "Les Ohabolana." *Cahiers Charles de Foucauld*, fifth series, no. 20, pp. 223–44. Paris, 1951.

Brunvand, Jan Harold. *The Study of American Folklore, an Introduction*. 3d ed. New York: Norton, 1986.

———. *The Vanishing Hitchhiker: American Urban Legends and Their Meanings*. New York: Norton, 1981.

Burke, Kenneth. *A Grammar of Motives*. New York: Prentice-Hall, 1945.

———. *The Philosophy of Literary Form*. New York: Vintage Books, 1957.

Cahiers Jean Paulhan, 1: Correspondance Jean Paulhan-Guillaume de Tarde. Paris: Gallimard, 1980.

Cahiers Jean Paulhan, 2: Jean Paulhan et Madagascar, 1908–1910. Paris: Gallimard, 1982.

Cailliet, Emile. *Essai sur la psychologie du hova*. Paris: Presses Universitaires de France, 1926.

Calame-Griaule, Geneviève. "L'art de la parole dans la culture africaine." *Présence Africaine* 47 (1963): 73–91.

———. *Words and the Dogon World*. Translation of *Ethnologie et langage* (1965) by Deirdre LaPin. Philadelphia: Institute for the Study of Human Issues, 1986.

Callet, R. P. *Tantara ny Andriana eto Madagascar*. Tananarive, 1908. Translated from reedition, *Tantaran'ny Andriana*, as *Histoire des rois* by G.-S. Chapus and E. Ratsimba. 4 vols. Antananarivo: Académie Malgache, 1953–58; reprint, Librairie de Madagascar, 1974.

Calvet, L.-J. *Langue, corps, société*. Paris: Payot, 1979.

———. *Linguistique et colonialisme*. Paris: Payot, 1974.

Catat, Docteur Louis. *Voyage à Madagascar*. Paris: Librairie Hachette, 1895.

Caussèque, R. P. Pierre. *Grammaire malgache*. Antananarivo: Imprimerie Catholique, 1886.

Chapus, G.-S. "Quatre-vingts années d'influence européenne en Imerina." *Bulletin de l'Académie Malgache*, n.s. 8 (1925):1–351.

Chapus, G.-S., and Mme. Dandouau. "Un chapitre de Hain-teny (Traductions)." *Bulletin de l'Académie Malgache*, n.s. 23 (1940): 89–122.

Chapus, G.-S., and Razanajohary. "Le sens de l'humour dans les proverbes malgaches." *Bulletin de l'Académie Malgache*, n.s. 29 (1949–50), 7–13.

Chauvicourt, J., and S. Chauvicourt. *Le fanorona, jeu national malgache*. Antananarivo: Imprimerie Centrale, 1972. Edited and translated by Leonard Fox as *Fanorona, the National Game of Madagascar*. Charleston, S.C.: International Fanorona Association, 1984.

Chomsky, Noam. *Aspects of the Theory of Syntax*. Cambridge, Mass.: MIT Press, 1965.

Clark, Henry E. "The Ancient Idolatry of the Hova." *Antananarivo Annual* 11 (1885): 78–82.

Clemes, S. "Malagasy Proverbs." *Antananarivo Annual* 3 (1877): 431.

Clifford, James. *The Predicament of Culture: Twentieth-Century Ethnography, Literature, and Art*. Cambridge, Mass.: Harvard University Press, 1988.

Clifford, James, and George E. Marcus, ed. *Writing Culture: The Poetics and Politics of Ethnography*. Berkeley: University of California Press, 1986.

Colançon, M. M. See Rasamuel 1928.

Coleridge, Samuel Taylor. *Selected Poetry and Prose*. New York: Modern Library, 1951.

Condominas, Georges. *L'Espace social à propos de l'Asie du sud-ouest*. Paris: Flammarion, 1980.

———. *We Have Eaten the Forest*. New York: Hill and Wang, 1977. Translation of *Nous avons mangé la forêt de la pierre-génie Gôo*. Paris: Mercure de France, 1957.

Cotte, P. Vincent. *Regardons vivre une tribu malgache, les Betsimisaraka*. Paris: La Nouvelle Edition, 1946.

Cousins, George. *Gramara Malagasy*. Antananarivo: London Missionary Society Press, 1882.

Cousins, William E. "The Ancient Theism of the Hova." *Antananarivo Annual*, vol. 1 (1875).

———. *A Concise Introduction to the Study of the Malagasy Language*. Antananarivo: London Missionary Society Press, 1873; 2nd ed., in J. Richardson, *A New Malagasy-English Dictionary*. Antananarivo: London Missionary Society Press, 1885, xi–lix. Unacknowledged reprint as G. W. Parker, *Concise Grammar of the Malagasy Language*. London: Trübner and Co., 1883.

———. *Madagascar of Today: A Sketch of the Island, with Chapters on Its Past History and Present Prospects*. London: Religious Tract Society, 1895.

Cousins, William E., and John Parrett. *Ny ohabolan'ny ntaolo (proverbes des anciens)*. 1877, 1885. Reprint, Tananarive: Trano Printy Loterana, 1939, 1963.

Crowley, Daniel J. "Plural and Differential Acculturation in Trinidad." *American Anthropologist* 59 (1957): 817–24.

Culler, Jonathan. *On Deconstruction: Theory and Criticism After Structuralism*. Ithaca: Cornell University Press, 1982.

Dahle, Lars. *Anganon'ny Ntaolo. Tantara mampiseho ny fomban-drazana sy ni finoana sasany nananany*. Edited by John Sims. Antananarivo: Trano Printy Loterana, 1971.

———. *Specimens of Malagasy Folk-lore*. Antananarivo: A. Kingdon, 1877.

Dalmond, Abbé. *Vocabulaire et grammaire pour les langues malgaches sakalava et betsimisaraka*. St. Denis, La Réunion, 1842.

Dama-Ntsoha. *La Bouddhisme malgache ou la civilisation malgache*. Tananarive: Imprimerie Antananarivo, 1938.

———. *La Langue malgache et les origines malgaches*. Tananarive, 1928.

———. *La Technique de la conception de la vie chez les malgaches révélée par leurs proverbes*. Tananarive: Masoandro, 1953.

Dandouau, André. "Chansons tsimihety." *Bulletin de l'Académie Malgache* 11 (1913): 49–149.

———. *Contes populaires des sakalava et des tsimihety de la région d'Analalava*. Publications de la Faculté des Lettres d'Alger; Bulletin de Correspondance Africaine, 58. Alger: Jules Carbonel, 1922.

Decary, Raymond. "Animaux et plantes de légende." *Revue de Madagascar* 20 (1954): 14–21.

———. *La divination malgache par le sikidy*. Paris: Librairie Orientaliste Paul Geuthner, 1970.

———. "Un jeu d'échecs tanala." *Bulletin de Madagascar* 9 (1959): 639–40.

———. *Moeurs et coutumes des malgaches*. Paris: Payot, 1951.

———. "Notes ethnographiques sur les populations du district de Maromandia (sakalava et tsimihety)." *Revue d'Ethnographie et des Traditions Populaires* 5 (1924): 343–67.

Decary, Raymond, and R. Castel. *Modalités et conséquences des migrations intérieures récentes des populations malgaches*. Tananarive, 1941.

Delivré, Alain. *L'histoire des rois d'Imerina*. Paris: Klincksieck, 1974.

———. "Oral Tradition and Historical Consciousness: The case of Imerina." Translated by Raymond K. Kent. In *Madagascar in History: Essays from the 1970's*, edited by Raymond K. Kent, pp. 123–44. Albany, Calif.: The Foundation for Malagasy Studies, 1979.

Derrida, Jacques. *Of Grammatology*. Translated by Gayatri Chakravorty Spivak. Baltimore: Johns Hopkins University Press, 1976.

Deschamps, Hubert. "Les Antaifasy. Origines, guerres avec les tribus voisines. Proverbes." *Bulletin de l'Académie Malgache*, n.s. 22 (1939): 1–40.

———. "Folklore antaisaka." *Bulletin de l'Académie Malgache*, n.s. 22 (1939), 113–29.

———. *Histoire de Madagascar*. 4th ed. Paris: Berger-Levrault, 1972.

Dez, Jacques. "A propos de quelques cas de synonymie en merina." *Bulletin de Madagascar* 283 (1969): 993–99.

———. "Le malgache." *Inventaire des études linguistiques sur les pays d'Afrique noire d'expression française et sur Madagascar*. Paris: CILF, 1978.

———. "Portée des pratiques ostentatoires." *Annales de l'Université de Madagascar*. Sér. Lettres et Sciences Humaines, 11 (1973): 93–114.

Domenichini, Jean-Pierre. "Regard sur la civilisation malgache." In *Malgache, qui es-tu?*, pp. 24–37. Neuchâtel: Musée d'Ethnographie, 1973.

———. "Une tradition orale: l'histoire de Ranoro." *ASEMI* 8, nos. 3–4 (1977): 99–150.

Domenichini-Ramiaramanana, Bakoly. *Du ohabolana au hainteny: langue, littérature, et politique à Madagascar*. Paris: Karthala, 1983.

———. *Hainteny d'autrefois, Haintenin'ny fahiny*. Tananarive: Librairie Mixte, 1968.

———. *Le malgache, essai de description sommaire*. Langues et civilisations de l'Asie du sud-est, de l'Océan Indien et de la Réunion. Paris: SELAF, 1977.

———. *Ohabolan' ny Ntaolo. Exemples et proverbes des anciens*. Mémoires de l'Académie Malgache, fasc. 44. Tananarive: Imprimerie Nationale, 1970.

———. "Première expérience de la littérature orale merina." *ASEMI* 5, no. 4 (1974): 31–66.

———. "Les traductions poétiques des hainteny." *Colloque sur la traduction poétique*, edited by Etiemble, pp. 107–50. Paris: Gallimard: 1978.

Dorson, Richard M. Foreword to *Folktales of Ireland*, by Sean O'Sullivan, pp. v–xxxix. Chicago: University of Chicago Press, 1966.

Dorst, John D. "Neck-riddle as a Dialogue of Genres: Applying Bakhtin's Genre Theory." *Journal of American Folklore* 96 (1983): 413–33.

Dournes, Jacques. *Le parler des jorai et le style oral de leur expression*. Paris: Publications Orientalistes de France, 1976.

Drury, Robert. *Madagascar, or Robert Drury's Journal during Fifteen Years of Captivity on that Island*. London, 1729.

DuBois, Ellen Carol. "Historians of Resistance." *The Nation*, February 25, 1984, pp. 228–30.

Dubois, Henri. *Monographie des Betsileo*. Paris: Institut d'Ethnographie, 1938.

Dundes, Alan. *Interpreting Folklore*. Bloomington: Indiana University Press, 1980.

————. "Metafolklore and Oral Literary Criticism." *Monist* 50 (October 1966): 505–16.

————. *The Morphology of North American Indian Folktales*. FF Communications no. 195. Helsinki: Suomalainen Tiedeakatemia, 1964.

————. "On the Structure of the Proverb." In Alan Dundes, *Analytic Essays in Folklore*, pp. 103–18. The Hague: Mouton, 1975.

————, ed. *The Study of Folklore*. Englewood Cliffs, N.J.: Prentice-Hall, 1965.

Dundes, Alan, Jerry W. Leach, and Bora Özkök. "The Strategy of Turkish Boys' Verbal Dueling Rhymes." In *Directions in Sociolinguistics*, edited by John J. Gumperz and Dell Hymes, pp. 130–60. New York: Holt, Rinehart and Winston, 1972.

du Picq, Ardant. "Le Samantsy, jeu d'echecs des tanala de l'Ikongo." *Bulletin de l'Académie Malgache* 10 (1912): 267–68.

Ellis, Bill. "De Legendis Urbis: Modern Legends in Ancient Rome." *Journal of American Folklore* 96 (1983): 200–208.

Emeneau, Murray B. "Oral Poets of South India—the Todas." In *Language in Culture and Society: A Reader in Linguistics and Anthropology*, edited by Dell Hymes, pp. 330–41. New York: Harper and Row, 1964.

Esoavelomandroso, Manassé. "Religion et politique: l'évangelisation du pays betsimisaraka à la fin du XIXème siècle." *Omaly sy Anio* 7–8 (1978): 7–42.

Faublée, Jacques. "Démographie de Madagascar." *Journal de la Société des Africanistes* 13 (1943): 209–10.

————. *L'Ethnographie de Madagascar*. Paris: Ed. de France et d'Outre-Mer, 1946.

————. "Haïnteny merina et pantun malais." *Cahiers Jean Paulhan 2: Jean Paulhan et Madagascar, 1908–1910*, pp. 397–408. Paris: Gallimard, 1982.

————. "Jean Paulhan malgachisant." *Journal de la Société des Africanistes* 50 (1970): 151–59.

————. *Récits Bara*. Paris: Institut d'Ethnologie, 1947.

Feeley-Harnik, Gillian. "Divine kingship and the meaning of history among the Sakalava (Madagascar)." *Man*, n.s. 13 (1978): 402–17.

————. "Issues in Divine Kingship." *Annual Review of Anthropology* 14 (1985): 273–313.

Ferrand, Gabriel. *Contes populaires malgaches*. Paris: Ernest Leroux, 1893.

————. *Essai de phonétique comparée du malais et des dialectes malgaches*. Paris: Geuthner, 1909.

————. "Note sur les *hain-teni* merina." *Journal Asiatique*, 11th ser. (1914): 151–57.

Fine, Elizabeth C. *The Folklore Text, from Performance to Print*. Bloomington: Indiana University Press, 1984.

Finnegan, Ruth. *Oral Literature in Africa*. Oxford: Oxford University Press, 1970.

Firth, Raymond. "Speech-making and Authority in Tikopia." In *Political Language and Oratory in Traditional Societies*, edited by Maurice Bloch, pp. 29–43. London: Academic Press, 1975.

Fischer, J. L. "Meter in Eastern Carolinian Oral Literature." *Journal of American Folklore* 72 (1959): 47–52.

Fish, Stanley E. *Is There a Text in This Class? The Authority of Interpretive Communities.* Cambridge, Mass.: Harvard University Press, 1980.

Flacourt, [Sieur] Etienne de. *Histoire de la Grande Isle de Madagascar.* Paris: Gervais Clouzier, 1658, 1661.

Foley, John Miles. "The Oral Theory in Context." *Oral Traditional Literature, a Festschrift for Albert Bates Lord*, pp. 27–122. Columbus, Ohio: Slavica Publishers, 1980.

———. *The Theory of Oral Composition, History and Methodology.* Bloomington: Indiana University Press, 1988.

Fontoynont, Dr. Maurice. "Une demande en mariage au temps passé." *Revue de Madagascar* 30 (July 1941): 77–82.

Fontoynont, Dr. Maurice, and Raomandahy. "Les Antaifasy: origines, guerres avec les tribus voisines, proverbes." *Bulletin de l'Academie Malgache*, n.s. 22 (1939): 1–40.

———. "Proverbes du Vakinankaratra." *Bulletin de l'Académie Malgache*, n.s. 21 (1938): 201–21.

Fox, Leonard, ed. and trans. *Hainteny, the Traditional Poetry of Madagascar.* Lewisburg, Pa.: Bucknell University Press, 1990.

Freeman, J. J., and David Johns. *English-Malagasy Dictionary* and *Malagasy-English Dictionary.* Antananarivo: London Missionary Society Press, 1835.

Gaignebet, Claude. "Le chauve au col roulé." *Poétique* 8 (1971): 444.

———. "L'Homme qui'a vu l'homme, qui'a vu l'homme, qui'a vu. . . . " *Poétique* 45 (1981): 1–8.

Gaster, Theodor H. *Thespis: Ritual, Myth, and Drama in the Ancient Near East.* New York: Doubleday, 1950.

Gauvin, Axel. *Du Créole opprimé au créole libéré.* Paris: L'Harmattan, 1977.

Geertz, Clifford. "Deep Play: Notes on the Balinese Cockfight." *Daedalus* 101 (1972): 1–38, reprinted in Clifford Geertz, *The Interpretation of Cultures*, pp. 412–453. New York: Basic Books, 1975.

———. *Local Knowledge: Further Essays in Interpretive Anthropology.* New York: Basic Books, 1983.

Genette, Gérard. *Palimpsestes: la littérature au second degré.* Paris: Editions du Seuil, 1982.

Georges, Robert A., and Alan Dundes. "Toward a Structural Definition of the Riddle." *Journal of American Folklore* 76 (1963): 111–18.

Gerbinis, Ernest. *La langue malgache.* Paris: Chassany, 1949.

Gerbinis, L. *La langue malgache, enseignée suivant la méthode directe.* Tananarive: Imprimerie Officielle, 1946.

Glassie, Henry. *Passing the Time in Ballymenone: Culture and History of an Ulster Community.* Philadelphia: University of Pennsylvania Press, 1982.

Glazier, Jack, and Phyllis Gorfain Glazier. "Ambiguity and Exchange: The Double Dimension of Mbeere Riddles." *Journal of American Folklore* 89 (1976): 189–238.

Goffman, Erving. *Frame Analysis.* New York: Harper and Row, 1974.

Gombrich, E. H. *The Sense of Order, A Study in the Psychology of Decorative Art.* London: Phaidon, 1979.

Goodman, Paul. *The Structure of Literature.* Chicago: University of Chicago Press, 1954.

———. *Utopian Essays and Practical Proposals.* New York: Random House, 1962.

Goody, Jack, ed. *Literacy in Traditional Society.* Cambridge: Cambridge University Press, 1968.

Gow, Bonar A. *Madagascar and the Protestant Impact.* London: Longman, 1979.

Gowlett, D. F. "Some Lozi Riddles and Tongue-Twisters Annotated and Analysed." *African Studies* 25, 3 (1966): 139–58.

Grandidier, Alfred. *Ethnographie de Madagascar.* Vol. 4 of *Histoire physique, naturelle, et politique de Madagascar.* Paris: 1908.

———. "Note sur les vazimba de Madagascar." *Mémoires publiés par la Société Philomathique à l'occasion du centenaire de sa fondation, 1788–1888,* pp. 155–161. Paris, 1888.

Grandidier, Alfred, and Guillaume Grandidier, eds. *Collection des ouvrages anciens concernant Madagascar.* 9 vols. Paris, 1903–20.

Grandidier, Guillaume. *Bibliographie de Madagascar.* 3 vols. Paris and Tananarive, 1905–57.

Granet, Marcel. *Fêtes et chansons populaires de la Chine.* 2d ed. Paris: E. Leroux, 1929.

Gratiant, Gilbert. "La place du 'Créole' dans l'expression antillaise." *Présence Africaine,* n.s. 14–15 (June–September 1957): 252–55.

Gray, Hanna Holborn. "Renaissance Humanism: The Pursuit of Eloquence." *Journal of the History of Ideas* (1967): 497–514.

Gray, Thomas. Letter to Richard West (1742), quoted in "Poetic Diction" by Bernard Groom. In *Princeton Encyclopedia of Poetry and Poetics,* edited by Alex Preminger. Princeton: Princeton University Press, 1965.

Griaule, Marcel. *Conversations with Ogotemmêli: An Introduction to Dogon Religious Ideas.* Translation of *Dieu d'eau* (1948). Oxford: Oxford University Press, 1965.

Gueunier, Noel J. "Chansons populaires rija des betsileo." *ASEMI* 4, no. 4 (1973): 135–67.

———. "La tradition du conte de langue malgache à Mayotte (Comores)." Dissertation, University of Paris VII, 1985. Abstract in *Cahiers de Littérature Orale* 20 (1986): 205–12.

Gunson, Niel. *Messengers of Grace: Evangelical Missionaries in the South Seas, 1797–1860.* Oxford: Oxford University Press, 1978.

Haas, Mary R. "Thai Word-Games." *Journal of American Folklore* 70 (1957): 173–75. Reprinted in *Language in Culture and Society: A Reader in Linguistics and Anthropology,* edited by Dell Hymes, pp. 301–4. New York: Harper and Row, 1964.

Hamnett, Ian. "Ambiguity, Classification and Change: The Function of Riddles." *Man,* n.s. 2 (1967): 379–91.

Haring, Lee. "The Classification of Malagasy Narrative." *Research in African Literatures* 11, 3 (Fall 1980): 342–55.

———. "The Folklore Component in Malagasy History." In *Madagascar in History: Essays from the 1970's*, edited by Raymond K. Kent, pp. 148–67. New York: Holt, Rinehart and Winston, 1970.

———. "Folklore and the History of Literature in Madagascar." *Research in African Literatures* 16, 3 (Fall 1985): 297–315.

———. "Interperfomance." *Fabula* 29, nos. 3/4 (1988): 365–72.

———. *Malagasy Tale Index*. FF Communications no. 231. Helsinki: Suomalainen Tiedeakatemia, 1982.

———. "On Knowing the Answer." *Journal of American Folklore* 87 (1974): 197–207.

———. "Performing for the Interviewer." *Southern Folklore Quarterly* 1972, 383–98.

———. Review of *Du Ohabolana au Hainteny*, by Bakoly Domenichini-Ramiaramanana (Paris, 1983). *Research in African Literatures* 16 (Fall 1985): 415–20.

Harries, Lyndon. "The Riddle in Africa." *Journal of American Folklore* 84 (1971), 377–93.

Harris, Marvin. *The Rise of Anthropological Theory*. New York: Thomas Y. Crowell, 1968.

Harrison, Jane Ellen. *Themis, A Study of the Social Origins of Greek Religion*. Cambridge: Cambridge University Press, 1912.

Hébert, J.-C. "Filan'ampela, ou propos galants des sakalava." *Journal de la Société des Africanistes* 34 (1964): 227–53.

Herzfeld, Michael. *Anthropology through the Looking Glass: Critical Ethnography in the Margins of Europe*. Cambridge: Cambridge University Press, 1987.

———. *Ours Once More: Folklore, Ideology, and the Making of Modern Greece*. Austin: University of Texas Press, 1982.

Heseltine, Nigel. *Madagascar*. New York: Praeger, 1971.

Houlder, J. A. "Proverbial Illustrations of Malagasy Life and Character." *Antananarivo Annual* 10 (1884): 86–99.

———. *Ohabolana, ou proverbes malgaches*. Trans. H. Noyer. Antananarivo: Imprimerie Luthérienne, 1960.

Howell, P. P. *A Manual of Nuer Law*. London: Oxford University Press for International African Institute, 1954.

Huizinga, Johan. *Homo Ludens*. Boston: Beacon Press, 1955.

Huntington, Richard. *Gender and Social Structure in Madagascar*. Bloomington: Indiana University Press, 1987.

Hyman, Stanley Edgar. *The Promised End*. Cleveland: World Publishing Company, 1963.

Hymes, Dell. "Directions in (Ethno-)Linguistic Theory." *American Anthropologist* 66 (1964): pt. 2, pp. 6–56.

———. "Folklore's Nature and the Sun's Myth." *Journal of American Folklore* 88 (1975): 345–69.

———. *Foundations in Sociolinguistics, an Ethnographic Approach*. Philadelphia: University of Pennsylvania Press, 1974.

———. *"In Vain I Tried to Tell You": Essays in Native American Ethnopoetics.* Philadelphia: University of Pennsylvania Press, 1981.

———. *Language in Education: Ethnolinguistic Essays.* Washington, D.C.: Center for Applied Linguistics, 1980.

———. "Models of the Interaction of Language and Social Life." In *Directions in Sociolinguistics: The Ethnography of Communication*, edited by John J. Gumperz and Dell Hymes, pp. 35–71. New York: Holt, Rinehart and Winston, 1972.

———. "Two Types of Linguistic Relativity." *Sociolinguistics*, edited by William Bright, pp. 114–58. The Hague: Mouton, 1966.

———, ed. *Pidginization and Creolization of Languages.* Cambridge: Cambridge University Press, 1971.

Jacobs, Melville. *Pattern in Cultural Anthropology.* Homewood, Ill.: Dorsey Press, 1964.

Jakobson, Roman, and Bogatyrev, Petr. "On the Boundary between Studies of Folklore and Literature." Translated by Herbert Eagle. In *Readings in Russian Poetics*, edited by Ladislav Matejka and Krystyna Pomorska, pp. 91–93. Cambridge, Mass.: MIT Press, 1971.

Jameson, Frederic. *The Political Unconscious.* Ithaca: Cornell University Press, 1981.

Jolles, André. *Formes simples.* French translation of *Einfache Formen* (1930) by Antoine Marie Buguet. Paris: Seuil, 1972.

Julien, Gustave. "Langage cérémonial chez les malgaches (procédés de tabouisation des mots réservés pour parler des chefs et des rois)." *L'Anthropologie* 36 (1926): 312–14.

———. "Pages arabico-madécasses." *Annales de l'Académie des Sciences Coloniales* (1929): 1–123; (1933): 57–83.

Julien, G. H. *Ibatoala, ou l'honneur de la brousse.* Paris: Emile Larose, 1923.

Jully, Antony. *Manuel des dialectes malgaches, comprenant sept dialectes . . . .* Paris: J. André, 1901.

Kaivola-Bregenhøj, Annikki. *The Nominatus Absolutus Formula, One Syntactic-Semantic Structural Scheme of the Finnish Riddle Genre.* FF Communications no. 222. Helsinki: Suomalainen Tiedeakatemia, 1978.

Keenan, Edward Louis, and Elinor Ochs. "Becoming a Competent Speaker of Malagasy." In *Languages and Their Speakers*, edited by Timothy Shopen, pp. 113–58. Cambridge, Mass.: Winthrop Publishers, 1979.

Keenan, Elinor Ochs. "Norm-Makers, Norm-Breakers: Uses of Speech by Men and Women in a Malagasy Community." In *Explorations in the Ethnography of Speaking*, edited by Richard Bauman and Joel Sherzer, pp. 125–43. New York: Cambridge University Press, 1974.

———. "A Sliding Sense of Obligatoriness: The Polystructure of Malagasy Oratory." *Language in Society* 2 (1973): 225–43. Reprinted in *Political Language and Oratory in Traditional Society*, edited by Maurice Bloch, pp. 93–112. London: Academic Press, 1975.

Kent, Raymond K. *Early Kingdoms in Madagascar, 1500–1700.* New York: Holt, Rinehart and Winston, 1970.

————. *From Madagascar to the Malagasy Republic*. New York: Praeger, 1962.

————, ed. *Madagascar in History: Essays from the 1970's*. Albany, Calif.: Foundation for Malagasy Studies, 1979.

Knappert, Jan. *Four Centuries of Swahili Verse, a Literary History and Anthology*. London: Heinemann, 1979.

Kodály, Zoltán. *The Selected Writings of Zoltán Kodály*. Budapest: Corvina, 1974.

Köngäs Maranda, Elli. "The Logic of Riddles." In *Structural Analysis of Oral Tradition*, edited with Pierre Maranda, pp. 189–232. Philadelphia: University of Pennsylvania Press, 1971.

————. "'A Tree Grows': Transformations of a Riddle Metaphor." In *Structural Models in Folklore and Transformational Essays*, with Pierre Maranda, pp. 116–139. The Hague: Mouton, 1971.

Koshland, Miriam. "The Poetry of Madagascar." *Africa South* (Cape Town), March 1960, pp. 114–19.

Kottak, Conrad P. *The Past in the Present: History, Ecology, and Cultural Variation in Highland Madagascar*. Ann Arbor: University of Michigan Press, 1980.

————. "The Process of State Formation in Madagascar." *American Ethnologist* 4, 1 (February 1977): 136–55.

Krappe, Alexander H. *The Science of Folklore*. 1930. Reprint: New York: Norton, 1964.

Krohn, Kaarle. *Folklore Methodology*. [*Die folkloristische Arbeitsmethode*, 1926]. Translated by Roger L. Welsch. Austin: University of Texas Press, 1971.

Kuhn, Thomas. *The Structure of Scientific Revolutions*. 2d ed. Chicago: University of Chicago Press, 1970.

Kuusi, Matti. *Ovambo Proverbs, with African Parallels*. FF Communications no. 208. Helsinki: Suomalainen Tiedeakatemia, 1970.

————. *Ovambo Riddles, with Comments and Vocabularies*. FF Communications no. 215. Helsinki: Suomalainen Tiedeakatemia, 1974.

————. *Towards an International Type-System of Proverbs*. FF Communications no. 211. Helsinki: Suomalainen Tiedeakatemia, 1972.

Labov, William. *Sociolinguistic Patterns*. Philadelphia: University of Pennsylvania Press, 1972.

Lanting, Frans. *A World Out of Time: Madagascar*. New York: Aperture, 1990.

Last, J. T. "Salutations and Other Customs Among the Malagasy, Chiefly the South-Western Tribes." *Antananarivo Annual* 23 (1889): 322.

Leaf, Murray J. *Man, Mind, and Science: A History of Anthropology*. New York: Columbia University Press, 1979.

Leblond, Marius-Ary. *La grande île de Madagascar*. 2d ed. Paris: Éditions de Flore, 1946.

Leenhardt, Maurice. *Do Kamo*. Paris: Gallimard, 1947.

Le Garreres, Roger, and Flavien Ranaivo. "Terre, langue et âme malgaches." *Revue de Madagascar*, n.s. 5 (April 1949): 75–91.

Lévi-Strauss, Claude. *The Naked Man. Introduction to a Science of Mythology, vol. 4*. Translated by John Weightman and Doreen Weightman. New York: Harper and Row, 1981.

————. *Structural Anthropology*. Garden City: Doubleday, 1967.

Lieber, Michael D. "Riddles, Cultural Categories, and World View." *Journal of American Folklore* 89 (1976): 255–65.

Linton, Margaret McIntosh. "Madagascar Proverbs." *Atlantic Monthly* 139 (1927): 352–54.

Linton, Ralph. *The Tanala, a Hill Tribe of Madagascar*. Anthropology Series, 22. Publication 317. Chicago: Field Museum of Natural History, 1933.

Lloyd, A. L. *Folk Song in England*. London: Lawrence and Wishart, 1967.

Lord, Albert B. *The Singer of Tales*. Cambridge, Mass.: Harvard University Press, 1960.

Mannoni, O. *Prospero and Caliban: The Psychology of Colonization*. 2nd ed. Translated by Pamela Powesland from *Psychologie de la colonisation*, Paris, 1950. New York: Praeger, 1964.

Marcus, George E., and Michael M. J. Fischer, *Anthropology as Cultural Critique: An Experimental Moment in the Human Sciences*. Chicago: University of Chicago Press, 1986.

Marre-de Marin, Aristide. *Grammaire malgache*. Paris, 1876.

Mattei, Louis. "Les Tsimihety." *Bulletin de l'Académie Malgache*, n.s. 21 (1938).

Mayer, Philip. "The Joking of 'Pals' in Gusii Age-Sets." *African Studies* 10 (1951): 27–41.

McDowell, John Holmes. *Children's Riddling*. Bloomington: Indiana University Press, 1979.

Medvedev, P. N./Bakhtin, M. M. *The Formal Method in Literary Scholarship, a Critical Introduction to Sociological Poetics*. Translated by Albert J. Wehrle. Baltimore: Johns Hopkins University Press, 1978.

Mercier, Paul. *Histoire de l'Anthropologie*. Paris: Presses Universitaires de France, 1971.

Messenger, John C., Jr. "Anang Proverb-Riddles." *Journal of American Folklore* 73 (1960): 225–35.

————. "The Role of Proverbs in a Nigerian Judicial System. In *The Study of Folklore*, edited by Alan Dundes, pp. 299–307. Englewood Cliffs, N.J.: Prentice-Hall, 1965.

Michel, Louis. "Essai sur la littérature malgache." *Revue de Madagascar* 28 (3d quarter 1956): 47–56.

————. *Moeurs et coutumes des bara*. Mémoires de l'Académie Malgache, fasc. 40. Tananarive: Institut Scientifique de Madagascar, 1957.

Michel-Andrianarahinjaka, Lucien X. "La poésie tsimihety." *Annales de l'Université de Madagascar*, sér. Lettres et Sciences Humaines 8 (1967): 17–37, 9 (1968): 73–96.

————. *Le système littéraire betsileo*. Fianarantsoa: Editions Ambozontany: 1986.

Mieder, Wolfgang. *International Proverb Scholarship: An Annotated Bibliography*. New York: Garland, 1982.

Mitchell, Joseph. *McSorley's Wonderful Saloon*. New York: Duell, Sloan and Pearce, 1943.

Molet, Louis. *Le Bain Royal à Madagascar*. Tananarive: Imprimerie Luthérienne, 1956.

———. *Le boeuf dans l'Ankaizinana*. Mémoires de l'Institut Scientifique de Madagascar, 2. Paris: P. André, 1953.

———. *La Conception malgache du monde, du surnaturel, et de l'homme en Imerina*. 2 vols. Paris: Éditions L'Harmattan, 1979.

———. "Esquisse de la mentalité malgache." *Revue de Psychologie des Peuples* 14 (January 1959): 25–41.

———. "Politesse malgache et jeux d'enfants." *Revue de Madagascar*, n.s. 35 (1966): 15–16.

———. "Le vocabulaire concernant l'esclavage dans l'ancien Madagascar." *Perspectives nouvelles sur le passé de l'Afrique noire et de Madagascar, Mélanges offerts à Hubert Deschamps*, pp. 45–65. Publications of the Sorbonne, series "Etudes," 7. Paris, 1974.

Mondain, Gustave. "Curieuses critiques proverbiales de certaines croyances malgaches." *Bulletin de l'Académie Malgache*, n.s. 31 (1953): 19–22.

———. "Un kabary inédit en usage dans l'Imerina du Sud." *Bulletin de l'Académie Malgache* 6 (1908): 99–114.

———. "Traditions et généalogies malgaches." *Bulletin de l'Académie Malgache*, n.s. 31 (1953): 13–17.

Montagné, Lucien. *Essai de grammaire malgache*. Paris: Société d'Éditions Géographiques, Maritimes et Coloniales, 1931.

Montgomery, W., Rev. "The Malagasy Game of Fanorona." *Antananarivo Annual* 10 (1886): 148–56.

Moore, John Robert. *Defoe in the Pillory*. Bloomington: Indiana University Press, 1939.

———. *Defoe's Sources for "Robert Drury's Journal."* Bloomington: Indiana University Press, 1942.

Morwitz, Ernst. "Stefan George." In *Poems*, by Stefan George, pp. 9–36. New York: Pantheon Books, 1943.

Navone, P. Gabriel. *Ny atao no miverina, ou ethnologie et proverbes malgaches*. Fianarantsoa: Librairie Ambozontany, 1977.

Needham, Rodney. *Circumstantial Deliveries*. Berkeley: University of California Press, 1981.

Nelson, Harold D., et al. *Area Handbook for the Malagasy Republic*. Washington, D.C.: United States Government Printing Office, 1973.

Nguyen van Huyen. *Les chants alternés des garçons et des filles en Annam*. Paris: Librairie Orientaliste Paul Geuthner, 1933.

O Súilleabháin, Seán. *A Handbook of Irish Folklore*. 1942. Reprint, Hatboro, Pa.: Folklore Associates, 1963.

Oliver, S. Pasfield, ed. *Robert Drury: Madagascar, etc.* London, 1890.

Olsen, Pastor. "Histoire des Zafindiamanana." *Bulletin de l'Académie Malgache*, n.s. 12 (1929): 57–60.

Osborn, Chase Salmon. *Madagascar: Land of the Man-Eating Tree*. New York: Republic Publishing Company, 1924.

Ottino, Paul. *L'Étrangère intime. Essai d'anthropologie de la civilisation de l'ancien Madagascar.* Paris: Editions des Archives Contemporaines, 1986.

———. "Le Moyen âge de l'Océan Indien et les composantes du peuplement de Madagascar." *ASEMI* 7, nos. 2–3 (1976): 3–8.

———. "La mythologie malgache des hautes terres. Le cycle politique des Andriambaoaka." In *Dictionnaire des mythologies et des religions des sociétés traditionnelles et du monde antique*, edited by Yves Bonnefoy. 2 vols, 2: 30–45. Paris: Flammarion, 1981. Translated by Gerald Honigsblum as "The Mythology of the Highlands of Madagascar and the Political Cycle of the Andriambahoaka," in *Mythologies*, compiled by Yves Bonnefoy, prepared under the direction of Wendy Doniger. 2 vols., 2: 961–76. Chicago: University of Chicago Press, 1991.

———. "Un procédé littéraire malayo-polynésien. De l'ambiguité à la plurisignification." *L'Homme* 6 (1966): 5–34.

Papen, Robert. "État présent des études en phonologie des créoles de l'Océan Indien." *Études Créoles* 1 (July 1978): 35–63.

Parker, G. W. *Concise Grammar of the Malagasy Language. See* Cousins.

Paulhan, Jean. "Expérience du proverbe." *Commerce* 5 (1925): 23–77.

———. *Les Hain-teny merinas, poésies populaires malgaches.* Paris: P. Geuthner, 1913.

———. *Les hain-tenys.* 1938. Reprint, Paris: Gallimard, 1960.

———. *Le repas et l'amour chez les merinas.* 1970. Reprint, Paris: Fata Morgana, 1987.

Pearse, J. "Leprosy and Lepers in Madagascar." *Antananarivo Annual* 22 (1898): 191.

Peek, Philip M. "The Power of Words in African Verbal Arts." *Journal of American Folklore* 94 (1981): 19–43.

Penfield, Joyce. *Communicating with Quotes: The Igbo Case.* Contributions in Intercultural and Comparative Studies, 8. Westport: Greenwood Press, 1983.

Permiakov, G. L. *From Proverb to Folk-Tale: Notes on the General Theory of Cliché.* Translated by Y. N. Filippov. Moscow: Nauka Publishing House, 1979.

Peukes, Gerhard. *Untersuchungen zum Sprichwort im Deutschen: Semantik, Syntax, Typen.* Berlin: Erich Schmidt, 1977.

Pfeiffer, Ida. *The Last Travels of Ida Pfeiffer, Inclusive of a Visit to Madagascar.* London, 1861. French translation, *Voyage à Madagascar, avril-septembre 1857.* Paris, 1862. Reprint, Paris, Editions Karthala, 1981.

Phillpotts, Bertha. *The Elder Edda and Ancient Scandinavian Drama.* Cambridge: Cambridge University Press, 1920.

Poirier, Jean. "Les hétéronymes malgaches." *Civilisation malgache* 1 (1964), 181–91.

Pound, Ezra. *Translations.* New York: New Directions: 1963.

Propp, Vladimir. *Morphology of the Folktale.* Translated by Laurence Scott and Louis A. Wagner. Austin: University of Texas Press, 1968.

Rabearivelo, Jean-Joseph. *J. J. Rabearivelo.* Littérature Malgache, 1. Paris: Fernand Nathan, 1967.

————. *Translations from the Night, Selected Poems*. Edited with English translations by John Reed and Clive Wake. London: Heinemann, 1975.

Raffel, Burton. *The Development of Indonesian Poetry*. Albany: State University of New York Press, 1967.

Rahidy, P. Basilide. *Cours pratique de langue malgache*. Tananarive, 1875.

Raison-Jourde, Françoise. "L'échange inégal de la langue. La pénétration des techniques linguistiques dans une civilisation de l'oral (Imerina, debut du XIXe siècle)." *Annales E.S.C* 32 (1977): 639–69.

————, ed. *Les souverains de Madagascar*. Paris: Editions Karthala, 1983.

Rajaona, Siméon. "Aspects de la psychologie malgache vus à travers certains traits des 'Kabary' et quelques faits de langue." *Annales Malgaches* 1 (1963): 23–37.

————. "Essai d'analyse de la structure de la pensée malgache, examen de quelques notions." *Bulletin de l'Académie Malgache*, n.s. 37 (1959): 75–79.

Ralinoro, Dr. Charles. "Développement et 'ohabolana.'" *Bulletin de Madagascar* no. 246 (November 1966): 1128–40.

Ranaivo, Flavien. "Les 'Hain-teny.'" *Revue de Madagascar* 7 (4th quarter 1949), 55–81.

————. *Hain-Teny, présentés et transcrits du malgache*. Série "D'Etranges Pays." Paris: Publications Orientaistes de France, 1975.

Randafison, Sylvestre. "Les mpihira gasy." *Ambario* 2, nos. 1–2 (1980): 189–194.

Randriamandimby, Bar-Jaona. "Le concept de hiérarchie en Imerina historique." *ASEMI* 4, no. 4 (1973): 3–16.

————. "La notion de double et la restauration de l'unité." *Archipel (Etudes interdisciplinaires sur le monde insulindien)* 9 (1975): 73–77.

Ranger, Terence O. "The Invention of Tradition in Colonial Africa." In *The Invention of Tradition*, edited by Eric Hobsbawm and Terence Ranger, pp. 241–62. Cambridge: Cambridge University Press, 1983.

Raphael, F. "De l'orthographe malgache." *Bulletin de l'Académie Malgache* 1, no. 4 (1904): 186–89.

Rasamuel, Maurice. *Ny fitenin-drazana*. Tananarive: Ny Antsiva, 1950.

————. *Kabary am-panambadiana sy amin' ny fanasana*. Antanimena: Imprimerie Catholique, 1973.

————. *Kabary am-panambadiana*. Translated by M. M. Colançon. *Bulletin de l'Académie Malgache*, n.s. 11 (1928, pub. 1929): 3–52.

Razafimino, Caleb. *La signification religieuse du fandroana, ou de la fête du nouvel an en Imerina*. Tananarive, 1924.

Reisman, Karl. "Contrapuntal Conversations in an Antiguan Village." In *Explorations in the Ethnography of Speaking*, edited by Richard Bauman and Joel Sherzer, pp. 110–24. New York: Cambridge University Press, 1974.

————. "Cultural and Linguistic Ambiguity in a West Indian Village." In *Afro-American Anthropology*, edited by Norman E. Whitten, Jr., and John F. Szwed, pp. 129–44. New York: Free Press, 1970.

Renel, Charles. *Contes de Madagascar*. Paris: E. Leroux, vols. 1 and 2, 1910, vol. 3, 1930.

Rey, H. "Le Folk-lore menabe." *Bulletin de l'Académie Malgache* 12 (1913): 57–63.

Richardson, John. "The Dialects of the Malagasy Language, Illustrated by Lists of

158 Common Words from Twenty-Four Different Localities." *Antananarivo Annual* 21 (1897): 105–15, 22 (1898): 208–14.

———. "Malagasy Conundrums." *Antananarivo Annual* 1 (1876): 247–48.

———. *Malagasy for Beginners*. Antananarivo: London Missionary Society Press, 1884.

———. *A New Malagasy-English Dictionary*. Antananarivo: London Missionary Society Press, 1885.

Roberts, John M., and Michael L. Forman. "Riddles, Expressive Models of Interrogation." In *Directions in Sociolinguistics, the Ethnography of Communication*, edited by John J. Gumperz and Dell Hymes, pp. 180–209. New York: Holt, Rinehart, and Winston, 1972.

Rogers, Alan D. "Human Prudence and Implied Divine Sanctions in Malagasy Proverbial Wisdom." *Journal of Religion in Africa* 15 (1985): 216–26.

Rolland de Renéville, A. *Univers de la Parole*. Paris: Gallimard, 1944.

Rorty, Richard. *Philosophy and the Mirror of Nature*. Princeton: Princeton University Press, 1979.

Rosaldo, Renato. *Culture and Truth: The Remaking of Social Analysis*. Boston: Beacon Press, 1989.

Rothenberg, Jerome, ed. *Shaking the Pumpkin: Traditional Poetry of the Indian North Americas*. New York: Doubleday, 1972.

———, ed. *Technicians of the Sacred: a Range of Poetries from Africa, America, Asia, and Oceania*. New York: Doubleday, 1968.

Rusillon, Henri. *Paganisme: observations et notes documentaires*. Paris: Société des Missions Evangéliques, 1929.

———. "De quelques differences entre la langue hova et le dialecte sakalava." *Bulletin de l'Académie Malgache*, n.s. 4 (1918–19, published 1921): 231.

Said, Edward. *Orientalism*. New York: Pantheon, 1978.

Sanches, Mary, and Barbara Kirshenblatt-Gimblett. "Children's Traditional Speech Play and Child Language." In *Speech Play*, edited by Barbara Kirshenblatt-Gimblett, pp. 65–110. Philadelphia: University of Pennsylvania Press, 1976.

Sankoff, Gillian. *The Social Life of Language*. Philadelphia: University of Pennsylvania Press, 1980.

Scheub, Harold. "A Review of African Oral Traditions and Literature." *African Studies Review* 28 (June–September 1985): 1–72.

———. "The Technique of the Expansible Image in Xhosa Ntsomi-Performances." *Forms of Folklore in Africa*, edited by Bernth Lindfors, pp. 37–63. Austin: University of Texas Press, 1977.

Schuchardt, Hugo. *Pidgin and Creole Languages: Selected Essays by Hugo Schuchardt*, edited and translated by Glenn G. Gilbert. Cambridge: Cambridge University Press, 1980.

Scott, Charles T. *Persian and Arabic Riddles: A Language-Centered Approach to Genre Definition*. Indiana University Research Center in Anthropology, Folklore, and Linguistics, Publication 39. The Hague: Mouton, 1965.

Secord, Arthur W. *Defoe's Sources for "Robert Drury's Journal."* Bloomington: Indiana University Press, 1942.

———. *Robert Drury's Journal and Other Studies*. Urbana: University of Illinois Press, 1961.

Seitel, Peter. "Saying Haya Sayings: Two Categories of Proverb Use." In *The Social Use of Metaphor, Essays on the Anthropology of Rhetoric*, edited by J. David Sapir and J. Christopher Crocker, pp. 75–99. Philadelphia: University of Pennsylvania Press, 1977.

Senghor, Léopold Sédar, ed. *Anthologie de la nouvelle poésie nègre et malgache de langue française*. Paris: Presses Universitaires de France, 1948.

Sherzer, Joel. "An Exploration into the Ethnography of Speaking of the Abipones." Thesis, University of Pennsylvania, 1967. Translated, somewhat abridged, by Nicole Belmont, "La parole chez les abipones." *L'Homme* 10 (1970): 42–76.

Sibree, James, Jr. *The Great African Island*. London, 1880.

———. *Madagascar Before the Conquest: The Island, the Country, and the People*. London: T. Fisher Unwin, 1896.

———. "The Oratory, Songs, Legends and Folk-tales of the Malagasy." *Folk-Lore Journal* (London) 1 (1883): 1–15, 33–40, 65–77, 97–106, 169–74, 201–11, 233–43, 273–79, 305–16, 337–43; 2 (1884): 45–57, 75–81, 129–38, 161–68. *Antananarivo Annual* 13 (1889): 28–38; 14 (1890): 171–81; 15 (1891): 357–68.

Silverman-Weinreich, Beatrice. "Towards a Structural Analysis of Yiddish Proverbs." *YIVO Annual of Jewish Social Sciences* 17 (1978): 1–20. Reprinted in *The Wisdom of Many, Essays on the Proverb*, edited by Wolfgang Mieder and Alan Dundes, pp. 65–85. New York: Garland, 1981.

Simmons, Donald C. "Cultural Functions of the Efik Tone-Riddle." *Journal of American Folklore* 71 (1958): 123–38.

———. "Possible West African Sources for the American Negro 'Dozens.'" *Journal of American Folklore* 76 (1963): 339–40.

Sims, John. *Angano'ny Ntaolo. Tantara mampiseho ny fomban-drazana sy ny finoana sasany nananany, nangonin-dRev. L. Dahle*. Antananarivo: Imprimerie F[riends] F[oreign] M[issionary] A[ssociation], 1908.

Sinclair, J. McH. and R. M. Coulthard. *Towards an Analysis of Discourse*. Oxford: Oxford University Press, 1975.

Southall, Aidan W. "The Illusion of Tribe." *Journal of Asian and African Studies* 5 (1970): 28–50.

———. "Madagascar." *Encyclopedia Britannica*, 15th ed. (1985), 21, 168.

Spivak, Gayatri Chakravorty. "Translator's Preface." In *Of Grammatology*, by Jacques Derrida, pp. ix–xc. Baltimore: Johns Hopkins University Press, 1976.

Stewart, Susan. *Nonsense: Aspects of Intertextuality in Folklore and Literature*. Baltimore: Johns Hopkins University Press, 1979.

Stocking, George W., Jr., ed. *Observers Observed: Essays on Ethnographic Fieldwork*. Madison: University of Wisconsin Press, 1983.

Sutton-Smith, Brian. *The Folkgames of Children*. Austin: University of Texas Press, 1972.

Tadié, Jean-Yves. *La critique littéraire au XXe siècle*. Paris: Pierre Belfond, 1987.

Taylor, Archer. *The Proverb*. Cambridge: Harvard University Press, 1931.

Taylor, Mark C. *Deconstruction in Context: Literature and Philosophy*. Chicago: University of Chicago Press, 1986.

Tedlock, Dennis. *Finding the Center: Narrative Poetry of the Zuni Indians*. New York: The Dial Press, 1972.

Thompson, Stith. *The Folktale*. New York: Holt, Rinehart and Winston, 1946.

———. *Motif-Index of Folk Literature*. 6 vols. Bloomington: Indiana University Press, 1955–58.

Todorov, Tzvetan. *Les genres du discours*. Paris: Seuil, 1978.

———. *Mikhaïl Bakhtine, le principe dialogique*. Paris: Éditions du Seuil, 1981.

Turner, Victor W. *Dramas, Fields, and Metaphors*. Ithaca: Cornell University Press, 1974.

———. *The Ritual Process*. Chicago: Aldine Press, 1969.

Urbain-Faublée, Marcelle. *L'art malgache*. Paris: Presses Universitaires de France, 1963.

van Gennep, Arnold. *Manuel de folklore français contemporain*. 6 vols. Paris: A. Picard, 1937–58.

———. *The Rites of Passage*. Translated by Monika B. Vizedom and Gabrielle L. Caffee. Chicago: University of Chicago Press, 1960.

———. *Tabou et totémisme à Madagascar. Etude descriptive et théorique*. Paris: Ernest Leroux, 1904.

Vérin, Pierre. "Madagascar." *Ancient Civilizations of Africa*. Vol. 2 of *UNESCO General History of Africa*, edited by G. Mokhtar, pp. 693–717. London: Heinemann, 1981.

———. *The History of Civilisation in North Madagascar*. Translated by David Smith. Rotterdam: A. A. Balkema, 1986.

Vérin, Pierre, Conrad Kottak, and P. Gorlin, "The Glottochronology of Malagasy Speech Communities." *Oceanic Linguistics* 8 (Summer 1969): 26–83.

Vérin, Pierre, and Narivelo Rajaonarimanana. "Divination in Madagascar: The Antemoro Case and the Diffusion of Divination." In *African Divination Systems: Ways of Knowing*, edited by Philip M. Peek, pp. 53–68. Bloomington: Indiana University Press, 1991.

Veyrières, P. Paul de. *Le livre de la sagesse malgache*. Paris, 1967.

Voigt, Vilmos. "Les niveaux des variantes de proverbes." *Acta Linguistica Academiae Scientiarum Hungaricae* 20 (1970): 357–64.

Volosinov, V. N. *Marxism and the Philosophy of Language*. Translated by Ladislav Matejka and I. R. Titunik. New York: Seminar Press, 1973.

Voorhoeve, Jan. "Varieties of Creole in Suriname." In *Pidginization and Creolization of Languages*, edited by Dell Hymes, pp. 299–322. Cambridge: Cambridge University Press, 1971.

Wallace, Anthony F. C. *Culture and Personality*. New York: Random House, 1961.

Webber, P. *Dictionnaire malgache-français*. Ile Bourbon, 1853.

Wellek, René. *History of Modern Criticism*. 6 vols. New Haven: Yale University Press, 1955–86.

Westermarck, Edward. *Wit and Wisdom in Morocco*. London: George Routledge and Sons, 1930.

Wilgus, D. K. *Anglo-American Folksong Scholarship Since 1898*. New Brunswick: Rutgers University Press, 1959.

Williams, Raymond. *The Long Revolution*. 1961. Reprint, New York: Harper & Row, 1966.

Wilson, William A. *Folklore and Nationalism in Modern Finland*. Bloomington: Indiana University Press, 1976.

Wolf, Eric. *Peasants*. New York: Holt, Rinehart and Winston, 1966.

Wolfenstein, Martha. *Children's Humor, a Psychological Analysis*. 1954. Reprint, Bloomington: Indiana University Press, 1978.

Wright, Henry T., and Susan Kus. "An Archaeological Reconnaissance of Ancient Imerina." In *Madagascar in History: Essays from the 1970's*, ed. Raymond K. Kent, pp. 1–31. Albany, Calif.: Foundation for Malagasy Studies, 1979.

Zahan, Dominique. *La dialectique du verbe chez les Bambara*. The Hague: Mouton, 1963.

Zumthor, Paul. *La lettre et la voix: de la "littérature" médiévale*. Paris: Éditions du Seuil, 1987.

Zumwalt, Rosemary Lévy. *American Folklore Scholarship: A Dialogue of Dissent*. Bloomington: Indiana University Press, 1988.

Index

This book has been set in Linotron Galliard. Galliard was designed for Mergenthaler in 1978 by Matthew Carter. Galliard retains many of the features of a sixteenth century typeface cut by Robert Granjon but has some modifications that give it a more contemporary look.

Printed on acid-free paper.